THE STORKS

**The Story of the Les Cigognes,
France's Élite Fighter Group of WW1**

Norman Franks and Frank Bailey

GRUB STREET · LONDON

Published by
Grub Street
The Basement
10 Chivalry Road
London SW11 1HT

A catalogue record is available on request from the British Library

ISBN 1-898697-81-7

Typeset by Pearl Graphics, Hemel Hempstead

Printed and bound in Great Britain by
Biddles Ltd, Guildford and King's Lynn

ACKNOWLEDGEMENTS

The authors wish to thank the following organisations and individuals for their generous help and
assistance: – Service Historique de l'Armée de l'Air; Service Historique de Terre; Escadron de Chasse
1/2 Cigognes; A.E. Clausen, Jr.; Mike O'Neal; Neal O'Connor; Peter Kilduff; George Williams;
Richard Duiven; Jon Guttman; Daniel Brunet; Nick Mladenoff; Dieter H.M. Gröschel, MD; Thomas
Nilsson; Keith Rennles, the late historians Paul Joly, Dennis O'Connell, Russell Manning and Iver
Penttenin.

Contents

CHAPTER ONE

Formation

Verdun; today Verdun is just a city. People of an older generation outside France may just about recall that name in connection with a battle fought in World War One. People in France, and especially its older generation, will know the tremendous significance of Verdun. In all probability some close or distant member of their family, or an old acquaintance fought at Verdun. There is also little doubt that the people of France immediately after World War One had a father, brother, uncle, cousin, friend, neighbour, school chum, family friend, or simply knew of someone, who had died at Verdun. Verdun was where the French army almost bled to death. Almost everyone in France was 'touched' by Verdun.

The bloody battle of Verdun began in February 1916 and lasted till early winter. The cost in human lives was appalling, even for WWI standards. Both the French and the Germans lost half-a-million men – 500,000 – quite apart from the wounded.

The battle has been recorded too as France's 'hinge of fate'; both sides saw that this was one city that had to be defended and not lost. The French knew that to lose Verdun would leave the road open to Paris, the Germans knew it too and also knew that in defending Verdun, the French army could be bled white. It didn't matter then that the British held the lines north of Amiens to the Channel coast. If Verdun fell, the British would be outflanked and have to fall back to the Channel, just as they would be 24 years later.

The task of attacking Verdun, situated on the River Meuse, was given to the German 5th Army, commanded by Crown Prince Wilhelm und Knobelsdorf. Verdun by this time was more than just a city, it was the Région Fortifée du Verdun – RFV – (Fortified Region of Verdun) a veritable citadel, commanded by Général Frédéric Georges Herr. On his left (ie. to the north) was the French III° Armée, under Général George Humbert, while to the south was Général Philippe Pétain's II° Armée. Pétain was in overall command, and during the period 25/26 February RFV was assimilated into the II° Armée, and ceased to exist.

The Germans launched their assault on 21 February 1916, knowing that they held complete control of the air over the sector in which the offensive was taking place. Even at this comparatively early stage of the Great War, the aeroplane had firmly established its place in modern-day warfare. Reconnaissance and artillery observation had become paramount to land battles, not only in finding and photographing the opposition, but in directing their own side's artillery fire, and locating the artillery – which would hopefully bring about its annihilation – of the enemy. Having control (ie. one's own aeroplanes dominating the sky thereby denying freedom of movement by the opposing aircraft, allowing the one side's aviators favorable conditions in which to carry out their tasks) was paramount. An aggressive land force needed its airmen if they were to succeed in an attack.

On the German side, a 48-year-old Colonel Hermann von der Lieth-Thomsen (he would be 49 in March), a thick-set, bald Prussian who had distinguished himself at the battle of Tannenberg at the start of the war, was head of the Luftstreitkräfte (German Air Force/Service). In February 1916 he could count 168 aircraft ready for operations, within Kagohl I and II (Kampfgeschwader der Obersten Herresleitung). These aircraft equipped ten Flieger-Abteilungen (FA – two-seater reconnaissance units), six Artillery Flieger-Abteilungen (FA(A)), plus a total of 21 Fokker Eindekker single-seat fighters, organized into three Kampfeinsitzer Kommandos (KEKs). In addition he had 14 observation balloon companies, not to mention the services, if required, of four Zeppelin airships.

Until now, the Fokker fighters had been distributed piecemeal among the various FA units as protection machines, but these Kek units – the forerunner of the famous Jastas that would be formed in the summer of 1916, were the first attempts at bunching fighters together as fighting units for a specific purpose, in this case, the Verdun offensive. Oberleutnant Oswald Boelcke, already an ace with nine victories, commanded one of the Kek units at Sivry, although he was officially within the aegis of FA62. The other Keks were at Arvillers.

At this stage the French Air Service was completely incapable of holding back the mass of German aircraft, or to carry out any offensive actions of their own. They were not able to send out any artillery observation planes, therefore the French artillery was blind as to the targets assigned them, and would not be made aware of enemy troop concentrations or movements. In order to remedy this situation, Colonel Joseph Barés, Chief of the French Air Service, ordered Chef des Escadrons Charles de Tricornot de Rose, to take command of all fighter forces in the area.

Jean Baptiste Marie Charles de Tricornot de Rose was born in Paris on 11 October 1876. He entered military service at the Special Military School at St. Cyr on 31 October 1895, shortly after his 19th birthday, and was promoted to Brigadier on 12 April 1896. He received a commission as a Sous-lieutenant on 1 October 1897, and was assigned to the 9° Régiment de Dragons and promoted to full Lieutenant on 1 October 1899. He was reassigned to the 19° Régiment de Dragons on 25 March 1909.

From here he was detached to the pilot's school and received Pilot's Brevet No. 330 on 23 November 1910, and Military Pilot's Brevet No. 1 on 7 February 1911. He was made a Chevalier de la Légion d'Honneur on 14 October of that year, and promoted to Capitaine on 24 June 1912. After the war began he was made Chef du Service Aéronautique de la V° Armée on 22 November 1914, the same date he was promoted to Chef d'Escadrons. He was made an Officier de la Légion d'Honneur on 13 July 1915, with the following citation:

> Head of an Army Air Service, rendering brilliant services in aviation each day.In command of a
> groupe of bombardement and chasse escadrilles (14 escadrilles). He obtains the most valuable results
> for the command by placing enemy aircraft and balloons under constant attack in co-operation with
> efficient bombing of enemy batteries that our artillery can't oppose.

To reinforce what air units were already on the Verdun Front, Colonel Barés sent additional Nieuport and Morane-Saulnier units together with some of the better pilots from other escadrilles. In one case, Escadrille N 3 sent a detachment under Capitaine Félix Antonin Gabriel Brocard, which included Sous-lieutenants Albert Deullin, Georges Guynemer and Jean Peretti, Adjudants Jules Védrines, Charles Haussemand and Louis Bucquet, and Sergent André Chainat. This groupe of pilots arrived on 12 March, and was based at Vadelaincourt, about 20 kilometres south-west of Verdun. Other fighter escadrilles known to have been in this sector are N 15, N 23, N 31, N 65, N 67, N 69 and N 124, the "N" denoting that each were equipped with the nimble Nieuport Scout single-seaters, mostly type XI. Of the N 3 pilots three were attached to N 67, Peretti, Haussemand and Bucquet.

The French commenced operating in flights of six or more aircraft, and escadrilles were assigned specific areas to patrol and ordered to keep aircraft in the air at all times. After a couple of weeks the Germans could see that they were losing the battle for air supremacy, and by 16 April the French had the situation well under control. From the beginning of the assault upon Verdun, the N 3 detachment had been credited with six German aircraft destroyed; Deullin had claimed three, Brocard and Chainat and Guynemer one each. However, Guynemer had been wounded on 17 March, followed by Brocard two days later and then Deullin on 2 April. Of the other units:

N 12	3 victories	Lt Georges Pelletier d'Oisy	2
		Adj Pierre Dufaur de Gavardie	1
	(One shared with Cdt du Peuty and Lt de Chivre of N 12)		

N 15	9 victories	Sgt Lucien Jailler	3
		S/Lt Raymond Lis	3
		Cpl Herman Hentsch	2
		S/Lt Paul Schneider	1

N 23	7 victories	Adj Edwards Pulpe	2
		Capt Louis Robert de Beauchamp	2
		Lt Jules de Boutiny	1
		Sgt Maxime Lenoir	1
		Sgt Théophile Ingold/Sgt de Ram	1

(one shared with Lt de Lage, his obsever)

N 31	7 victories	Capt Alfred Auger	2
		Sgt Jean Chaput	2
		S/Lt Leith Jensen	1
		Adj Jacques Ortoli	1
		Adj Pierre Touvet *	1

(* Shared with Asp Duchenois (P) and Sgt Balthasar (O) of Escadrille MF 44)

N 57	5 victories	Lt André Bubois de Gennes	1
		Lt Charles Dumas	1
		S/Lt Jean Chaput	1
		Lt Jean Robert	1
		Sgt Louis Coudouret	1

N 65	13 victories	S/Lt Charles Nungesser	7
		Capt Philippe Féquant	1
		Lt Georges Boillot	1
		S/Lt Sebastien de Neufville	1
		S/Lt Henri Reservat	1
		Adj Michel Leroy	1
		MdL Elloit Cowdin	1

N 67	10 victories	S/Lt Jean Navarre	7
		S/Lt Jean Peretti	1
		MdL Georges Flachaire	1
		Sgt Robert de Marolles	1

N 69	4 victories	Lt Henri Gilles de Chivre*	3
		Sgt Carlos des Allimes **	1

(* One shared with Cdt du Peuty and S/Lt Pelletier d'Oisy of N 12)
(** Shared with an aircraft from Escadrille C 27)

N 124	3 victories	Lt William Thaw	1
		Sgt Bert Hall	1
		Cpl Kiffin Rockwell	1

Jean Marie Dominique Navarre was called the *Sentinel of Verdun* at this time, and well known to the French public. The French tended to publicise their heroes. Postcards and magazine articles presented their feats and their faces to the French people. Escadrille N 124, of course, was the famous unit made up of American volunteers – the Lafayette Escadrille, although commanded and led by French officers.

The Battle of Verdun lasted virtually for the entire year of 1916, with the French suffering 543,000 casualties, the Germans over 434,000, with nothing of significance in the amount of ground taken. Verdun itself had little strategic value, other than a distant bastion for Paris, but had become a symbol of French nationalistic pride and resistance that had existed since Roman times. However, in the air, it had seen the first real use of massed fighter units brought together for a specific task.

*   *   *

The next extensive use of massed fighter units was during the Battle of the Somme, another Allied disaster that began on 1 July 1916 on the British Front, and lasted into November. While both the French and British had been planning offensive action for 1916, the Germans had got in first with their Verdun offensive, and the Somme attack had been launched in order to relieve pressure on the French south at Verdun.

Opposing them was General Sir Henry Rawlinson's British 4th Army, along with General Sir Edmund Allenby's 3rd Army on the left and the French VI° Armée under Général Marie Emile Fayrolle protecting the right flank, the dividing line being at Maricourt. On the first day, despite days of intense artillery bombardment, the British lost 60,000 men, with almost no ground gained. The famous 'walk up' to the German trenches, which everyone believed had been obliterated by shell-fire, resulted in a massive loss of lives. With six divisions, General Otto von Below's Second Army held off the attacks of eighteen Allied divisions, but it did take some of the pressure off Verdun.

The French Air Service started building up their fighter force at Cachy, about 15 kilometres south-east of Amiens, in the VI° Armée Sector, during April 1916. Félix Brocard's N 3 was the first to report on the 16th. Capitaine Henri Gallet's N 103, an Escadrille d'Armée with the VI° Armée, was already based at Cachy, and was assigned to the Groupe on the 28th. N 62, commanded by Capitaine Henri Horment, moved to Cachy from Moreuil, on 5 May, N 26, commanded by Capitaine Jacques de Plan de Sieyes de Veynes, arrived from Saint Pol-sur-Mer, on 5 June, while N 65, Capitaine Philippe Féquant commanding, moved from Lemmes, on the Verdun Front, during June.

All these units were available at the beginning of the Somme offensive and were supplemented by Capitaine Marcel Feierstein's N 37 on 2 July and the newly created N 73, commanded by Lieutenant Jean Richard, on the 22nd. During August 1916, N 67 arrived from Froidos, on the Verdun Front, commanded by Capitaine Henri Constans de Saint Sauveur. All these units came under the overall command of Félix Brocard, although N 62 was re-assigned to Chipilly during September, to become an Escadrille d'Armée for the VI° Armée, remaining in this capacity until the end of the war. (Note: an Escadrille d'Armée is a unit assigned permanently to a certain Armée that carries out the duties assigned by the commander of that armée. They handle photographic, reconnaissance, bombing and escort missions as well as any other kind of special duties assigned them, in addition to regular fighter patrols.)

From the time N 3 commenced operations at Cachy, until GC 12 started operations on 1 November the unit was credited with 52 victories, including two balloons. Four of these were shared by two pilots. Individual pilot's victories at Cachy, are as follows:

Adj René Dorme	15	S/Lt Georges Guynemer	10
Lt Alfred Heurtaux	10	Adj André Chainat	9
Lt Mathieu Tenant de la Tour	6	Lt Albert Deullin	4
S/Lt Georges Raymond	1	S/Lt Charles de Guibert	1

Of the other Escadrilles in the Cachy Groupe, the pilot's victories scored are as follows:

N 26 S/Lt Noël de Rochefort	4	Sgt Constant Soulier	2
Sgt Jean Sendral	2	Lt Victor Ménard	1
Capt Jacques de Plan de Sieyes de Veynes			1

N 37 S/Lt Roger Prudhommeux	2	Sgt Etienne Tsu	1
Sgt Aristide Jan	1	Sgt Georges de Geuse	1*
Sgt Fernand Garrigou	1*		

* Shared

N 62 Adj Paul Tarascon	6	Adj Marcel Bloch	5
MdL Célestin Sanglier	4	Adj Louis de Guibert	1
Adj Charles Borzecki (O)	2*	Sgt John Huffer	1*

* Shared

N 65 S/Lt Charles Nungesser	7	Sgt Paul Sauvage	5
Adj Robert de Bonnefoy	4	Capt Emile Billon du Plan	1
Lt J. d'Astier de la Vigerie	1	Lt Raymond Privat	1

N 67 S/Lt Marcel Viallet	4	MdL Georges Flachaire	3
Sgt Henri Massot	1		

N 73 Sgt Marcel Paris	1

N 103 Sgt André Steuer	2*	MdL René Ouvrard de Linière	1
Capt Jean d'Harcourt	1	Lt Jean Gigodot	1*
S/Lt Auguste Ledeuil	1		

* One shared

CHAPTER TWO

Groupe de Combat 12

Groupe de Combat 12 was authorized by Grand Quartier Général, Commandant de l'Aéronautique aux Armées document 17.007 dated 19 October 1916. The Groupe commenced operations from Cachy, on 1 November 1916.

Cachy village and airfield is right between two long, straight roads, one heading due east to St. Quentin, the other south-east towards Roye and Noyon. It is just about five kilometres from the Somme River and canal, and only a couple of kilometres from Villers-Bretonneux. Thus Cachy was right at the southern end of the British part of the Western Front.

Félix Brocard, or to give his full title, Chef de Bataillon Félix Antonin Gabriel Brocard, took command of the new formation. A career officer, he was born on 14 November 1885, at Briol (Isère region) and had volunteered for the Special Military School at St. Cyr on 25 October 1905. He became a Caporal on 8 April the following year, Sergent on 1 November and commissioned a sous-lieutenant on 1 October 1907, and assigned to the 30° Régiment d'Infanterie. He was promoted to full lieutenant two years later to the day and transferred to the 144° Régiment d'Infanterie.

On 10 October 1911 he was sent to Pau, as a student pilot and received his French Aero Club Pilot's Brevet on 17 February 1912, and Military Pilot's Brevet No. 123 on 6 July. He served as an instructor at Reims, until 1 August 1912, when he was assigned to Escadrille Dep 6 (Deperdussin machines). He was named commander of Escadrille MS 3 (then equipped with Morane-Saulnier aeroplanes) on 21 March 1915, and promoted to Capitaine the next day. Following the initial Verdun operations, Brocard assumed command of Groupement de Combat de la Somme, at Cachy. He was given a temporary promotion to Chef de Bataillon on 16 October 1916.

His GC 12 consisted of Escadrilles N 3, now commanded by Lieutenant Alfred Heurtaux, N 26 – Capitaine Victor Ménard, N 73 – Lieutenant Jean Richard, and N 103, Capitaine Jean d'Harcourt. GC 12 was assigned to Groupe des Armées du Nord and received logistical support from Parc 102, and later Parc 112 when that aeroplane park became established.

* * *

The Commanding Officer of a Groupe de Combat had the same prerogatives as the Air Commander of a Corps d'Armée or an Armée. A Groupe was attached to an Armée with which it was operating for tactical and administrative purposes. The orders from the Commanding Général of the Armée were issued through the Commandant de l'Aéronautique (Air Commander) of his armée who would coordinate the operations of the Groupe and the escadrilles assigned to the Armée to ensure there was no duplication of effort, and that proper cooperation between the Groupe and the reconnaissance and artillery observation units was observed.

Each Groupe had a Parc assigned to it and was identified by adding 100 to the groupe's number, thus Parc 112 was assigned to GC 12. The duties of the Parc were to ensure the repairs to aircraft airframes and motors were handled expeditiously and it also served as a supply depot for replacements and provisions. The commanding officer of Parc 112 was Capitaine Joseph Peralda, who had been born 21 February 1879, and had entered military service on 20 October 1897 with the 103° Régiment d'Infanterie. He had transferred to aviation on 20 December 1910 and had been made a Chevalier de la Légion d'Honneur on 11 July 1912. He came from Parc 4 to assume this command.

Until they became part of GC 12, the following escadrilles each had their own history. Before proceeding further we shall look at each unit and what they had achieved thus far.

Escadrille N 3

This unit was formed at Avord during July 1912, as Bl 3, equipped with Blériot XI aircraft (much the same type that Louis Blériot had used to fly across the Channel in 1909), under the command of Lieutenant Bellenger. When the war started, Bl 3 was stationed in the Alsace region, at Belford-Chaux, under the command of Lieutenant Georges Louis Auguste Bellamois, and now flying the Blériot two-seater variation of the Mark XI.

Lieutenant Bellamois was 34 years old, having been born in Paris on 21 June 1880, joining the military in 1900 and attending St. Cyr Military School the following year. Promoted to Sous-lieutenant in September 1903, he was assigned to the 1er Régiment d'Infanterie. Following promotion to full lieutenant he was sent to the 4° Régiment de Zouaves. Assigned to aviation in January 1911, his regimental affiliation was changed to the 144° Régiment d'Infanterie, the same as Brocard.

Completing his pilot training, he received the French Aero Club Pilot's Brevet No. 546 on 28 July 1911, and Military Pilot's Brevet No. 45 on 5 September. He was assigned to Escadrille Bl 3 on 1 October 1912 and made commanding officer on 27 May 1914. Promoted to Capitaine on 1 November of that fateful year, he retained command until relieved by Lieutenant Félix Brocard on 21 March 1915, and he took command of Escadrille C 43 in April 1915.

The unit's first war action was over the Vosges, while assigned to the Ier Armée des Vosges. Capitaine Tiersonnier was wounded by anti-aircraft fire on 6 August, just two days after war had been declared. Bl 3 moved about quite a bit in those first weeks of the war, operating on the Ier, VI°, and IV° Armée Fronts, seeing its first aerial combat on 20 October. On 18 March 1915, the unit was equipped with Morane-Saulnier two-seaters, and therefore changed its designation to MS 3.

Capitaine Félix Brocard now arrived to take command on 15 March and during July the first Nieuport two-seaters arrived. Brocard himself scored the Escadrille's first combat success by downing an Albatros two-seater at 17.25 hours on 3 July over Dreslincourt. MS 3 became N 3 in September even though the unit still had a mixture of machines; in December for instance it had ten Nieuport Xs, four Moranes and three Caudrons.

Sergent Georges Guynemer became the first pilot to achieve five confirmed victories by shooting down an LVG two-seater between Roye and Chaulnes, on 3 February 1916, the observer of this machine being named as Leutnant Heinrich Zwanger, of FA 27. On 12 March, the detachment of pilots referred to in chapter one was sent to the Verdun Front to help wrestle air superiority from the Germans, Brocard leaving Capitaine René Colcomb temporarily in command of N 3. Escadrille N 3, less the Verdun detachment, moved to Cachy on 16 April to become the first escadrille to make up the Groupement de Combat de la Somme, under Brocard, although he also retained command of N 3.

During June the first Nieuport 'Bébé' was received, then during August the first of the Spad VII fighters arrived. N 3 was cited in l'Ordre Général No. 391 de la VI° Armée on 13 September.

> Under the orders of its chief, Capitaine Brocard, has given proof of initiative and spirit of devotion beyond compare in the operations of Verdun and the Somme, having taken part, from 19 March to 19 August 1916, in 338 combats, downing 38 planes and three balloons, and obliged 36 others, badly damaged, to land.

By the time Escadrille N 3 became a part of GC 12 it had been credited with the destruction of 65 aircraft (five being shared) and three balloons, while suffering the loss of three pilots, two observers and one gunner killed in action, two pilots and two observers missing, ten pilots and one observer wounded (one pilot died of wounds), plus one pilot and one gunner injured in accidents.

The scoring pilots were:

S/Lt Georges Guynemer	18	Adj René Dorme	15
Sgt André Chainat	11	Lt Albert Heurtaux	10
Lt Albert Deullin	8	S/Lt Mathieu Tenant de la Tour	5
Capt Félix Brocard	3	S/Lt Georges Raymond	1
Adj Louis Bucquet	1	S/Lt Charles de Guibert	1

As a matter of interest, René 'Père' Dorme had flown a total of little more than 198 hours over the front, and engaged in 86 combats; in addition to his 15 confirmed victories he had seven more recorded as probables. All this in just four months, July to October, while his aircraft had received only two bullet holes and been hit by anti-aircraft shrapnel seven times – an outstanding record.

The casualties had been:

Lt Trétare, pilot, killed in an accident, 5 August 1914.
Capt Tiersonnier, observer, wounded in action 6 August 1914.
Soldat Dineaux, gunner, killed in action 19 June 1915.
Sgt Victor Grivotte, pilot
Lieut Grassel, observer } missing 2 February 1916.
MdL Richard, pilot
Soldat Pillon, gunner } killed in an accident 8 March 1916.
S/Lt Georges Guynemer, wounded in action 17 March 1916.
Capt Félix Brocard, wounded in action 19 March 1916.
Lt Albert Deullin, wounded in action 23 March and 2 April 1916.
Lt Jean Peretti, wounded in combat and died of wounds, 28 April 1916.
Caporal Antoine Chassin, pilot
Adj Paul Hatin, observer } missing 30 April 1916.
Lt Gabriel Foucault, pilot
Soldat Boreau, gunner } killed in an accident.
Sgt André Chainat, wounded in combat 16 June 1916.
Adj Joseph Guiguet, wounded in action 1 and 27 July 1916.
Sgt Dufresne, gunner, injured in an accident 3 July 1916.
Sgt André Chainat, injured in an accident 3 August 1916, and wounded again, 7 September 1916.

Escadrille N 26

Formed as Escadrille MS 26 at Saint-Cyr, on 26 August 1914, under the command of Capitaine Henri Louis Robert Jeannerod, with just four aircraft on charge.

Capitaine Jeannerod was born 21 April 1878, in Marseilles (Bouches du Rhône). He was yet another who entered the military school at St. Cyr, in October 1899, graduating as a sous-lieutenant on 1 October 1901, from where he was assigned to the 133° Régiment d'Infanterie. Promoted to lieutenant two years later, he also served with the 144° Régiment between 1911-12, reporting to the 1er Groupe d'Aviation (Section d'Aviation du Maroc Oriental [Morocco]) on 24 September 1912. A year later promoted to Capitaine and on the last day of 1913 he became a Chevalier de la Légion d'Honneur. He was campaigning in Africa when the war started, but returned to France to assume command of MS 26 on 26 August 1914.

On 21 September a move was made to the Flanders Sector in Belgium. The unit's first combat casualty occurred on 20 October, Lieutenant Happe being forced to land in Holland where he was interned. On 6 February 1915, Capitaine Marie Pierre René de Malherbe relieved Jeannerod as commanding officer.

Capitaine de Malherbe was born on 27 June 1881, and also entered St. Cyr, on 18 October 1902. Graduating as a sous-lieutenant on 1 October 1904, and assigned to the 17° Régiment de Dragons, he was then posted to the 14° Régiment de Dragons on 8 August 1905. Full lieutenant came on 1 October 1906 and on 26 October 1910, he became attached to the aviation service. He received French Aero Club Pilot's Brevet No. 334 on 23 December 1910, followed by Military Pilot's Brevet No. 2 on 7 February 1911. He was made a Chevalier de la Légion d'Honneur on 30 December of that same year, and when the war came he was assigned as a pilot to Escadrille C 4 (Caudrons), taking command and promoted to Capitaine on 1 November. His tenure was brief as he departed on 6 February 1915, to assume command of MS 26.

The man who gained some fame at this time, Sous-lieutenant Roland Garros, scored MS 26's first victory on 1 April 1915, by downing an Albatros two-seater over Westkapelle. (Probably Gefreiter August Spacholz and Leutnant Walter Groskopff of FA 40, killed this date over Oudekapelle). Garros was flying a Morane 'L' with metal deflector plates on both blades of the machine's propeller in order to deflect bullets fired by his fixed machine-guns, set to fire directly in the line of flight through the whirling blades of the propeller.

The Escadrille's designation was changed to N 26 on 20 September with the arrival of Nieuport aircraft, and on 25 November Capitaine de Malherbe was transferred to GDE. It is not known who the temporary commander was, but Capitaine Marcel Thobie arrived to take command on 25 January 1916. Then during May he was replaced by Capitaine Jacques de Plan de Sieyes de Veynes. On 5 June N 26 was transferred from Flanders to Cachy in the VI° Armée Sector, to join Brocard's Groupement de Combat de la Somme (see note 1). The commanding officer was shot down and taken prisoner on 3 July after flaming a balloon. Command of N 26 was assumed by Capitaine Victor Raphaël Ménard.

Capitaine Ménard, a career officer, was born on 8 June 1881, at Rochefort, entering the army on 13 July 1899. With the rank of adjudant he received the French Aero Club's Pilot's Brevet No. 199 during 1910, and after being commissioned on 19 January 1911, he received Military Pilot's Brevet No. 5 on 10 March.

He had been promoted to lieutenant during 1913, and after the war broke out he was on a special mission to Lille, but was taken prisoner on 12 October. During his imprisonment he was promoted to Capitaine in May 1915. Affecting a successful escape during 1916, and after a period of rest and recuperation, he was assigned to active duty once more. Ménard was to become well known amongst the French fighter fraternity in WWI.

On the day Ménard took command on N 26, Sergent Noël de Rochefort became the first ace of the Escadrille, downing an Aviatik two-seater at 18.45 east of Péronne. By the time the unit became a part of GC 12 , it had received credit for the destruction of 17 German aircraft (six shared) and three balloons, while losing one pilot killed, one missing and three wounded, with five more brought down and taken prisoner. Of the latter two died, one was interned. Two other pilots had been killed in flying accidents, two observers wounded in action, one dying of his injuries, and another killed in an accident. Personnel credited with victories were:

S/Lt Noël de Rochefort	7	S/Lt Roland Garros	3
Capt Perrin (O)	2	Sgt Constant Soulier	2
Adj André Simon	2	Lt Joseph Maria (O)	2
Sgt Jean Sendral	2	Lt Armand Pinsard	1
Capt Victor Ménard	1	Adj Henri Moutach	1
Soldat Murat (O)	1	Adj Maurice Faure	1
Lt Daniel Dumêmes (O)	1		

Casualties:

Lt Delaplane, pilot ⎫
Lt Barbier, observer ⎭ killed in an accident 27 August 1914.

Lt Happe, interned in Holland 20 October 1914.

Lt Radisson, killed in action 6 November 1914.

Sgt Jean Montmain, killed in an accident 14 January 1915.

S/Lt Roland Garros, prisoner of war 18 April 1915.

Adj André Simon, pilot ⎫
S/Lt Joseph Maria, observer ⎭ both wounded in action 19 December 1915.

Adj Maurice Faure, wounded in action 9 January 1916.

S/Lt Georges Momet, died of wounds 17 January 1916.

Capt Jacques de Plan de Sieyes de Veynes, prisoner of war 3 July 1916.

Cpl Martin Pelhat, prisoner of war 9 July 1916.

Sgt Auguste Pouchelle, wounded in action 18 August 1916.

S/Lt Noël de Rochefort, prisoner of war 15 September 1916, DOW 16th.

S/Lt Guy de Bammeville, prisoner of war 22 September 1916.

Sgt Rosenlecker, missing 23 September 1916.

Escadrille N 73

Formed originally as Détachement Nieuport de Corcieux, in the VII° Armée Sector, by Decision No. 294, issued by the Chef du Service Aéronautique, Grand Quartier Général on 1 April 1916. The unit was commanded by Lieutenant Honoré Baillardel de Lareinty Tholozan.

The Commander was born on 6 September 1887, at Guermantes (Seine et Marne) and entered military service as a Soldat de 2 Classe, assigned to the 124° Régiment d'Infanterie on 3 October 1905. He was promoted to Caporal on 20 September the following year, and to Sergent on 18 March 1907. Released to the reserves three years after his first assignment, he was commissioned on 20 December 1909. He took pilot training and received a Military Pilot's Brevet on 10 April 1912. Became a Chevalier de la Légion d'Honneur on 7 August 1913, and on 22 December was made a full lieutenant in the Reserves. Mobilized on 3 August 1914, he was posted to Escadrille Bl 9 (Blériots) on 20 September. Leaving this unit in February 1915 he joined Escadrille MF 14 (Maurice Farmans) on 1 April until sent to the Nieuport Detachment at Corcieux.

Three days after this unit's designation was changed to N 73 on 19 April, Baillardel de Lareinty Tholozan was promoted to Capitaine but he was killed during a take-off accident on 3 May. Temporary command was probably assumed by Lieutenant Jean de Limier, the next senior officer in the Escadrille. N 73's first combat victory came on 17 May, Sergent Théophile Funck-Bretano and Caporal Robert Sabatier downing an Aviatik two-seater over Chatas. Lieutenant Jean Richard, from N 3, was assigned as commander on 1 June, pursuant to GQG Télégramme No. 425.

Lieutenant Richard was born on 19 September 1889, in Paris, and joined the military on 7 October 1908, with the 20° Régiment d'Artillerie and promoted to Brigadier on 7 May 1909. After attending a special military school he was promoted to sous-lieutenant as assigned to the 6° Régiment d'Artillerie in August 1912. Transferred to the 26° Régiment d'Artillerie in July 1913, and promoted to Lieutenant on 2 September 1914. He was assigned to RGAé at Lyon in October to commence pilot training, then to Le Plessis-Belleville on 17 April where he was awarded his Pilot's Brevet two days later. Posted to MS 3 on 22 June he remained with this unit, receiving the Croix de Guerre with one palme and one étoile de bronze, before reassignment to command N 73.

The first combat casualty occurred on 25 June, Sergent Funck-Bretano being killed during a combat with three German aircraft, his machine falling in French lines. When Escadrille N 73 became established on 4 July, by GQG Télégramme No.2959, with Lieutenant Richard in command, they prepared to move to their base to Cachy, which took place in the 22nd, at which time they became part of Groupement de Combat de la Somme.

Up to the time N 73 joined GC 12 it had been flying Nieuport XIs and XVIIs, and credited with three aircraft destroyed for the loss of one pilot killed, one missing, one wounded plus another killed in a flying accident. Victories had been claimed by Sergent Funck-Bretano, and Caporal Sabatier (one), Funck-Bretano, one on his own, and Sergent Marcel Paris one (plus another forced to land). The losses had been:

Capitaine Honoré Baillardel Lareinty Tholozan, killed in an accident on 5 May 1916.
Sgt Théophile Funck-Bretano, killed in combat 23 June 1916.
Sgt Bordes, missing 7 September 1916.
Adj Robert Bruneau, wounded in combat 20 October 1916.

Escadrille N 103

This unit was mobilized on 2 August 1914 as Bombardement Escadrille Br 17 (Bréguets) at Longvic, near Dijon, with Capitaine Georges Benoist commanding. During November it was re-equipped with Voisins, and on 23 November assigned to Groupement de Bombardement No.1 under the command of Commandant Joseph Barés, who answered to Commandant Louis de Goys de Mezcyrac. On 5 January 1915, while stationed at Toul, the designation was changed to VB 3, having ben equipped with six Voisin aircraft, while still under Capitaine Benoist. On 4 March the designation was changed again, this time to VB 103, and Capitaine Max Boucher assumed command of the Escadrille on 25 May.

Capitaine Boucher was born on 11 April 1879, entering St. Cyr on 27 October 1900. He graduated as a sous-lieutenant on 1 October 1902 and was assigned to the 19° Régiment de Chasseurs. In August 1903 he went to the 11° Régiment de Hussards, with promotion to lieutenant coming on 1 October 1904. On 26 December the following year he was assigned to the 7° Régiment de Chasseurs, followed by a posting to the 23° Régiment de Dragons at the beginning of 1908. From August 1909 to June 1911 he saw service in the French colony of Madagascar, and returning to France, joined the 11° Régiment de Dragons.

This experienced cavalry officer entered the aviation service on 23 October 1912, promoted to Capitaine on 1 July 1913 and received Military Pilot's Brevet No.413 on 15 December. On 10 April 1914 he assumed command of Escadrille Bl 18. He was made a Chevalier de la Légion d'Honneur on 1 February 1915, his citation reading:

Cavalry Captain, aviator, commander of an escadrille: although commanding an escadrille, he has taken part, since the start of the war, in numerous reconnaissances in the rear of the enemy lines, sometimes as an observer, sometimes as a pilot, often under very perilous conditions. He constantly sets an example of audacity and composure to the young pilots of his escadrille. He particularly distinguished himself on 25 December in the initiation of bomb dropping on important enemy positions.

On 25 March Boucher took command of MS 15, a position he held until he was given command of VB 103 two months later.

Groupement de Bombardement No.1 was cited by Général Joseph Joffre in l'Ordre de l'Armée No.995 on 7 June 1915, which resulted in VB 103 receiving its first citation:

The eighteen pilots and bombardiers of the 1er Groupe de Bombardement have successfully carried out a bombardment over important factories, accomplished over a route of more than 400 kilometres over enemy territory.

Further recognition came following another citation received by GB 1 on 19 October, again by Joffre, in l'Ordre de l'Armée No.1549 "D" thereby giving VB103 the right to display a pennant of the Croix de Guerre on the unit's colours, in recognition of having been cited twice:

1er Groupe de Bombardement, since the expedition of .... under the energetic influence of Lieutenant de Vaisseau Cayla, its chief, and the escadrille commanders, Capitaines Boucher, de la Morlais and Féquant, has executed military raids of great distance over the enemy lines.

However, Capitaine Boucher was transferred on 21 October, command of VB 103 passing to Lieutenant Guy Gaborit de Montjou. VB 103 moved to Cachy on 19 February 1916, and with a change of aircraft, its designation became N 103, command going to Capitaine Henri Gallet. Now an escadrille de chasse (fighters) for the VI° Armée, it was then assigned to Brocard's Groupement de Combat de la Somme on 28 April. On 1 July Lieutenant Jean d'Harcourt took command of N 103, being promoted to Capitaine on the 14th.

Capitaine d'Harcourt was another career officer, born in Paris on 17 December 1885. He enlisted on 29 September 1906, and was assigned to the 9° Régiment de Dragons. During 1910 he entered officer training and was commissioned Sous-Lieutenant in October 1911, going to the 5° Régiment de Chasseurs à Cheval. On 23 October 1912 he was detached to aviation service where he received Military Pilot's Brevet No.390 on 31 October the following year, and was promoted to Lieutenant in December. He rejoined his regiment when the war started and was twice cited before being posted back to aviation in January 1915. He was assigned to Escadrille MS 38, where he was made a Chevalier de la Légion d'Honneur on 10 April. His citation read:

A pilot of the highest order. Having left aviation before the war, he requested a return because the role of the cavalry, to him, seemed to diminish in importance. He renders the best services to his escadrille which he commands and trains.

His escadrille was redesignated N 38 with the arrival of Nieuport machines, from February 1916. Then at the end of June came his posting to N 103. Capitaine d'Harcourt himself scored the first victory credited to N 103, on 3 August. Up to the time the unit joined GC 12, it had been credited with the destruction of five German aircraft (one shared) while losing six pilots and one bombardier missing, plus two pilots and one bombardier killed in accidents. Victories had gone to:

Sgt André Steuer	2*	Capt Jean d'Harcourt	1
MdL René Ouvrard de Linière	1	S/Lt Auguste Ledeuil	1
Lt Jean Gigodot	1*		
* shared.			

Casualties were:

Sergent Bridou, pilot
Soldat Vinal, bombardier } killed in an accident 13 August 1914.
Sgt Mallinger, pilot
Cpl Vailatoux, bombardier } missing 31 July 1915.
MdL Seigneurie, missing 2 July 1916.
MdL Debrod, missing 3 August 1916.
Cpl Jean Maffert, missing 3 August 1916.
Sgt André Steuer
Sgt François Roman } missing 24 September 1916.†
MdL Alfred Bazot, died of injuries in an accident 1 October 1916.

† possibly shot down by Oblt R Berthold of Jasta 4, an unconfirmed claim.

* * *

Groupe de Combat 13 was formed at the same time as GC 12 and occupied the same airfield for a little over two months, and its operations are included in the daily reports of patrols, combats, etc, which were reported as operations of the Groupe de Combat de Cachy. At this time, GC 13, commanded by Chef de Bataillon Philippe Féquant, was made up of the following units:

Escadrille N 65 commanded by Capitaine Emile Billon du Plan.
Escadrille N 67 commanded by Capitaine Henri de Saint Sauveur.
Escadrille N 112 commanded by Lieutenant Mangien.
Escadrille N 124 (Lafayette) commanded by Capitaine Georges Thenault.

* * *

The star of the new Groupe was, of course, Georges Guynemer, who had brought his score to 18 on 23 September. N 3 had started to receive the new SPAD VII fighters, and Guynemer had been one of the first to have one – No. S113. In the event it only last ten days – until 23 September.

He had fought some Fokkers in the late morning, claiming two with another probable, but he had been plagued by French AA fire. Despite firing off a flare as a signal for them to cease they had not done so, perhaps not identifying the new French type, which looked very different from the sesquiplane (the lower wing having far less chord than the upper wing) Nieuport.

In any event, Guynemer's new Spad was finally hit by a shell which smashed through both right-hand wings, fortunately without exploding. Spinning down out of control, he gingerly regained control, although expecting the whole thing to collapse at any moment, and almost succeeded before he hit the ground. Contacting mother earth at full speed, the Spad was badly damaged but he survived serious injury, with just a badly bruised knee, which caused him to hobble about for the next week.

CHAPTER THREE

Cachy, VI° Armée Sector

As the war in the air had progressed from its first faltering steps in the late summer of 1914, each side had to come to terms with the increase in the numbers of their own and hostile aircraft, which in turn led to an increase in aviation logistics. Therefore, by 1916 it had become necessary to augment the command structures also.

By the summer of 1916 the Germans had begun to form their Jagdstaffeln, hunting squadrons, or Jastas as they were usually known. The British had formed Wings and Brigades, while the French had their Groupements. It should be remembered, however, that in the main these formations were mostly for administration and command purposes. It did not mean that the French and British had begun to fight in units any larger than a squadron; that was still in the future. Even the Germans did not group their Jastas together until mid-1917, and even then they rarely operated all their grouped Jastas at once. Most of the British and French squadrons usually operated only in flight size of four or five machines, and only flew in squadron strength on special sorties.

The first victory for the embryo GC 12 came on 1 November, and fell to Lieutenant Armand Pinsard of N 26. Pinsard was a 29-year-old former soldier from Nercillac, having served with a Spahis Régiment in Algeria and Morocco long before the war in Europe. He had transferred to aviation in 1912. Flying with MS 23 he had been commissioned but it then looked like his military career was at an end, for on 8 February 1915 he was forced to land in enemy territory and became a prisoner. However, he managed to escape in March, along with Capitaine Victor Ménard, the same man mentioned earlier as commander of N 26.

Now back in harness, Pinsard shot down a German aircraft over Lechelle at 15.25, actually between Bus and Mesnil-en-Arrouaize. It was the first day of operations by the Groupe, a day of hazy skies, wind and rain. Twelve patrols were flown resulting in four combats, and one pilot also carried out a strafing run over German trenches near Chaulnes from a height of 200 metres.

However, the next day saw the first casualty. Under misty and cloudy conditions, Caporal Ravel of N 103, flying a Nieuport XI, failed to return from a patrol over the Chaulnes – le Transloy area, that afternoon. It would appear that he was brought down by a crew from Kampfstaffel 25, which claimed two Nieuports this day. One at Bouchavesnes and one at Manancourt, both near le Transloy. Either Vizefeldwebel Beiser and Leutnant Prechter, a Nieuport at Manancourt, about 9 kilometres south-east of le Transloy, or Leutnant King and Offizierstellvertreter Koch – a Nieuport at Bouchavesnes, about 10 kilometres south-south-east of le Transloy. GC 12 flew 12 patrols resulting in 16 combats none of which was conclusive.

The Groupe flew 21 patrols on the 3rd, in hazy conditions with low clouds in the morning with strong winds. They engaged in combat 58 times, three ending in conclusive claims with two more probables. Alfred Heurtaux of N 3 claimed his 11th personal victory, downing an Aviatik two-seater in flames over Rocquigny, while Georges Guynemer claimed a probable. The other confirmed victories were by GC 13's N 65 and a patrol of the other units. One of Heurtaux's victims was probably Unteroffizier Ernst Hanold, unit unknown, who was killed over Rocquigny on this date.

The poor weather continued on the 4th, with more wind, low clouds and haze, but the two Groupes had four combats between them, GC 13 downing a German machine, and although more patrols were undertaken the next day, strong winds on the 6th kept the machines in the hangars for most of the time, although the Cachy Groupes managed a few sorties and one combat. Despite the bad weather, Sergent Baron of N 103 seriously damaged a German aircraft between Ligny and Baulencourt, and Adjudant Hall, of N 103, another over Buire on the 6th.

Bert Hall was an American (not to be confused with James Norman Hall, another American volunteer flying with the French in N 124) from Kentucky or Missouri, whichever he chose to name at the time. According to his own press, he had served in the Turkish-Bulgarian War of 1912, then with the British Army, then with the French Foreign Legion. He had flown with MS 38 before being accepted for the Escadrille Lafayette, but towards the end of 1916 moved to N 103. He was only with this unit until early 1917, at which time he volunteered to go with the French Mission to Romania and Russia. He was certainly a colourful and adventurous character.

Weather improved somewhat on 9 November, allowing more serious flying, the two Groupes completing 30 patrols and engaging in 58 combats. Sous-lieutenant Ledeuil of N 103 gained his second victory, claiming an aircraft down east of Manancourt, while Bert Hall was credited with a probable between Fonche and Sailly-Saillisel. Albert Deullin, N 3, seriously damaged three German aircraft on one patrol.

Caporal Léon Millot of N 103, flying a Nieuport XVII, was killed during an air fight, evidently shot down by a pilot from Jasta 2 just before 11.00. Leutnants Walter Höhne and Hans Wortmann both claimed Nieuports, one over Flers the other south-west of le Transloy. Millot was born on 12 July 1896, at Gondrecourt by the Meuse River. He had received the French Aero Club Pilot's license No.3373 on 22 June 1916.

The Groupes also dropped 12,000 flechettes over Misery, Moislains and Péronne as well as the Bois de Vaux. These were nasty metal pencil-shaped darts, slightly fatter on one end for balance, and sharply pointed. Some were slightly corkscrew-shaped for downwards stability. They were designed for dropping on cavalry horses, or any horse-drawn vehicles or guns. How accurately they could be dropped was open to question, but if on target, could be devastating to close-ranked animals, or men! GC 13 also received credit for a probable aircraft victory.

Groupe aircraft were again in evidence on the 10th, during 45 combats. At 10.15, Maréchal-des-Logis Soulier of N 26 gained his second victory east of Péronne, downing an Aviatik two-seater. He found five two-seaters and despite fire from all of them, went down on one, firing 30 rounds into it, whereupon the machine burst into flames and crashed, killing both occupants. Bullets from the other four riddled Soulier's Nieuport, but he was not hit.

Sous-lieutenant Guynemer claimed his 19th and 20th victories at 12.15 and 12.25. On patrol he spotted four German aircraft, an Albatros two- seater and three single-seater scouts. He went for the two-seater first, a 220-hp Mercedes-engined Albatros, which came down in French lines after his attack south of Nesle. Guynemer had killed the observer after firing just three bullets, and after six further rounds, the pilot was dead. The men were reported as being Leutnants de Reserve Karl Staemm and Albert Eder, of FA 13.

Engaged by the scouts, Guynemer shot one down in flames near Morcourt, probably Vizefeldwebel Christian Kress of Jasta 6, who was reported down in flames at around 13.00 hours near Morcourt, which is north of Chaulnes. Kress had been credited with four victories[1].

At 13.40, Albert Deullin registered his ninth kill over Péronne. Two N 103 pilots, Sergents Baron and Lutzius, each seriously damaged German machines in the vicinity of Saint Pierre Waast, while Sergents Prou and Lannes of N 26, did likewise over Athies. However, Sergent Roxas-Elias of N 73, who had taken off at 08.30, was reported missing in a Nieuport XXI, probably falling to Oberleutnant Erich Hahn of Jasta 1, who claimed a French machine down at Rocquigny at 12.30 German time. Although the time is questionable, this is the only French loss and German victory claim in this area this date.

Another casualty this morning was Sergent Bourdarie of N 103, injured in a crash whilst taking off on a dawn patrol. Other Groupe activities covered 3,000 flechettes dropped on the Bois de Vaux

---

[1] All these and others following are referred to in *Carre d'As* by Jacques Mortane, Editions Baudinière, 1934.

at 16.00 (presumably someone had reported cavalry or horse-drawn vehicles amongst the trees), while GC 13 claimed two combat victories.

More flechettes went down between late morning/early afternoon of the 11th, again on the woods at Vaux, Péronne, Misery and St. Christ. Alfred Heurtaux claimed victory number 12, an Albatros two-seater in flames over Sailly-Saillisel at 09.00, one of the crew believed to have been Uffz Karl Münster who was killed this date at this locality. Over the next two days, high winds and bad weather stopped all operational flying. However, Heurtaux and Deullin were cited in l'Ordre de la VI° Armée No.60, for achieving their 9th, 10th and 9th victories respectively. Another piece of information that came down on the 14th, was that the Groupe d'ordres Escadrilles de Chasse of the Groupe des Armées du Nord (GAN), had destroyed 106 German aircraft and 14 balloons, and probably downed or seriously damaged a further 171 others, during the period 1 July to 14 November 1916.

GC 12 added to this total on 15 November, during 15 patrols, and despite low clouds and haze. At 10.15, Adjudant Jeronnez of N 26 registered his first victory east of Chaulnes, probably Vzfw Hermann Michel and Oberleutnant Heinrich Bauer of FA 7 who were both killed over Chaulnes this day. Caporal Laulhe (N 3), who had strafed Chaulnes the previous day, went down again today, shooting up the railway station from 100 metres. Another patrol let go 4,000 flechettes between Bussu and Doingt.

Heurtaux got his 13th the next morning at 09.30, one of three German aircraft claimed on 16 November. It was a Fokker D-type, probably that flown by Leutnant Ernst Wever of Jasta 6, who fell in flames over Pressoir Wood. Heurtaux, now aged 23, came from Nantes on the Atlantic coast by the Loire. Another graduate of St. Cyr and a former Hussar, he had gained his flying Brevet in 1915 and had flown with MS 38. His eighth victory had been over the German ace Kurt Wintgens back on 25 September, who had scored 19 victories and won the Pour le Mérite before his death.

The mercurial Georges Guynemer today gained his 21st victory, another Fokker scout, at 13.40 to the south of Pertain, while another ace of the Escadrille, affectionately known as 'Père' Dorme shot down a Rumpler two-seater for victory No.16, east of Marchélepot at 15.16 hours. N 26's Sergent Sendral was credited with a probable at 11.45 over Barleux, while GC 13 claimed one destroyed and another possibly so.

Obviously the activities of the units at Cachy were exercising the minds of the Germans, for on the night of 16/17 November, the airfield was bombed. N 3's hangar was completely destroyed along with six of their aircraft, plus several others from N 26 and N 65 being damaged by explosions and rendered unfit for use. One ground crewman, Soldat Mechanic Besseir, was killed and seven others received various wounds.

Despite these problems and the high winds, N 3 wreaked some revenge on the 17th. Guynemer found a two-seater and attacked, seeing his fire knock out the observer. As the machine pulled up, Adjudant Bucquet attacked and set the aircraft on fire and both watched as it crashed near Liancourt-Fosse. The crew was probably from FA(A)226, who lost Leutnant Karl Germer and Oberleutnant Roland Müller (1 ibid). At 15.20 'Père' Dorme seriously damaged an LVG two-seater over Malancourt by firing 200 rounds into it at close range. Leutnant Walter Andrae was killed at Ytres this date, possibly the observer. (1ibid). Sergent Georges Sendral of N 26 was wounded in combat this date, and more flechettes (3,000) were dropped on Morchain.

The Groupes had a break between 19 and 21 November due to the weather, and it had not improved over-much on the 22nd, but Guynemer was airborne and claimed victories 22 and 23, downing two Halberstadt Scouts. One fell at 14.45, east of St. Christ and for once, the Frenchman had been surprised by four of them, his Spad was hit twice, but they failed to do him or his machine serious injury – and paid the price.

He turned on two of his adversaries, both of whom dived away, then he took on a flight of three, firing at one from as close as five metres. This fighter went down to 3,700 metres and ground observers saw it crash. The second Halberstadt went down over Falvy at 15.10. One of the victims has been reported as Gefreiter Robert Michaelis of Jasta 12, who was noted as killed over Guedecourt, which is some distance north of where Guynemer claimed his victories, but only one of the two German pilots was lost in this area this day. Guynemer also heavily damaged another Scout near St. Christ at 15.55.

If the Germans had hoped to knock-out the hornets at Cachy, they had failed. On 23 November more success came to the Groupes, Adjudant Bergot of N 73 claiming his first victory at 09.35, over Fins; his victims were probably Vzfw Friedrich Schwain and Oberleutnant Johann Kohn of FA(A)221, lost over Etricourt, about 5 kilometres west of Fins.

Sous-lieutenant Ledeuil, N 103, claimed his third victory over Marchélepot at 14.35, and Deullin continued his scoring with his tenth victory, at 15.50 over the Bois de Vaux. It seems possible that his victims were Hauptmann Hans Linke and Leutnant Wilhelm Stainbrenner of KG 5, who were both killed over Vaux on this date. GC 13 also put in claims for six victories of which four received confirmation.

Following two further days of poor weather, Bert Hall gained his third victory on 26 November (his first two had been scored with the Escadrille Lafayette). More patrols were flown on the 27th and more flechettes went down on Fins, while a pilot strafed the railway station at Chaulnes once more. There followed almost a week of no flying weather but on 4 December, Heurtaux got a probable Aviatik mid-morning over Rocquigny while Dorme put in a similar claim over Hyencourt at 13.50. Dorme followed this by crashing one of two Fokkers he fought north of St. Cren at 14.25. This was probably flown by OfStv Karl Ehrenthaller of Jasta 1, who was killed operating from Pronville (1 ibid)

One of the greater aces of GC 13, Charles Nungesser, flying with N 65, downed his 19th and 20th victories on the 4th, a Halberstadt at noon and an LVG two-seater at 13.05. Oberleutnant Hans Schilling and Leutnant Rosenbachs of FA22 were shot down this day, Schilling being a two-seat ace with eight victories. In the past both Heurtaux and Nungesser have been credited with their loss, but it would seem that Nungesser probably got them.

Weather once more restricted flying until 10 December, but on the 8th, N 3 was cited for a second time by Général Ferdinand Foch, commander of the Groupe d'Armées du Nord, and with it N 3 was allowed to display the fourregère of the Croix de Guerre on its own colours.

Under the command of commandant Brocard, always ardent, showing exceptional qualities of audacity and skill in combat, particularly formidable towards the enemy. From 19 August to 19 November 1916, it downed thirty-six enemy aircraft.

It must be stated that Chef de Bataillon Brocard was very strict before giving confirmation of victories to his pilots, requiring three independent witnesses for each claim. He also frowned on 'shared' victories as can be seen in the Groupe's Combat Log. (Although other units allowed share victories much more readily). During his ten and one-half months tenure as CO of GC 12, only five shared victories were allowed, and three of these were shared with other escadrilles, so in effect only two shared victories within the Groupe were allowed. However, in contrast, during the last thirteen and one-half months of the war a total of 32 shared victories were allowed by the subsequent GC 12 commanders.

It had become apparent to Brocard that, as many of his pilots' victories were achieved far over the lines, out of sight of the French ground forces, a strict code of confirmation needed to be implemented. On the face of it it almost seems as if he didn't trust his élite bunch of flyers, or perhaps he did not want any fingers of suspicion pointed at them. Therefore, his pilots had to furnish him with type of enemy aircraft, time and locality of the action or crash, how it had fallen (in flames, in pieces or crashed), and he also needed three witnesses from ground units and/or other flying units. Other members of the patrol were disqualified from being accredited witnesses. This seems harsh; if two or more other patrol pilots witnessed a sure kill but if nobody else did, confirmation was not approved.

One example of this was given by Louis Risacher long after the war. He recalled his first patrol with Guynemer during which Risacher attacked and shot down a two-seater. Guynemer attacked first and missed. Risacher stated: 'I was at his right, I shot the German and brought him down. He went to pieces, but he was far inside the German lines. Guynemer came back to the escadrille and said to Brocard, "It's a shame. I just saw a plane shot down, but I can only confirm it alone." You couldn't get a confirmation for one lone witness. But they gave me the Croix de Guerre and two days' leave in Paris.'

In this way, some of the big aces of GC12 had almost as many probables as confirmed victories; Dorme may have had as many as 70, and Guynemer himself had around 35. All the more galling for the pilots was that other escadrilles did not have such tough rules imposed upon their pilots.

* * *

On 11 December eleven patrols and six combats took place, one enemy machine being probably destroyed at 08.45 north of the Bois de Vaux, by Capitaine Ménard of N 26. Lieutenant Armand Pinsard, also of N 26, who had been credited with one confirmed victory, assumed command of Escadrille N 78 on 12 December. He would hold this position until wounded in combat on 12 June 1917. During this time he would bring his score to 16. Upon recovery he took command of Escadrille N 23 during September 1917, and promoted to Capitaine. Commanding this unit till the war's end, his personal score rose to 27. Pinsard had received Military Pilot's Brevet No.210 on 3 September 1912, and the French Aero Club Pilot's Brevet No.1108 on 8 November 1912. He had been decorated with the Médaille Militaire during 1913 for exceptional skill as a military pilot during manoeuvres. He became a Chevalier de la Légion d'Honneur on 7 September 1917, and an Officier of the Ordre on 30 August 1918.

Following more winter weather, operating continued on 15 December despite a day of mixed rain and mist. Adjudant Guiguet of N 3 downed his second victim between Barleux and Belloy. Little further flying was achieved until the 20th, but on this date, 20 patrols and 24 combats were noted. Guiguet registered his third victory at 14.50 over Marchélepot, his victim probably being Leutnant Kurt Haber, a five-victory ace from Jasta 3, who was shot down in flames at 15.45 (G) near Omiécourt, about 5 kilometres south-south-west of Marchélepot. Brigadier Lemelle of N 73 got his first, south-east of Devise, at 09.10. Adjudant Bucquet, N 3, probably downed two enemy machines, the first at 14.15 over Lihons and the other immediately afterwards over Chaulnes. Sergent Baron of N 103 probably another German at 15.25 near Rancourt. The day was marred through, 'Père' Dorme being severely wounded in the right arm during a combat with two Halberstadts over Athies. An explosive bullet sent seven shards of shrapnel into the limb. Fortunately he managed to land and was immediately taken to Lariboisière Hospital. Just over a month later he was commissioned Sous-lieutenant. Also GC 13 claimed three probables and Nungesser got his 21st, an enemy aircraft near Rouy-le-Grand. One of the probables was by Maréchal-des-Logis Viallet of N 67 who claimed an enemy aircraft at 13.15 near St. Christ. His victims were probably Vzfw Karl Bucher and Ltn Erich Sauerbray, of KG 4, who were reported as killed near Licourt, about 3 kilometres south-west of St. Christ.

Some flying was achieved over the next three days but poor weather precluded any real action and it wasn't until Christmas Eve that the next successful combat took place. At 11.20, Lieutenant Heurtaux claimed his 14th victory over Liancourt, while Sous-lieutenant Raymond scored his second above the German lines, possibly Leutnant Lothar Erdmann of Jasta 20, who was killed in the St. Quentin area. Heurtaux also claimed a probable ten minutes later after his first kill over Omiécourt. Sergent Bourdarie, N 103, was killed in an accident flying a Nieuport XVII, one of the few remaining Nieuports in the Groupe, the rest having been re-equipped with Spads. Nor was there any amnesty on Christmas Day. MdL Soulier of N 26 engaged a two-seater north-east of Cernay-en-Dormois, and was credited with a probable.

Perhaps the Mess wine made the pilots more aggressive than mellow, for on the 26th, under cloudy skies with some rain, twenty patrols were flown and ten combats registered, which meant the

Germans were also far from under-the-weather! Heurtaux attacked an Aviatik at 09.45 over the Bois de Vaux, victory No. 15, then severely damaged a scout that tried to intervene a few minutes later, which appeared to crash near Misery. This two-seater may have been that flown by Vzfw Friedrich Rau and Ltn Karl Steinmetz, of FA6, lost this day over Vaux Wald. At the same time Guynemer attacked a scout, firing three bursts from 25 metres into the Halberstadt, causing it to crash east of Misery, for his 24th victory.

Georges Guynemer scored again on the 27th, downing an Albatros two-seater at 11.45 over La Maisonnette. He had fired at it from ten metres and return fire from the observer had cut two cables on his Spad. However, the C-type fell, taking the crew to their deaths – thought to be Vzfw Ernst Dorner and Ltn August Gulting of KG 4, shot down at Barleux, about five kilometres south of Guynemer's combat area. (1 ibid) Then at 11.50 Sous-lieutenant Mathieu Tenant de la Tour of N 3 shot down a Halberstadt over Péronne, thereby achieving his eighth official victory. De la Tour was a Parisian, a 33-year-old former cavalryman and had been with N 3 since the summer following a wound whilst flying with N 57. He was a Chevalier de la Légion d'Honneur and in the coming spring would take command of N 26.

Heurtaux, meantime, had scored his 16th victory, a Rumpler observation machine which crashed west of Misery. The last victory of the day was gained by Lieutenant Gigodot of N 103, his second, at 14.45 over Omiécourt – probably Ltns Erich Jungmann and Albert Holl of FA(A)287, who were killed north of Fonchette, which lies about five kilometres south of Omiécourt. A patrol also dropped 3,000 flechettes over Lechelle and another 2,000 over Curchy.

GC 13 claimed four victories, one of which was reported to have been Leutnant Gustave Leffers, although it is now understood that he was shot down and killed in combat with a FE2b of No. 11 Squadron, RFC.

Winter weather curtailed operations on the 28th although some flying took place, but the weather effectively ended all further activity till the turn of the year. The year ended on a happy note for Georges Guynemer with his promotion to full Lieutenant on 31 December. GC 12 completed its first two months of operations with 31 aircraft destroyed while suffering the loss of just one pilot killed, two missing and two wounded, with two others injured in flying accidents. The year 1917 would bring further challenges.

CHAPTER FOUR

1917 – A New Year

The momentous year of 1917 opened, as had been expected, with bad weather which curtailed aerial operations for anyone, not only the pilots of Groupe de Combat 12. The only significant flying came on 4 January, patrols being sent out to locate two anti-aircraft batteries, which were found at Marchélepot and to the north of Curchy. The first combats came the next day.

Adjudant Lemelle of N 73 intercepted a German machine over Nurlu at 11.30, his fire seriously damaging it. At 13.00, Joseph Henri Guiguet of N 3 damaged another over Roye and a third machine was damaged by Lieutenant Auguste Ledeuil of N 103 to the north-east of Manancourt, at 16.00 hours. Shortly afterwards, Lieutenant Pierre Marie Henri Joseph Hervet, another pilot with N 103, received credit for his first victory over Falvy. Hervet would claim two victories with N 103 and still be flying fighters with the French Air Force in the 1920's aged 39.

Three days later Guynemer attacked a two-seater, one of 14 combats this day by the Groupe. The observer stopped firing and dropped out of sight in his rear cockpit as the pilot took his machine down to land near Ablaincourt – credited as a probable victory. It will be noted by now that French victory claims differed from the British system. Until early 1917 the British often credited a 'victory' if a pilot forced a German aeroplane to land within its own territory. The British would never know if the pilot or a crewman was wounded, mortally wounded, or just getting out of trouble, or if the machine was damaged to any degree or not. The French too acknowledged probable victories but unlike the RFC, who noted them usually as 'out of control', did not allow a pilot to count them in his score. Thus a British pilot who had destroyed two German aircraft, claimed two more out of control and another as forced to land, might note his score as five, whereas the Frenchman's score was only noted as two. After the early weeks of 1917, RFC, and later RAF, pilots could only record destroyed and out of control victories in their score. It follows, therefore, that RFC, RNAS or RAF pilots did not actually 'destroy' a given number of enemy machines, but rather they destroyed a lesser number plus those deemed out of control.

Meantime, bad weather again stopped much of the action until the 20th. However, on the 18th GC 13 was detached from Cachy, moving to Ravenel, situated about 18 kilometres south-south-west of Montdidier in the III Armée Sector.

Two pilots were cited in VI Armée Ordres on 20 January, Heurtaux for his 13th and 14th victories, Guiguet for his second. Guynemer scored his 26th and 27th victories on 23 January, a day of sudden clear skies. On patrol near Péronne he spotted an Albatros two-seater at 10.30 between Misery and Chaulnes and shot it down. This was probably the machine of FA(A)269 lost this date whose observer, Hauptmann Martin Korner, was killed. Forty minutes later he went down on another two-seater, this time a Rumpler, above the train depot at Maurepas. It caught fire and crashed in flames, taking the crew of Leutnants Bernard Roder and Otto von Schanzenbach of FA(A)216 to their deaths. (1 ibid)

Guynemer was in his element this morning. Not satisfied with these two kills, he also engaged an Albatros Scout, forcing the pilot to dive away from the combat, then went after two more two-seaters, again knocking out the man in the rear cockpit of one, and putting several shots into the second. Out of ammunition he saw another German machine over Marceleau and forced it to land inside its own lines through his fake attacks. Having the 'wind up', as the Royal Flying Corps men would call it! Guynemer didn't get away Scott free from these five combats – his mechanics found a single bullet hole through one blade of his propeller! The other bit of news this day was that 'Père' Dorme, still recuperating from his wound of 20 December, received a commission, albeit a temporary one despite his 17 confirmed victories and at least five probables so far, a Croix de Guerre and palmes, Médaille Militaire and Légion d'Honneur awards; one couldn't rush these things.

Due to the fact that the fighting on the Somme had decreased somewhat because of the general German withdrawal on this front, GC 12 received orders to depart Cachy, as GC 13 had just done, for Manoncourt-en-Vermois, about ten kilometres south-south-west of Nancy. N 26 was the first Escadrille to depart, leaving on 23 January.

The great Heurtaux claimed two Germans on the 24th, in two of nine combats fought by the Groupe. The first went down at 11.30 between Rocquigny and the Bois de Vaux, while the other fell between Parvillers and le Quesnoy, at 14.25 that afternoon. The latter was probably Gefreiter Franz Budny and his observer, Sgt Gottfried Kort, killed over le Quesnoy this date. Not to be outdone, Guynemer raised his tally by two also. His first action came at 11.25, diving upon five German machines over Roye, but he was having engine trouble and the motor stopped as he got on the tail of one and he had to let it go. With his engine back on line he fought a two-seater which he forced to land, damaged, near Goyencourt. Although he noted it as only damaged it became the first confirmed kill of the day (see below), a Rumpler two-seater at 11.45. Even so, the two-seater was so nearly saved by Guynemer's motor which stopped again suddenly as he closed in for the kill. Most pilots would have broken away and down quickly in order to save themselves, but not Guynemer. With still just enough flying speed and still close enough to get in a good burst, the Frenchman opened fire and sent the hostile machine down to crash. Only then did he break off and see to his problem engine.

Getting his engine going at full power again, he climbed up and found another Rumpler which was under French AA fire. He attacked and shot it down over Etelfay. His fire hit the pilot, Gefreiter Heinrich Bauer, through the lungs, and his observer, Anton Haschert, in one knee. The Rumpler then caught fire and crashed, at Molleville Farm, both men being killed. Falling inside French lines enabled Guynemer to land near his victims. However, when he came to take off a wheel was broken by the rough, hard ploughed ground. When the ground personnel came to take the damaged Spad away they managed to damage it further and it had to be sent to Paris for major repairs.

Another victory was claimed this day by a Russian pilot attached to N 3 for experience of combat on the Western Front. Lieutenant Ivan Orloff had celebrated his 22nd birthday just five days earlier and was one of the Russian nobility, from St. Petersburg. As a boy he had built several gliders followed in 1913 by his own aircraft which he constructed and named, quite rightly, 'Orlov No. 1'. By June 1914, virtually self-taught, he received his pilot's license while a member of the Russian Aero Club of St. Petersburg. Flying at the front between 1915-1916 he saw a good deal of operational service, both on two-seaters and later fighters. In Nieuport XIs with the 7th Fighter Detachment he had gained three aerial victories over two-seaters in 1916. Later he would return to the Russian Front and the 7th Detachment to gain his fifth victory in May 1917, but he fell in combat with four enemy aircraft on 4 July. For his one victory in France, he received the Croix de Guerre and Palme.

Following a 'forced to land' victory by Caporal Achille Papeil of N 3 at 09.40 near Nesle on the 25th, Heurtaux brought his score to 19. It was a two-seater, downed east of Puzeaux at 10.00, possibly crewed by Ltn Ewald Erdmann and Günther Kallenbach, of FA(A)216, who were bought down this date. At 11.40 André Chainat of N 3 probably scored over Varlencourt, south-west of Bapaume, duplicated by Alfred Auger at 14.30 near Ham. Also, N 73's Caporal Adolphe Lemelle received a promotion to Sergent this day.

During one of three patrols by GC 12 on 26 January, Georges Guynemer, who was without his usual Spad due to the broken wheel and other damage, borrowed the Spad of Adjudant Bucquet and garnered his 30th victory. Intercepting an Albatros two-seater, he discovered his gun would not fire but nevertheless forced the pilot to make a landing at the airfield of R 209 (Caudron R.4s) at Monchy, where the occupants were taken prisoner. Guynemer also landed at the airfield. The aircraft and crew were reported to have been from FA(A)266. (1 ibid) As can be imagined, the Germans were embarrassed to discover their adversary's gun would not fire, while the observer mentioned he in turn had fired over 200 rounds at the Frenchman. The captured pilot also told his captors that a two-seater forced down at Goyancourt two days earlier had its observer killed and the pilot had to have his leg amputated above the knee, which was why Guynemer's recent victory was confirmed. The observer is reported to have been Leutnant Kurt Just of FA(A)234. (1 ibid) Also on 26 January Caporal Martin Pelhat of N 26, who had been shot down and taken prisoner on 6 July 1916, was awarded the Médaille Militaire with this citation:

> An energetic pilot imbued by the highest spirit of sacrifice. He executed two particularly dangerous reconnaissances. During the course of the last one he fell into the hands of the enemy, after having destroyed his aircraft and accomplished his mission.

Guynemer, the hero and darling of France, was the leading French ace by a long way. Nungesser had 21, Heurtaux 19, and Dorme had 17 by this time and were his nearest rivals, but they would never reach his score. Only Fonck, who had yet to become a chasse pilot and had only one victory at this time, would score more than Guynemer eventually achieved, and that wouldn't be until the summer of 1918. Guynemer was still only a Lieutenant with just the Médaille Militaire and a Chevalier de la Légion d'Honneur to his name, yet his name was on everyone's lips in France. He dined with Generals and Royalty.

In the air Spa 3, and probably the other escadrilles in the Groupe, pilots were identified by the number of their aeroplane which adorned the rear fuselage sides. As far as is known pilots kept their individual number while with the unit, although they would change as a pilot was lost. And of course, it was probably not always possible to fly one's own machine if it needed repair or overhaul, the pilot 'borrowing' another machine. However, in the early part of 1917 the following numbers were assigned to these pilots:

No. 2 – Guynemer; No.3 – Brocard; No.4 – Bozon-Verduraz; No.6 – Auger; No.9 – Raymond; No.10 – Rabetel; No.11 – Heurtaux. Later some Spad numbers indicated: No.13 – Guillamet; No.14 – Moulines; No.16 – Bozon-Verduraz; No.17 – Risacher.

* * *

On 28 January Escadrilles N 3 and N 103 made the move N 26 had made on the 23rd, from Cachy to Manoncourt-en-Vermois, in the VIII° Armée Sector, commanded by Général Augustin Grégoire Arthur Gérard, and on the 29th N 73 followed.

Sous-lieutenant Dorme had just arrived back from the hospital and had to catch up with his Escadrille, which took some effort. After a brief welcome back from the other members of the Groupe, he took off at 09.30 in his Spad and landed at le Plessis-Belleville an hour later, then on again to Monte Fourmois, near Rilly-la-Marque, where he had to put down short of fuel at 15.45. The next afternoon at 13.35 he took off for Bar-le-Duc which he reached at 14.15, taking off again at 15.45 to land at Manoncourt at 16.55. Still not fully fit for operations, he continued to convalesce for most of February, but nevertheless managed to fly. Between 3 and 20 February he reached a total of nine hours, ten minutes in the air.

Manoncourt-en-Vermois, VIII° Armée Sector

Groupe de Combat 12 completed its move to Manoncourt-en-Vermois by the end of January, situated about ten kilometres south-south-east of Nancy, in the VIII° Armée Sector, commanded by Général Gérard. The city of Nancy had been subjected to some recent bombing and the Groupe were being sent there to help protect it.

For the first few days of February high winds kept most pilots on the ground, although Heurtaux probably shot down an enemy machine near Embermebil on the afternoon of the 4th. It was the Groupe's first success over Lorraine. Two days later he was again in combat, damaging three German machines, followed by his 20th confirmed kill at 13.25 over the Bois de Faulx. Guynemer damaged a German machine late morning of the next day over the Forêt de Bezange.

The Groupe's first big test came on the 8th. At about 10.30 a force of some 15 German aircraft, comprising eight twin-engined bombers and seven fighters were observed crossing the front lines at Moncel-sur-Seille and their presence was reported. They were heading for Nancy. The Storks were ordered up and in the ensuing combat, Guymener downed one of the Gotha bombers, which fell at Bouconville at 11.15, the crew being taken prisoner. Guynemer's fire had scored 180 hits on the bomber which was later displayed in La Place Stanislas Leczinski, by the latter's statue, in Nancy in order to show the population up close the sort of aircraft that had been harassing them of late.

The Germans returned the next afternoon, 15 aircraft being encountered over Nancy, one of which – an Albatros – Heurtaux sent down in flames at 15.30 between Tremblecourt and Rogéville. OfStv Richard Krone, unit unknown, was reported killed this date at Pont-à-Mousson which is about ten kilometres north-east of Rogéville.

Escadrille N 3 was now mostly equipped with the Spad VII, but its designation would not change until later in the year. The most famous and most photographed Spad was, of course, Guynemer's "Vieux Charles" – Old Charles, this name being painted beneath the cockpit on the fuselage of each of Guynemer's fighting machines, just as it had been on his earlier Nieuports. At one time his Spad also had a red-white-and-blue stripe diagonally across the fuselage.

Capitaine Alfred Auger of N 3 gained his third victory at 15.30 on 9 February by crashing an Albatros near Rogéville. February 10 saw Guynemer in action once more and although the result of the combat was only a probable victory, Guynemer felt sure he had hit the pilot and the fuel tank. It went down over Nomeny at 11.15 but the machine righted itself at about 500 metres only to crash in the Bois de Ressaincourt, about 15 kilometres east-north-east of Pont-à-Mousson. In this case it was probably because nobody witnessed the action that led even the great Guynemer to fail in receiving confirmation. Albert Deullin downed his 11th, a two-seater in flames near Champenoux at 13.40 that afternoon, probably Uffz Hermann Heilte and his observer Ltn Otto Michaelles of FA(A)257 who were both killed near this location.

Guynemer and Heurtaux were both cited in VIII° Armée Ordre No.130 on 12 February confirming their 25th, 26th and 15th and 16th. The following day Guynemer was cited in l'Ordre de la VIII° Armée No. 131 for his 27th and 28th, and Heurtaux for his 17th and 18th victories.

On the 14th, during some fine weather, 16 patrols were flown and six combats took place. Adjudant Bucquet of N 3 scored a probable at 10.00 hours between Domevre and Blamont, while Lieutenant Ledeuil of N 103 downed his 4th official victory in flames, at 10.35 between Custines and Morey. This was probably the FA39 machine crewed by Ltns Max Rolzshoven and Wilhelm Sievert. Meantime, Guynemer and Heurtaux were cited in l'Ordre de la VIII° Armée No. 132 for the 29th, 30th and 19th victories.

During this period from 1 to 15 February 1917, Groupe de Combat 12 had flown 130 sorties, engaged in 70 combats which resulted in five German aircraft being downed inside French lines and another nine probably destroyed inside German lines. Capitaine Auger of N 3 was wounded on the 16th during a combat with four German scouts, being hit in the right side, but the injury did not prove too serious.

In recognition of its recent victories, an important award was made to the Groupe commander and promotions followed. Chef de Bataillon Félix Brocard was made an Officier de la Légion d'Honneur on 18 February, his citation noting:

Chef de Bataillon (TT), commander of a groupe de combat: An elite officer having a high regard of duty besides professional competency beyond compare, and the rare qualities of audacity and composure. As an example, he made the escadrille and the groupe de combat, which he commanded successfully, into elite units that have been rendered formidable to the enemy, and have contributed in large part to the success of the Somme operations by ardent pursuit without respite, against enemy aircraft. One wound, five citations.

Alfred Heurtaux and Georges Guynemer were promoted to Capitaine the same day, and on the 22nd, Lieutenant Jean Richard, Commanding Officer of N 73, was transferred to the staff of GC 12 by GQG Ordre No. 1825 of 19 February. Command of N 73 passed to Lieutenant Albert Deullin of N 3.

Deullin had been born on 24 August 1890, at Epernay (Marne). He entered military service and was assigned to the 31° Régiment de Dragons. Released from active duty in October 1912, he was recalled when the war broke out, returning to his former unit. He received a promotion to sous-lieutenant during December 1914. Entering aviation during April 1915, he received Military Pilot's Brevet No. 2078 on 14 June and after further schooling he was assigned to Escadrille MF 62 on 2 July. He was awarded the Médaille de Saint Georges on 11 February 1916 but was wounded in the arm during a combat on 2 April, keeping him out of action until the 30th. Transferring to fighters, he was posted to N 3. On 4 June 1916 he was made a Chevalier de la Légion d'Honneur, his citation recording:

> Sous-lieutenant of N 3. A pilot of exceptional initiative and composure, ceaselessly looking for combat with enemy aircraft. Wounded on 2 April 1916, during the course of an aerial combat, he returned to his escadrille before being fully recovered, and has had, since his return, 12 new difficult combats. On 30 April 1916, he attacked and downed an enemy aircraft behind our trenches. Already cited twice in l'Ordre de l'Armée.

By the time GC 12 was formed, Deullin had been credited with eight confirmed victories and been cited in orders on at least six occasions.

To indicate the size of GC 12 in February 1917, according to the VIII° Armée Compte-Rendu des Operations on 27 February, it had 26 aircraft available for operations.

* * *

March 1917 began with the Groupe having 28 aircraft serviceable, which was increased to 30 by the 3rd, the date Caporal Vincent Scalingi of N 73 was promoted to Sergent. N 3's Père Dorme was also fully recovered and put into full combat status as March began. During 21 patrols carried out by the Groupe, he engaged a Rumpler two-seater between Lunéville and then Forêt de Parroy at 10.15 on the morning of the 3rd, although he failed to bring it down.

There were two casualties on the 3rd. Sous-lieutenant Auguste Constant Ledeuil of N 103, flying a Spad VII, was found to be missing and was later reported to have been taken prisoner. Ledeuil, an excellent pilot with four confirmed victories, somehow became disoriented and came down inside the German lines. He had been born on 18 October 1887, at Saint Suzanne (Mayenne). He entered military service during 1907, and after the war broke out he was assigned to the 2° Trailleur de Marche as a Maréchal-des-Logis on 9 November 1914, and during December he was promoted to Adjudant. Ledeuil was promoted to Adjudant-Chef during February 1915, and given a temporary promotion to Sous-lieutenant on 6 September. Wounded that same month and unfit for further duty as an infantryman he volunteered for aviation, going to the flight school at Pau as a student pilot on 10 April 1916, receiving Pilot's Brevet No. 3578 on 17 May. Assigned to N 103 on 10 September he was soon in the thick of combat action for which he became a Chevalier de la Légion d'Honneur on 30 December:

> Enlisted voluntarily for the duration of the war, and has always given an example of bravery and the spirit of sacrifice, severely wounded on 20 September 1915, while training his section for an assault and became unfit for further infantry duty, passing to aviation service at his request, where he has shown himself to be a brilliant pilot. He downed a German aircraft on 31 October 1916, and another in flames on 9 November, and a third on 23 November.

Lieutenant Richard Robert of N 73, and also flying a Spad VII, was severely injured in a flying accident on 3 March. Capitaine Victor Ménard, the commander of N 26, claimed his second victory – a two-seater – on 4 March, at 15.10 over the Forêt de Bezange.

Groupe serviceability at this time was about 22 to 24 aircraft, the former being the figure on 6 March that led to 12 patrols being flown. This produced six combats and one that saw Capitaine Auger, in company with Sous-lieutenants Raymond and Dorme of N 3, engage a two-seater at 14.15 over the Forêt de Parroy. Dorme fired 25 rounds from 15 metres, causing the German to spin down, but confirmation was not received and they had to be satisfied with a probable. A further decoration was announced on 8 March, this time the Médaille Militaire awarded Maréchal-des-Logis Constant Soulier, flying with N 26. His citation read:

> Voluntarily enlisted for the duration of the war. He has shown himself to be an excellent pursuit pilot, skilful as well as audacious. He has had numerous combats during the course of which he has downed three enemy aircraft and forced four others to fall disabled. Cited four times in l'Ordre de l'Armée.

Men noted as enlisting for the duration of the war, of course, were the wartime volunteers as opposed to those who had joined pre-war or in the war, as regular service (career) personnel. Mention of someone being cited in orders usually meant that the Croix de Guerre had been awarded with either a palme, étoile de vermeil, étoile d'argent, or an étoile de bronze depending on the level the citation was issued, Armée, Corps, Division, Régiment, etc.

Capitaine Jean d'Harcourt, the CO of N 103, had a lucky escape on 9 March. Engaged in combat shortly before midday his aircraft became riddled with bullets, forcing him to make a landing near Lunéville, but although his machine looked a sorry mess, he was unharmed.

The Groupe was now averaging 25 serviceable aircraft, almost equally divided between Nieuports and Spads. It should be noted that the Escadrille designation did not change (in the Groupe's case) from N to Spa, until the unit had been totally re-equipped with the new type, even though an escadrille might operate with both types for some time. The Groupe had also been busy this first half of March, having achieved 122 sorties over the Front, and engaged in at least 14 combats.

Of the 27 available machines on 16 March, Capitaine Guynemer put his to good use. This day three German aircraft were to fall to his gun. The first, in collaboration with Lieutenant Georges Raymond, was an Albatros two-seater that went down in flames at 09.08 hours near Serre. This was probably that flown by Uffz August Reichenbach and Obltn Wilfried Buchdracker of FA12. (1 ibid) In fact Guynemer related how exploding AA shells awoke him in his bed, sending him running for his fighter. What is not recorded is why he was still abed at 09.00!

The second victory was a Roland single-seater scout, which came down intact 22 minutes later, north of Horville – Leutnant Lothar von Hausen, of Jasta 32. (1 ibid) The third was another Albatros C-type, which fell in flames over Regneville-en-Haye, at 14.30 that afternoon. This time the crew was probably Fliegern Josef Fruendorfer and Franz May. (1 ibid) Guynemer later noted that von Hausen was the nephew of General von Hausen. As all three victories came down inside French lines, Guynemer was able to meet von Hausen after the capture although he had been seriously wounded, and in fact died of his injuries on 15 July, the day before his 23rd birthday.

In the same fight that von Hausen was brought down, Albert Deullin shot down another single-seater, this time in flames. This was flown by the Staffelführer of Jasta 32, Oberleutnant Heinrich Schwandner, who had taken command of his unit on 23 February. He came down near Athienville, north of Lunéville at 10.30 German time.

Dorme and Auger had also sent down a two-seater this morning but it was not confirmed. For Guynemer, however, came further reward for his labours. The President of France, Raymond Poincairé, had actually witnessed his three combats from the ground, so it was a joyous President who was able to present Guynemer with the Russian Ordre of Saint George, 4th Class.

* * *

Groupe de Combat 12 was on the move again. This time it left Lorraine and went to la Bonne-Maison, about 30 kilometres west-north-west of Reims, in the X° Armée Sector (Général Denis Duchène). The move was made in support of the Nivelle Offensive, known as the Second Battle of the Aisne, which would start on 16 April and end 20 May.

On 17 March, Guynemer made it 35, with another two-seater in flames at 1330 hours between Attilloncourt and Attancourt. This was believed to have been Uffz Karl Mauer and his observer Ltn Eduard von Marcard of FA12, killed at Ebelinghofen this day. (1 ibid)

On the 18th the Groupe now sent one of its experienced pilots, Lieutenant Guy Tourangin of N 26, to accept the command of Escadrille N 89. Tourangin was born 22 December 1888, at Vingt Hanaps (Orne) and entered military service on 11 October 1909, assigned to the 8° Régiment de Cuirassiers. Promoted to Brigadier on 27 February 1910, and to Maréchal-des-Logis on 21 September. Named as Aspirant, he was sent to the Special Military School on 15 October, graduating as a sous-lieutenant on 1 October 1912, being assigned to the 24° Régiment de Dragons. Tourangin, like so many cavalry men made redundant by trench warfare, entered the aviation service on 6 February 1915. After leaving GC 12 he was given a temporary promotion to Capitaine on 22 July 1917 and later made a Chevalier de la Légion d'Honneur. By the end of the war he had been credited with four aerial victories.

La Bonne-Maison: Groupe des Armées de Réserve

Pursuant to Grand Quartier Général, Service Aéronautique Note No.16266 of 19 March 1917, Groupe de Combat 11 (commanded by Capitaine Edouard Duseigneur) which was comprised of Escadrilles N 12, N 31, N 48 and N 57; Groupe de Combat 12 of N 3, N 26, N 73 and N 103; Groupe de Combat 14 (commanded by Capitaine Robert Massenet Royer de Marancour), N 75, N 80, N 83 and N 86, were assigned to the Groupe des Armées de Réserve (GAR) commanded by Général Joseph Micheler. The GAR consisted of the V° Armée (N 76), VI° Armée (N 62) and X° Armée (N 69), plus all the above air units, under the command of Commandant Auguste Le Reverend. To the right of GAR was the IV° Armée with Groupe de Combat 15 and N 38, while to the left was the GAN with Groupe de Combat 13.

Lieutenant Mathieu Tenant de la Tour, N 3, was assigned as commanding officer of N 26 on 21 March replacing Capitaine Victor Ménard, who had been credited with two victories, and who was named as the new commander of Groupe de Combat 15 on 19 March. Ménard would later be promoted to Chef de Bataillon and command the newly created Escadre de Combat No.1 established in February 1918, and the Groupe Ménard which also added Groupement de Bombardement 12 to its formation. When the 1er Division Aérienne was created on 14 May 1918, he reverted to the command of Escadre de Combat No.1 until assigned as commanding officer of the Centre d'Instruction de Chasse at de Bombardement (CIACB) on 17 October. He had been made an Officier de la Légion d'Honneur on 22 October 1917, having already received the Croix de Guerre with at least seven palmes. He ended the war with four confirmed victories, and was one of the most illustrious commanders who had served in GC 12 prior to assuming higher commands.

Tenant de la Tour was born in Paris on 5 December 1883. He had served with cavalry prior to transferring to aviation. He received Military Pilot's Brevet No.1919 on 6 May 1915, and was assigned to RGAé where he was injured in a flying accident on 30 October. Assigned to Escadrille N 57 on 29 December, he immediately distinguished himself and was made a Chevalier de la Légion d'Honneur on 1 February 1916, with this citation:

Sous-lieutenant of Escadrille N 57. On 25 January 1915, he was surprised by a sea of fog, from which emerged a German observation balloon, which he decided to attack. He approached it and duelled with the passenger in the basket succeeding in silencing the enemy's gun. He continued to fire at the balloon until he was within 30 metres of the ground. Completely lost and with his motor acting up, he returned by dint of his coolness and strength, landing behind the British lines.

Père Dorme encountered an AEG C two-seater that was engaged on photographing French positions at 1100 hours on 25 March, between Reims and Soissons. He forced it down north-east of Fismes where the occupants were taken prisoner. This was his 18th victory and his first confirmed kill since 4 December 1916.

Pilots known to have been assigned to GC 12 Escadrilles on 31 March 1917 were:

N 3

Capt Albert Heurtaux – CO
Capt Alfred Auger
Capt Georges Guynemer
Lt Albert Deullin
Lt Georges Raymond
Adj Adrien Fétu
Adj Joseph Guiguet

Others unknown.

N 26

Capt Jean Perrin – CO
Capt Kiyotake Shigeno
Lt Mathieu Tenant de La Tour
Lt Daniel Dumêmes
S/Lt André Dezarrois
S/Lt René Dorme
Sgt Constant Soulier
Adj Charles Jeronnez
Sgt Léon Barés
Sgt Marcel Boileau
Sgt Jean Dedieu
Sgt Benjamin de Tascher
Cpl Pierre Devaulx

N 73

Capt Jean Lamon
Lt Albert Deullin – CO
Lt Jean Verdié
S/Lt François Battesti
S/Lt Jacques Ouvrard de Linière
S/Lt Louis Pandevant
Adj-Chef François Bergot
Adj Albert Barioz
MdL Vincent Scalingi
Sgt Adolphe Lemelle
Sgt Marcel Paris
Sgt Roger Tassou

N 103

Capt Jean d'Harcourt
Lt Pierre Barbey
Lt Jean Gigodot
Lt Pierre Hervet
S/Lt Tournier
Sgt Joseph Baron
Sgt Marcel Haegelen
Sgt Georges Lutzius
Brig Chapel
Cpl Degorce
Cpl René Lecomte
Cpl Watrin

CHAPTER FIVE

Spring 1917

On the northern British Front, at Arras, the British commanders were making final arrangements for their spring offensive, planned to start on 9 April. The attack would be along a one-hundred-mile section on the lines from Arras to the Aisne River in the south. The object was to take the high ground of Vimy Ridge and put the pressure on the German Sixth Army positions. Once this was underway and the enemy's attention focused along these sectors, the French under Général Robert Nivelle, the hero of Verdun, would make an attack along the French Front. There was nothing massively new in the idea of a breakthrough into German-held territory, but is was the first major assault since the disastrous Somme battles of the previous year. It was also one planned so that the Germans would be battling hard in the north and hopefully be surprised by a subsequent assault from the French in the south.

The British Royal Flying Corps would support its field armies although in the main they were still flying much the same aircraft as the previous year. The new machines were promised but had yet to materialize although the Bristol Fighter and SE5 (just one squadron of each) would see action in April. The French fighter escadrilles were somewhat better off with their two main single-seater types, the Nieuport and the Spad VII, but many of the reconnaissance and bombing aircraft were still the tired Farmans, Caudrons and Voisins.

Opposing the British and the French were the newly established German Jastas that had already begun to cut their teeth since the previous autumn and whose pilots were simply praying for the chance to show their mettle. The Royal Flying Corps would call the month not just April but Bloody April. Opposite the French was known to be Jastas 9, 13, 14, 17, 19, 22 and 36.

Escadrille C 46, a Caudron triplace unit, commanded by Capitaine Didier Lecour-Grandmaison, was temporarily assigned to GC 12 for these operations. C 46 had been established during March 1915, at Dijon, under the command of Capitaine Legardeau and equipped with the Caudron G.III. It operated on the fronts of the II° and VI° Armées, and during March 1916 was re-equipped with the Caudron G.IV. Capitaine Legardeau was replaced by Lieutenant Didier Grand-maison, and during March 1917, the unit was given the Letord aircraft. By the time C 46 joined GC 12 it had been credited with the destruction of 19 enemy aircraft, while suffering the loss of three killed and eight wounded in combat, and four injured in accidents.

Didier Lecour-Grandmaison was born on 18 May 1889, at Nantes (Loire Atlantique) and entered the Special Military School at St Cyr during 1907. Upon being commissioned a sous-lieutenant he was assigned to the 26° Régiment de Dragons in 1910. During early 1915, he requested a transfer to aviation and on 15 May 1915, he was issued Military Pilot's Brevet No.1977 and assigned to Escadrille C 47. After training on the Caudron G.IV he was transferred to C 46 where he distinguished himself and was made a Chevalier de la Légion d'Honneur on 1 October 1916.

As the preparations continued, it was a cloudy day on the 6th as Adjudant Jeronnez of N 26, following orders to 'blind' the Germans, attacked and flamed the balloon at Veslu at 1805 hours, the observer being keen to take to his life-saving parachute. Inclement weather on the 7th did not keep the Frenchmen on the ground and Adjudant Bucquet of N 3 chased a German aircraft down to 90 metres above Breuil-les-Vesles, forcing the pilot to make a rapid landing near Hourges. No sooner had it set down than it caught fire; probably a Rumpler CI of Schutzstaffel 7.

The weather all along the lines was pretty bad, even snow and fog in the north. The French found clouds on the 8th although it cleared slowly in the afternoon to be a beautiful day. The Groupe flew 28 patrols using 56 aircraft and had many combats. An R.IV from C 46, which was temporarily assigned to GC 12, crewed by Caporal Damanez and his two gunners, Caporal Rivière and Maréchal-des-Logis Theron were in action with a German machine at 15.30, and although Theron was hit in the chest and killed, the German appeared to go down near Orgeval. Another of the unit's R.IV crews shot down a German near the Ferme de Godat – Lieutenant Bloch, Caporal Boye and Sergent Joussen. Joussen was later injured in a heavy landing at Aguilcourt. C 46 also had a casualty at 16.00, one of its R IVs being shot down during combat with four enemy aircraft near Villers-Franqueux, to the north-west of Reims, but not before they had probably downed one of their adversaries over Orainville. Its pilot, Sergent Gendronneau was not hurt but the observer, Lieutenant René Wilmes was killed and gunner Adjudant de Cuypers severely wounded. They were probably the victims of Oberleutnant Erich Hahn, Staffelführer of Jasta 19, who claimed his second victory in the vicinity of Loivre, about five kilometres north-east of Villers-Franqueux.

On this day, Caporaux André Pernelle, Degorce, Watrin, and René Lecomte of N 103 were all promoted to Sergent.

* * *

The Battle of Arras opened on the dawn of 9 April despite poor weather. On the French Front it rained off and on all day until about 17.00 and GC 12 flew little and had no combats. The next day it even snowed. Heavy wind with clouds made things difficult on the 11th, but 22 patrols were flown. Sergent Paris of N 73 severely damaged a German aircraft at 11.10 above Soissons, although he was wounded in the face and shoulder during the engagement. Paris and Adjudant Albert Barioz, the latter in Spad VII No.370, had departed on patrol at 10.00. Barioz did not return. The two probably met up with aircraft of Jasta 14, led by Oberleutnant Rudolf Berthold. He and Offizierstellvertreter Hüttner each claimed a Spad at about 11.45 German time, south of Corbeny and at Berry-au-Bac, for their 11th and second victories respectively.

Oberleutnant Rudolf Berthold was already a successful fighter pilot and would eventually score 44 confirmed victories despite several crippling wounds and injuries. He would also win the Ordre Pour le Mérite; Hüttner would gain three victories.

Adjudant Jeronnez, N 26, downed his third victim at 1050 at Cerny en-Laonnois, and Sergent Haegelen of N 103 attacked a kite balloon at Chavaille, and forced it to be pulled down. Claude Marcel Haegelen was 22 years old and following infantry service he came into aviation and received Military Pilot's Brevet No.2309 on 10 January 1916. After serving in Escadrille F 8 he became a fighter pilot and assigned to N 103 on 8 March 1917. Whether this was his first brush with a balloon is uncertain but by 1918, and then flying with Spa 100, he burned 12 of these dangerous targets, plus ten aircraft before the war's end.

On 12 April N 26 suffered one of those stupid casualties due to pilot error. Maréchal-des-Logis Benjamin de Tascher flying Spad VII No.184, became lost while on patrol and finally landed inside German territory to be taken prisoner. De Tascher was born 22 February 1886, in Paris, and entered military service during 1906. On 1 October 1907 he was sent to the 4° Régiment de Hussards and on 3 August 1914 was reassigned to the 23° Régiment de Dragons. Transferred to the 6° Régiment as a machine-gunner on 18 September he finally requested a move to aviation on 21 September 1915, receiving a Military Pilot's Brevet on 11 January the following year. His first assignment was to Escadrille C 30 on 10 March, then to the school at Buc on 6 October. Now a fighter pilot he was sent to N 26 on 29 November. He had survived just over four months.

Guynemer was back in action on the 13th. Under partly cloudy skies but with good visibility he attacked an Albatros Scout over Betheny which resulted in a probable victory, then damaged another. Maréchal-des-Logis Soulier of N 26 also seriously damaged a German machine, at 10.30 near Cerny-en-Laonnais.

On the morning of 14 April there were a few clouds but by mid-afternoon the weather was clear with excellent visibility. Forty patrols involving 96 of the Groupe's aircraft had numerous combats. At 05.45 Adjudant Jeronnez, N 26, flew over the German trenches at 100 metres north of the Chemin-des-Dames, between Cerny-en-Laonnais and Ailles. He got back but his Spad had been hit six times.

Escadrille C 46 sent one EA into the French lines at 1210 – Capitaine Lecour-Grandmaison, Adjudant Vitalis and Sergent Rousseaux. It was Lecour-Grandmaison's fifth victory, the seventh for Marie Gaston Vitalis, and the fifth for Achille Rousseaux. This was probably Leutnant Otto Weigel of Jasta 14.

Guynemer gained his 36th victory, shooting down an Albatros in flames over La Neuville at 1030. He gained two probables the next day while another pilot of N 3 damaged one and Adjudant Jeronnez, who seemed to be in the thick of the recent fighting, seriously damaged another over Chamouille. Albert Deullin of N 73 gained his 13th victory by downing an aircraft over Festieux, with a second probably destroyed, and Brigadier Rigault of the same escadrille forced a balloon down near Festieux. N 3 lost Sergent Papeil in Spad VII No.117. He had taken off on a dawn sortie at 0520 hours and was shot down and taken prisoner. The details of his being shot down is mentioned by the German pilot who received credit for downing him, Julius Buckler, in his book *Malaula*. In general this what was printed: Papeil had spotted German aircraft over the lines and attacked one flown by Vizefeldwebel George Strasser of Jasta 17. The attack was seen by another Jasta 17 pilot, Julius Buckler, who went down to save his comrade. At first Buckler thought it was two friendly aircraft; several moments elapsed before he realized it was a French Spad chasing an Albatros. Buckler's guns jammed after his first attacking burst. Strasser, now fully aware of the danger, turned to attack the Frenchman, but his guns jammed too. The two German pilots now pursued Papeil but without the means to engage him. However, Papeil's machine had been badly hit in the fuel tank while another bullet had grazed his cheek. His gun had likewise jammed, so all three pilots were unable to fire their armament! Papeil, his fuel having drained away, attempted a forced landing six kilometres behind the front lines, near Prouvais, but somersaulted. Both Buckler and Strasser landed close by, finding the French pilot had already been taken prisoner by nearby German soldiers. In a borrowed car, they took him to Jasta 17's airfield, but the next day Papeil headed for prison camp. He was lucky to survive. Not only because both German pilots had gun problems but also because he was up against two future aces. Buckler, whose fourth official victory this was, would go on to score a total of 36, while Strasser, with two victories already would end the year with seven kills before a wound put him out of action. Achille Louis Papeil was born 27 July 1890, and entered military service in October 1910 in the Reserves. A mechanic in civil life he was mobilized on 2 August 1914, in an artillery unit, and transferred to aviation during October 1915, and had been assigned to N 3 since 21 February 1917. Just after the end of the war Buckler ran into Papeil again shortly after his release from captivity.

Also on 15 April, Chef des Escadrons du Peuty, Chef du Service Aéronautique aux Armées, issued an ordre to Groupes de Combat 12 and 14, and to Commandant Le Reverend, the overall commander of both Groupes. It read, that as of noon this day, the Groupes de Combat shall again, without restriction, resume their offensive tactics, with the aim of the destruction of enemy aircraft, and that all patrols were to be of ten or more aircraft. This was the start of the French support offensive.

And not before time. Général Nivelle had promised an attack by the 14th but word came to General Haig that he was not ready. Five days had now elapsed during which Vimy Ridge had been secured and other gains made, but with the pressure on the Front building, Haig was now expecting Nivelle to honour his pledge to attack the German trenches in the south in order to help take the strain. German reinforcements were already heading for the Arras Front.

On the morning of the 16th Nivelle finally made his move. This was to be the first day of the Second Battle of the Aisne (Offensive du Chemin-des-Dames). The French V° Armée, under Général Oliver Mazel, and the VI° Armée, Général Charles Mangin, with Général Denis Duchène's X° Armée in reserve, went *over the top* at 06.00 hours against the German's Seventh Army, commanded by General von Bohm. By the time the operation stopped on 20 May they had made some minor gains. They had taken 20,000 prisoners and about 150 artillery pieces not to mention heavy casualties inflicted on the German troops. However, the French lost 118,000 men and failed to obtain the original objective of a complete breakthrough. After the hell of Verdun, this fiasco broke the morale of the French troops and many mutinies occurred involving about 200,000 men. Général Nivelle, who had planned the operation, was relieved of his command and replaced by Général Philippe Pétain, who eventually restored the morale of his troops by giving them a rest through inducing the British to carry out attacks on their northern fronts to draw the German troops from the French sectors. This was exactly what Haig had done prior to Nivelle's attack and now the British, Canadian and Australian soldiery had to continue their pressure to help the French rest and restore order. Had the Germans become aware of the desperate plight of the French Armée, and taken advantage of it, the outcome of the war might have been very different. Luckily it was kept quiet, some of the mutineers were shot, and order was re-established.

* * *

Meantime, the French Air Force had done what it could to support the battle. Visibility had been bad on the first morning with low clouds and rain starting at 17.00 hours. At 10.25 in the morning, however, Brigadier Rigault of N 73 claimed a German machine destroyed north of Comicy – his first victory. Brigadier Edmond Thomassin of N 26 claimed another at 14.30 west of Juvincourt, although he was wounded. This may have been Leutnant Werner Utermann, an observer with FAA 218 who was killed over this town on this date. At 1445 Capitaine Auger of Spa 3 claimed a probable over Xures.

Visibility prevented the confirmation of a claim by Sous-lieutenant Dorme of Spa 3. He had engaged a two-seater at 1505, firing 20 rounds into it from a range of 40 metres and it fell in flames about ten kilometres inside German lines near St Etienne-sur-Suippe. The crew were probably Unteroffizier Walter Köppen and his observer, Leutnant Heinrich Wiecke of FA(A) 248 (1 ibid).

Capitaine Perrin of N 26 flew a reconnaissance mission on the 18th, flying low over the front lines in the vicinity of Braye-en-Laonnais, at 16.15. He was met by intense small arms fire and a bullet went through his fuel tank, forcing him to return without completing his assignment.

Dorme brought his score to 19 on the 19th. He got into a fight with six German single-seaters north-east of Brimont at 14.51 and shot one down, which appears to have been Leutnant Paul Hermann of Jasta 31, who was reported as killed near the Bois de Malval this day in a fight with a Spad. He was the Jasta's first combat loss. (1 ibid) In addition, Auger claimed a probable west of Orainville at 1450. On the 20th, there were no victory claims made, but Lieutenant Jean Verdie of N 73 was wounded during a combat.

It was cloudy most of the 22nd, but after clearing skies at around 17.10, Adjudant Bergot of N 73 claimed a probable over Auménancourt and five minutes later, C 46 claimed another over Berry-au-Bac. Then at 17.50 Lieutenant Deullin of N 73 claimed his 14th victory, west of Craonne, which was probably Unteroffizier Gustav Richter and Leutnant Erich Bersau of FA(A) 212 who were killed at Chrevigny, about 15 kilometres west-north-west of Craonne. (1 ibid) Sous-lieutenant Dorme followed this by claiming his 20th during an attack on what was described as three small two-seaters, at 18.35. His burst of 30 rounds from 40 metres caused it to crash near Berrieux. Capitaine Auger gained his fourth kill, a two-seater, over Lierval at 1910, while MdL Soulier of N 26 forced a balloon down near Bruyères. All in all not a bad evening's work.

René Dorme had a very productive day on the 23rd, a beautiful day with good visibility. He claimed four probables. The first, an Albatros two-seater at 07.15 received 50 rounds from his gun, hitting the observer and puncturing the fuel tank, causing the pilot to head rapidly for his airfield. Twenty-five minutes later he encountered an AEG two-seater over Witry-les-Reims and 100 rounds caused the machine to dive steeply. The third combat was with a Roland Scout at 16.38 that afternoon which went down over Coucy-les-Eppes. The final claim was over another Roland D-type over Festieux. He fired 50 rounds into this machine from 100 metres and it went down lost from view. However, Gefreiter Gustav Siebel was killed over Festieux this date. (1 ibid)

Dorme claimed two more probables the next day under clear skies. The first at 09.30 was a Roland Scout over Brimont and his second was during an afternoon patrol, a two-seater he found in the vicinity of Vaucelles- Montbavin , that may have been Leutnant Werner Hecht and his observer, Leutnant Hugo Schneider, of FA(A) 222 who were killed over Coucy-le-Château. (1 ibid) Sous-lieutenant Battesti of N 73 claimed his first victory on the 24th, at 1800 hours over Ste Croix. N 26 and C 46 also claimed probables this day as did Capitaine Lecour-Grandmaison and his crew. Sous-lieutenant Bucquet of Spa 3, forced a German aircraft to land disabled near Chivy-les-Etouvelles at 18.40.

The skies were covered with low clouds on 25 April and nothing of note occurred. The following day Adjudant-Chef René Fonck was assigned to N 103, a significant happening in view of his distinguished future. He had already seen action as a pilot with Escadrille C 47 and had achieved two victories.

René Paul Fonck was just barely past his 23rd birthday, having been born on 27 March 1894, in Saulcy-sur-Meurthe, at the foot of the Vosges Mountains, a part of France that had suffered badly following defeat in the 1870 Franco-Prussian War. Fonck, a farmboy, had dreams of righting the wrongs heaped upon his countrymen although he could not have dreamed how well he was to achieve his ambition. When war came in 1914, he went to Dijon to enlist on 22 August and was assigned to the 1er Groupe d'Aviation. Unknown to his family he had already been taken aloft in an aeroplane and he had ardently followed the early exploits of such French aviation heroes as Védrines, Pégoud and Garros.

Progress and training were slow in coming, and his basic military training was with an engineers' regiment, but by the spring of 1915 he was on his way. Military Pilot's Brevet No.1979 was awarded him on 15 May and then he was assigned to C 47 the following month. His two victories which came on 6 August 1916 and 17 March 1917, gave him four citations and the Médaille Militaire, the citation for the latter recording:

> A pilot of remarkable bravery, skill and spirit, who has already engaged in a great number of aerial combats. On 6 August 1916, he resolutely attacked two strongly armed enemy aircraft and pursued one of them, and by a series of bold and skilful manoeuvres, forced it to land uninjured in our lines. Twice cited in orders.

His aggressiveness brought him onto single-seaters and to Escadrille N 103 of Groupe de Combat 12. He arrived with the rank of Adjudant-Chef, and most unusually, he had also been decorated by the British, with the Military Medal.

The skies were cloud covered during the morning of the 26th, but cleared in the afternoon. C 46 scored a victory over Brimont at 17.20. The next morning, a German aircraft was attacked by Capitaine Georges Matton, commander of N 48, and the chase was taken up by Capitaine Auger of Spa 3. His attacks forced the pilot to land near Bétheniville at 08.00. Auger had four victories to date, with at least three more forced to land and four probables. Under the British system, he would have had 11 victories thus far.

A probable by N 3 on the 28th was followed by Dorme gaining his 21st victory on the 29th. He engaged a German Scout at 10.25, north of Amifontaine, but despite another pilot seeing it he did not receive confirmation because of a lack of ground witnesses, which shows how stringent were the French rules on confirming victories. However, at 1343 in the afternoon, he attacked an Albatros C-type over Fleuricourt and shot it down for number 21.

An aircraft of C 46 was shot down in flames at 18.45 near Brimont, taking Lieutenant Campion, MdL Lamy and Caporal Bousque with it. The Caudron was the victim of Leutnant Walter

Böning of Jasta 19, who claimed his third victory – a Caudron over Brimont on this day.

On the last day of April at 17.05 Capitaine Kiyotake Shigeno, a Japanese pilot with N 26, probably downed an enemy aircraft between Juvincourt and Prouvais. Baron Shigeno was born on 6 October 1882, in Nagiya, Japan, and became interested in aviation. Deciding to fly he gained International Pilot's License No.744 on 26 January 1912. He entered the French military service on 20 December 1912, as a pilot, assigned to the 1er Régiment Étranger. After the war erupted he was serving with Escadrille V 24 where he was made a Chevalier de la Légion d'Honneur on 28 September 1915. He was transferred to Escadrille N 12 on 1 June 1916, but remained there only until 15 June when he was made available for additional training, being reassigned to N 26 on 17 September 1916.

CHAPTER SIX

May 1917

The month began with hazy weather conditions over the Front which made for bad visibility. This probably hindered several combats on the 2nd, for only probable victories were claimed by Dorme at 09.05 hours over Montchâlons, Adjudant Bergot (N 73) at 15.10, between Berrieux and Aizelles, while Claude Haegelen had damaged another over Neufchâtel at 08.05. That evening, Auger seriously damaged another near the Réservoir at 18.40.

The only confirmed victory was scored by Guynemer. He had attacked a group of four Albatros Scouts at 19.15, in the same area as Auger's fight. He damaged one before his gun jammed, but clearing the problem, attacked another which fell in flames between Courtecon and Ailles at 19.35. MdL Soulier smashed his Spad completely in a night landing but he scrambled clear without injury – other perhaps than his pride.

Day three of the month was beautiful but brought only probable victories for Dorme (09.12), Heurtaux (09.53 and 19.35), Guynemer (11.20) and a crew of C 46 at 17.10. However, Heurtaux fared better on the 4th by gaining his 21st confirmed victory, shooting down an Albatros two-seater over Berrieux at 07.15 hours. René Dorme should have received credit for a scout he shot down at 14.00 hours near Amifontaine. Although witnessed by two other pilots, lack of ground witnesses again precluded confirmation. However, not to be outdone, he attacked a German three-seater north-west of the same location five minutes later, thus gaining his 22nd kill.

Guynemer also scored – his 38th – at 15.08, an Albatros C-type between Courtecon and Braye. It appears he took out the pilot with his first burst, but the observer put up a good fight, several bullets hitting the Frenchman's Spad. Guynemer later stated that it was a miracle he was not hit himself. His opponents were probably Flieger Johann Weidmann and Vizefeldwebel Walter Lagerhausen, who were killed over Courtecon this date. The only casualty this day was Sergent Pierre Devaulx of N 26, who was wounded in combat and had to make a forced landing in the front-line trenches near Juvincourt.

On the 5th, Fonck and Lieutenant Gigodot, N 103, attacked two enemy machines near Berry-au-Bac and downed one – a Rumpler – at 07.30. Fonck shot it up and it headed down and east. Gigodot then got in the fatal 20 rounds at point-blank range as he chased it back over the lines at 200 feet and sent the German down to crash despite heavy ground fire. The shared kill was Fonck's third official victory. In the evening, at 19.15 hours, Adjudant Guiguet of Spa 3 downed another German between Bruyères and Montchâlons for his fourth victory.

The Groupe suffered a serious blow this day. Capitaine Alfred Heurtaux, commander of Spa 3, was severely wounded in combat with Jasta 15 at 19.30 (German time) – giving Ernst Udet, who was to end the war with the second highest score on the German side (62), his sixth victory. Heurtaux came down inside French lines and was taken to a hospital. Alfred Auger took temporary command of the Escadrille. On the 6th Capitaine Jean Jacques Perrin of N 26, who had been credited with two victories, was designated as the commanding officer of Escadrille N 76. He had been born 15 November 1885, in Paris, and when he entered military service he was assigned to the 48° Régiment d'Infanterie on 1 October 1906. After the war started he served on the staff of the 63° and 37° Divisions d'Infanterie and was promoted to Capitaine on 20 September 1915. He entered aviation as an observer on 4 December 1915, and then received pilot training and was awarded his brevet on 21 October 1916. He had been made a Chevalier de la Légion d'Honneur on 7 April 1916 and was assigned to N 26 on 18 March 1917.

This same day Lieutenant Tenant de la Tour of N 26 claimed his ninth victory, at 09.55 between Brimont and Orainville. As it was to transpire, this was his final combat success, although he severely damaged a German on the 9th. Although he continued combat flying for the rest of the year, he did not score again before his death in December, in a crash at Auchel.

Dorme was back in action on the 10th during a windy morning. At 10.05 he engaged a two-seater, sending it down in flames near Sivry-le-Etouvelles two minutes later – his 23rd victory. Unteroffizern Max Kandler and Wilhelm Scheffel were killed near Sailly this date. Adjudant Lemelle of N 73 scored his second official victory this day too, at 13.10 between Bievres and Montchâlons. Jasta 15 picked off another of the Groupe's pilots on the 10th. Adjudant Céléstin Eugène Jules Sanglier of Spa 3, took off on patrol at 10.40 flying a Spad VII. He fell in combat to Heinrich Gontermann, who claimed a Spad at 12.30 north of Berry-au-Bac, for his 19th victory.

Sanglier had been born on 30 March 1889 in Paris, and had entered aviation as a mechanic in 1911. When the war came he was called to service with a Régiment de Chasseurs à Cheval (light cavalry), then volunteered for pilot training beginning 22 December 1914. He received Pilot's Brevet No.1895, on 29 April the following year. During his time at the front he had been credited with four official victories and eight probables, and had been awarded the Médaille Militaire on 15 August 1916, with this citation:

> Assigned to Escadrille N 62, an audacious and adroit pilot who has carried out numerous long distance reconnaissances and has had fifteen aerial combats. On 15 July 1916, he downed an Aviatik de chasse in enemy territory.

Gontermann followed up this victory over a Groupe aircraft by gaining another that evening. Escadrille C 46 lost one of their Caudron R IVs which fell into the French lines. However, the occupants were the ace pilot Capitaine Didier Lecour-Grandmaison, who was also the CO, together with Caporal Crozet, his gunner, who were both killed, and Sergent Alfred Boye, who survived although wounded.

Capitaine Lecour-Grandmaison, who had been credited with five victories, had been born on 18 May 1889, in Nantes (Loire Atlantique) and had entered the Special Military School at St Cyr in 1907; after graduation he was assigned to the 26° Régiment de Dragons. After the war was declared he requested transfer to aviation and was issued Military Pilot's Brevet No.1977 on 15 May 1915. His first posting was to Escadrille C 47 before joining C 46. He had been made a Chevalier de la Légion d'Honneur, and also held the Croix de Guerre with five Palmes. Gontermann's claim over a 'large Caudron' at 1820 over Berry-au-Bac netted him his 20th victory. He would shortly receive the Ordre Pour le Mérite – the famed Blue Max.

* * *

Another fine day on the 11th brought several combats and several probables and damaged German aircraft. Confirmed kills were claimed by Auger and de Sevin of N 3 and N 12, their combined efforts sending down a two-seater at 11.25 near Vailly-sur-Aisne. It was Auger's fifth and de Sevin's third. In the afternoon, Deullin of N 73 brought his score to 15 by claiming an Albatros, and at 18.50 Fonck achieved his fourth victory – another Albatros, in flames at Aguilcourt. One crew lost to the Germans this date was that of Vizefeldwebel Breidenbach and Leutnant Adelbert Rossbach of FA(A)237, killed over St Croix.

Also on the 11th, Adjudant Charles Jeronnez of N 26 was decorated with the Médaille Militaire; his citation read:

> After being very seriously wounded in the infantry, and being declared unfit, transferred to aviation where he has shown a magnificent temperament as a soldier. An ardent and tenacious *pilote de chasse*

he volunteers for all missions, and downed and enemy aircraft in our lines on 15 November 1916, a balloon in flames on 6 April 1917, and an enemy plane on 11 April 1917. Already cited in orders.

Fonck gained his fifth victory on 13 May to put him in the league of aces, a Fokker (Albatros?) crashed at Nogent l'Abbesse at 18.30 hours. His first burst disabled the machine and it went down with Fonck following. He was not sure if the German was pretending or not for he could see some slight movement of the rudder, indicating the pilot was alive and well. As he neared the ground the German pilot suddenly pulled up and headed for the lines, but Fonck was ready and another burst sent him crashing.

Twenty-five patrols were flown on the 14th, from the 55 Spads available to the Groupe. These resulted in one confirmed victory, the fourth of MdL Soulier of N 26, a two-seater between Neuville and Chemizy.

According to GQG Aéronautique Note No.14716 of 16 May, GC 12 was to operate in the area between Rethel and St Quentin as needed and requested by the Commanding Generals of the GAN and GAC, but was assigned to the X° Armée for administrative purposes.

Promotions at this time came for two of Spa 103's pilots, Caporal Pierre Schmitter to Sergent, while Brigadier Chapel became a Maréchal-des-Logis on 21 May. Two days later Adjudant Joseph Guiguet, Spa 3, was commissioned but on the same date he was severely wounded in the head by shrapnel over Bazoches. His controls were shot through and his right femur broken in the resultant crash-landing. At 18.30, Lieutenant Hervet of N 103 crashed his second victim near Bouconville. Possibly this was Gefreiter Anton Niemczik who was killed at Festieux this date, less than 10 km north of where Hervet claimed.

Dorme was unlucky again on 25 May. It was another beautiful spring day with a few clouds and light breeze. Dorme attacked a two-seater north-east of Reims and sent it down to crash between Berru and Epoye, but he did not receive confirmation. His probable victims were Vizefeldwebel Ferdinand Wens and Unteroffizier Wilhelm Miltner of Schusta 24b, reported lost near Flers. (1 Ibid)

The day, however, went to Georges Guynemer with four victories, numbers 39 to 42. The first two were in the morning at 08.30 and 08.31, with an LVG two-seater losing a wing and crashing into some trees to the north-east of Corbeny. (Possibly Leutnants Georg Feldmann and Georg Oehler of FA(A)257, who went down near Malmaison, ten kilometres NNW of Guynemer's claim) (1 Ibid). The second was a two-seater near Juzancourt.

At 09.15 Lieutenant Rabatel of Spa 3 gained his second victory by downing a two-seater near Berry-au-Bac. Then at 12.15, Guynemer struck again, this time a DFW two-seater down in flames near Courlandon. That evening at 18.30, he crashed a Fokker (but more probably another two-seater) between Guignicourt and Condé-sur-Suippe, then dispersed a flight of six German fighters while in company with Capitaine Auger. (1 Ibid).

To mar this day came the loss of the great Père Dorme. He had flown out on another patrol in company with Chef de Bataillon Brocard and Albert Deullin at 18.40. Later Deullin reported they had met a group of scouts and a fierce fight began. He saw Dorme send one down in flames before Deullin was attacked by four others, causing him to lose sight of Dorme. We know now that the Germans were of Jasta 9 and that Dorme fell to Heinrich Kroll, an up-and-coming German *kanone* whose fifth victory this was. He would later achieve a total of 33 victories and survive the war. Deullin, as he flew back, saw a burning Spad on the ground. Reporting back with Brocard, neither man, nor the Groupe personnel could believe Dorme had fallen. To date he had been in over 120 combats and survived.

Dorme had been born on 30 January 1894, in Abaucourt-les-Souppleville (Meuse). He was inducted into military service in 1913 and assigned to the 70° Groupe d'Artillerie à Pied in North Africa. When the war started he was a Maréchal-des-Logis, and later requested a transfer to the Air Service. Following various assignments he was sent to pilot school as a student on 13 February 1915, and received Military Pilot's Brevet No.1935 on 6 May. His first posting was to Escadrille C 94, Camp

Retranché, Paris (CRP). He was seriously injured on 9 January 1916, but returned to duty on 1 March and had his first combat on the 13th. His first victory claim came on 3 April for which he was cited. Then came his transfer to N 3 and the *Cigognes* (Storks) on 25 June.

During his time on the Front Dorme had flown a total of 623½ hours. During his 120 combats he was credited with 23 confirmed victories and a further 20 probables. Dorme has been variously credited to Kurt Wolff of Jasta 11 and to Emil Thuy of Jasta 21, but Kroll's claim over the Fort de Pomacle (Fort de la Pompelle), about ten kilometres NNE of Reims, at 20.15 hours German time, which was one hour ahead of French time (19.15 hours), is the most likely. Kroll's report stated:

> I shot him down near Fort de Pompelle near Reims. It was a very fierce circling fight that started at
> 6,300 metres and went down to 800 metres. He suddenly dived vertically and burst into flames when
> he hit the ground.

Dorme's identity was confirmed by a watch he was wearing with the inscription *'Presented by the Lip Factory at Besançon, to M. René Dorme in remembrance of his heroic achievements during the war.'* (1 Ibid)

* * *

Guynemer claimed his 43rd victory on 26 May under beautiful skies, an Albatros two-seater at 10.00 hours west of Condé-sur-Suippes. A probable followed on the 27th, the same day as Sergent Claude Marcel Haegelen of Spa 103 gained his first confirmed victory, east of Nauroy. It would not be his last, although his fame would come with Escadrille Spa 100 in Groupe de Combat 17.

Later in the day, at 18.35, Constant Soulier of N 26 became an ace by crashing a DFW two-seater near Pont Faverger. Soulier would be the youngest ace to survive the war at the age of 19 years, eight months and 22 days. The youngest French pilot to achieve acedom at the age of 18 years, seven months and 27 days, was Sergent Paul Johannes Sauvage of Escadrille N 65, who reached that plateau on 2 October 1916. Unfortunately, he did not survive the war, being killed by AA fire on 7 January 1917.

Soulier had been born on 5 September 1897 – yet another Parisien, and had volunteered for military service on 12 March 1915, being assigned to the 21° Régiment d'Artillerie. On 15 October he was sent to Dijon as a student pilot and received a Military Pilot's Brevet on 11 March 1916. Promoted to Brigadier on 15 April, he arrived at N 26 on 18 June, where he became a Maréchal-des-Logis on 15 August.

The 28th day of May saw Marcel Haegelen of N 103 claim his second confirmed kill, shared with Sergent Félix Durand of N 80, a two-seater down over Chenay at 10.45. Both occupants were taken prisoner. The event was marred by Haegelen being severely injured as he attempted a landing and crashed his Spad VII, causing him to be hospitalized until 21 September.

The stringent confirmation system denied MdL Soulier of N 26 two kills on this day, even though the first, a scout, went down on fire at 08.10; the second 15 minutes later was also logged as a probable – both over Pont Faverger. Deullin killed the observer of a two-seater he attacked over Neufchâtel at 08.45 and claimed the machine as damaged.

The Groupe and Spa 3 lost a pilot on the 29th. Caporal Lucien Perot departed on patrol at 18.25 and did not get back. M/Flakzug 34, commanded by Leutnant Meyer, claimed a Spad over Montchâlons for the first victory of his anti-aircraft unit which was probably Perot. Two days later, the 31st, MdL Auguste Pouchelle of N 26, flying a Spad VII, was wounded in the right thigh during a fight with four German scouts – his machine being riddled with bullets, but he got back.

Two more decorations for the Groupe came on the last day of May, Médaille Militaire to Maréchal-des-Logis Adolphe Lemelle and Sergent Pierre Devaulx. The former's citation read:

> A *pilote de chasse* of exceptional initiative and strength who has constantly rendered the highest

services. On 10 May 1917, he downed his second enemy aircraft in its lines. Wounded during the course of the war.

Devaulx's citation read:

> He departed, as a volunteer, on 4 March 1917, to attack a balloon; he sustained a combat with several enemy pursuit aircraft. Very seriously wounded, he had the strength to return his aircraft by virtue of his great courage and succeeded in regaining our lines under violent enemy machine-gun fire.

* * *

June began with the Groupe having a total of 44 serviceable aircraft, and on the first day they carried out 18 patrols. During a patrol on 3 June, a two-seater was shot down by three pilots, Soulier of N 26 (his sixth victory), Lieutnant de Bonald of Spa 69 (his third) and Sergent Chapelle of Spa 31 (his third too). It was a DFW and went down over Muizon at 18.50.

June 4th saw Deullin of N 73 achieve his 16th victory, which he shot down between Fismes and Bovelle at 09.40 hours. Guynemer was in combat with a German machine over Craonne at 10.30 but had his controls damaged and a longeron completely shot in two, forcing him to break off and fly home. However, Capitaine Auger shot down his sixth opponent over Grandelain at 20.05. During the night of 4/5 June the Germans bombed GC 12's airfield during which two mechanics – Royal and Roche – were killed.

Back in action on the 5th, Guynemer had much better fortune, gaining his 44th and 45th victories. The first, an Albatros two-seater, he attacked over Berry-au-Bac at 3,600 metres; it crashed at Loivre at 17.15. (Possibly Unteroffizier Karl Weingarten and Leutnant Franz Wenninger of FA(A) 287 who were killed over Vendeuil. 1 Ibid). He then attacked a second DFW at a height of 4,500 metres to the east of Reims, but his guns jammed. However, the observer signalled their surrender and Guynemer indicated they should land in French territory. He shepherded them down, clearing his guns while doing so, and when down to about 2,200 metres, the German pilot seemed reluctant to land so Guynemer fired a burst of about 15 rounds. The pilot turned sharply, so sharply it caused the observer to lose balance and fall overboard. The two-seater finally crashed near the Forêt de Berru at 17.30. (Possibly Leutnant Hans Philler, of FA(A) 267, an observer who was killed near Berru this date.) Guynemer is also understood to have engaged a new type of German fighter which was very badly handled, and is said to have been flown by Ernst Udet. Is it possible this was the incident mentioned by Udet in which he confirmed that chivalry in the air was practiced even by the great pilots? Udet recalled engaging in combat with Guynemer in 1917 and at the height of the combat his guns jammed, Guynemer seeing Udet hammering desperately on his guns, refrained from shooting, banked and headed for home raising his arm and waving at Udet. If this is in fact true, many Allied airmen lost their lives because of it.

A few patrols were flown on the 6th and 7th but then inclement weather curtailed war flying until the 12th. This latter date Adjudant Fétu of N 26 gained his first confirmed victory, destroying a scout near Laon. Fonck also notched up another kill, crashing an Albatros at 0900 hours between Cauroy-les-Hermonville and Comicy, bringing his score to six.

In Fonck's book *Mes Combats* he states that his victim was a Captain von Baer, the commanding officer of one of the best German fighter squadrons who had been credited with 12 victories. This has to be an error, as there was no German pilot lost this date of that name. However, the most likely victim was Hauptmann Eberhard von Seel, the CO of Jasta 17 who was shot down by a Spad and killed this day and in this sector – at Montigny. Seel had previously been with Jasta 2 but had not scored any victories.

June 14 saw Guynemer, Heurtaux and Dorme all cited in orders (l'Ordre de la VI° Armée No.486) for their recent (and for Dorme his last) successes in air combat. Three days later Lieutnant

Jean Gigodot of Spa 103, who had achieved two victories so far, left to take command of the newly established Escadrille N 153 and was promoted to Capitaine (TT) on 8 November, and the following day he would become a Chevalier de la Légion d'Honneur. He would end the war with four official victories and have been awarded the Croix de Guerre with four Palmes and two Étoiles de Bronze, and the Italian Croix de Guerre. Gigodot had been born 20 December 1893, at Villebois (Ain) and volunteered for military service 12 August 1914, assigned to the 13° Bataillon de Chasseurs. Then he was promoted to Caporal and transferred to the 22° Bataillon de Chasseurs on 12 October. He was named an Aspirant on 12 August 1915, and became a student pilot on 26 November, receiving a promotion to Sous-lieutenant (TT) on 5 December. Gigodot was issued Military Pilot's Brevet No.2763 on 23 February 1916. His first assignment was to Escadrille N 103 on 21 June, where he was promoted to lieutenant (TT) two days later. On this latter date, the 17th, Sergent Brière of Spa 3 achieved his first confirmed victory.

Over the next week several more clashes came with German aircraft and a number of them were damaged or claimed as probables, but the next confirmed kill came on the 28th, Capitaine Auger sending down his seventh enemy aircraft, a two-seater at 17.00 hours near the Château de Blanc Sablon, west of Pontavert. The crew of Vizefeldwebel Grabow and Leutnant Cassel, of KG2, were both wounded.

The Groupe lost the services of one of their aces on 29 June; Maréchal-des-Logis Constant Soulier of N 26, was re-admitted to hospital and did not return to front-line flying. In addition to the Médaille Militaire, he had received the Croix de Guerre with seven Palmes and one Étoile de Bronze, and the Croix de la Vertu Militaire of Roumania. After discharge from hospital he was assigned to a Military Mission to the United States of America to demonstrate combat flying.

At the end of June Marcel Haegelen was decorated with the Médaille Militaire, the citation reading:

A pursuit pilot of exceptional courage and of the highest military spirit. On 27 May 1917, he downed an enemy aeroplane. On the 28th he was seriously wounded during the course of a combat which ended in the fall of the enemy aircraft in our lines. One wound, two citations.

At the end of June pilots known to have been assigned to GC 12 were as follows:

N 3
Capt Alfred Auger (CO)
Capt Georges Guynemer
Lt Jean Bozon-Verduraz
Lt Gustav Lagache
Lt Henri Rabatel
Lt Georges Raymond
S/Lt Louis Bucquet
Sgt Robert Brière
Sgt Gaillard
Sgt Louis Risacher

N 73
Capt Jean Lamon
Lt Albert Deullin (CO)
Lt Charles de Guibert
Lt Louis Pandevant
Lt Jean Verdié
S/Lt François Battesti
Adj Marcel Paris

MdL Pierre Jolivet
Sgt Gaston Dron
Sgt Adolphe Lemelle
Sgt Vincent Scalingi
Sgt Roger Tassau

N 26
Capt Kiyotake Shigeno
Lt Mathieu Tenant de la Tour (CO)
Lt Jean de Moulignon
Lt André Dezarrios
Lt Daniel Dumêmes
S/Lt Emile Letourneau
Adj Adrien Fétu
Adj Charles Jeronnez
Sgt Léon Barés
Sgt Jean Dedieu
Sgt Pierre Prou
MdL Noël Fontaine

N 103

Capt Jean d'Harcourt (CO)	Sgt Joseph Baron
Lt Pierre Barbey	Sgt René Lecomte
Lt Paul Dumas	Sgt André Pernelle
Lt Pierre Hervet	Sgt Camille Pietri
S/Lt Desquenne	Sgt Watrin
Adj-Chef René Fonck	MdL Chapel

* * *

Albert Deullin wrote a monograph on combat flying which was published in June 1917 under the title of *Pursuit Work in a Single-Seater*, which was later adopted as a combat doctrine and training manual by the United States Air Service.

There are some interesting facets in the paper, recording this experienced air fighter's thoughts on the development of air fighting on the French Front, which was duplicated in much the same fashion on the British Front. In it, for instance, he notes the change from the lone flyer to the small formation as air fighting developed.

One observation concerned the area of patrols, in that Deullin – and presumably others – found that by increasing the number of scouts in a patrol it appeared to frighten off the opposition. "The French patrols succeeded only in creating an empty sky." he wrote. "Everything disappeared before them, only to come back on their [the French] departure. They were hardly ever able to bring down a *Boche*."

The fascinating thing here is that as a fighter pilot he seems much more interested in being able to shoot down the enemy than merely ensuring this same enemy is kept from flying above the battle front, which in reality, was surely the prime directive so as to protect the troops on the ground from observation, artillery fire and possible ground attack and bombing.

Duellin went on to record that following the demise of the lone hunter, patrols of three became the norm in late 1916 early 1917. He recognised too the problems associated with close escort of two-seaters where the scout is hampered by the slow speed of his charge "... because this paralyses the single-seater and obliges it, often at low altitude, to follow the wake of a comrade who is slow and cannot manoeuvre quickly ..." This is exactly what faced the Luftwaffe during the Battle of Britain in 1940 – 23 years after Deullin wrote these words.

July 1917

There was something of a lull on the French Front at this time. On the northern British Front the Battle of Messines had ended with a British victory but the war was no real way forward. On the French Front GC 12 continued its daily round of patrols, initial successes this month going to Lieutenant François Battesti of Spa 73. On the 2nd he seriously damaged a German machine while on the 4th he sent one down to crash near Berry-au-Bac for his second confirmed kill.

In contrast, Guynemer, who engaged in combat with three DFW two-seaters on the 5th, had trouble with the controls of his Spad. While trying to do his best, return fire from one of the C-types hit his machine, one bullet smashing into the engine and another the radiator. Far from being in a happy frame of mind he found upon returning there was a ceremony awaiting him. Général Louis Franchet d'Espérey had arrived and Guynemer was presented with the Rosette d'Officier de la Légion d'Honneur, to rank with effect from 11 June 1917. The citation for this decoration stated:

> An élite officer, a fighter pilot as skillful as he is audacious, he has rendered brilliant service to his country, as much by the number of his victories, as by his daily keenness and ever-growning mastery.

Heedless of danger he has become for the enemy, by the sureness of his methods and by the precision of his manoeuvres, the most redoubtable adversary of all.

On 25 May 1917, he accomplished one of his most brilliant exploits in downing in one minute, two enemy planes, and reporting the same day two other victories. By all his exploits he contributes to the excitement, courage and enthusiasm of those who, in the trenches, are witnesses to his triumphs. Forty-five planes downed, twenty citations, two wounds.

The next day the Groupe had 41 machines available, and those participated in 18 patrols during which 15 combats took place. Guynemer, flying his cannon-armed Spad XII, blasted his 46th adversary during a combat with five DFW two-seaters, sending it down with just three rounds from the gun, at 10.55 hours near Brimont. There was a reason he took only three rounds – his gun jammed after the third! The probable victims were from FA(A) 278 who had observer Leutnant Martin Heiber killed this day (1 ibid). That afternoon Guynemer almost made it 47 but he could only claim a probable aircraft over Craonne at 16.45.

One of the most short-lived of postings to the Groupe was that of Sergent Georges Silberstein who reported to Spa 3 on this day, only to die in a crash during a training flight at 17.00 hours that afternoon. During the morning, Sergent Lecomte of the same escadrille had to make a forced landing after a combat due to his engine being hit at around 10.30. The Spad overturned but Lecomte was not hurt.

Guynemer raised his score on the 7th. At 11.10 he scored Spa 3's 127th and 128th confirmed victories, his own 47th and 48th. The first, an Albatros Scout, went down over Villers-Franqueux, possibly that flown by Leutnant Reinhold Oertelt of Jasta 19 who was killed over Hermonville, situated only about two kilometres north of Guynemer's claim area. (1 ibid) His 48th, another DFW two-seater, was achieved at 12.30 over Moussy, possibly the crew of a FA(A) 280 machine, whose officer observer Leutnant Walter Ghers was mortally wounded over Monssy (Chemin des Dames) this date. (1 ibid)

Lieutenant Joseph Point-Dumont joined the staff of GC 12 as Armament Officer on 8 July. He was born 28 January 1890 and entered military service on 22 January 1909, and was with the 159° Régiment d'Infanterie when the war broke out. He was wounded in action on 17 September and was made a Chevalier de la Légion d'Honneur on 24 September. After recovery from his wounds he transferred to aviation and after being breveted a military pilot was assigned to Escadrille VC 116 on 30 December 1916, then after training on scouts he transferred to Escadrille N 37 on 28 April 1917 where he remained until this assignment.

Sous-lieutenant Georges Raymond, also of Spa 3, was made a Chevalier de la Légion d'Honneur on 10 July, his citation reading:

A remarkable officer. He had distinguished himself many times at the start of the war at the head of his troops. After transferring to aviation he has continued to give proof of a magnificent spirit, combined with brilliant bravery and the highest qualities of intelligence and initiative. Three citations.

On the same date, Adjudant-Chef François Bergot of Spa 73 was awarded the Médaille Militaire. His citation recorded:

A first rate pilot, full of initiative and composure. He has distinguished himself during the course of numerous meetings with enemy aircraft, by downing two and forcing two others to land disabled. One citation.

The Groupe moved north. It commenced its move from Bonne-Maison, on the X° Armée Front, on 11 July, going to airfields at Bergues, Bierne and Coudekerke, all near to the port of Dunkerque on the Channel Coast, opposite the Flanders Front. Here GC 12 joined the Ier Armée under Général François Anthoine, in preparation for the Third Battle of Ypres. In fact the area had already seen an attack on the Nieuport Sector on the 10th which precipitated the move north.

The Groupe would work in close liaison with GC 11, commanded by Capitaine Edouard Duseigneur. It was composed of Escadrilles N 12 (Capitaine Raymond de Pierre de Bernis), N 31 (Capitaine Lucien Couret de Villeneuve), N 48 (Capitaine Georges Matton), and N 57 (Capitaine Georges Herbulot), all of which transferred to this Sector at the same time. The two Groupes were to enhance the efforts of Escadrille N 102, an Escadrille d'Armée under Capitaine Jean Derode, which was permanently attached to the 1er Armée.

On the first day of action on the new front (the 12th), Sergent Naudin of Spa 26 attacked a formation of three German aircraft and shot down one. However, later in the day he was wounded by a sliver of shrapnel from AA fire while out on an aircraft spotting patrol, but he accomplished his mission in spite of his wound. Also on the 12th Lieutenant Georges Raymond of Spa 3 was made a Chevalier de la Légion d'Honneur.

The next day, Lieutenant Jean Gigodot of Spa 103 transferred to the command of the newly forming N 153, equipped with the Nieuport XXIVs at Etamps-Montdesir. Gigodot would gain two more combat victories and be promoted to Capitaine on 8 November. The following day he became a Chevalier de la Légion d'Honneur. At the war's end he had also received the Croix de Guerre with four palmes and two étoiles de bronze, as well as the Italian Croix de Guerre, or to be exact, the *Croce al Merito di Guerre*.

Gigodot was born on 20 December 1893, at Villbois (Ain), and volunteered for military service on 12 August 1914. Assigned to the 13° Bataillon de Chasseurs, he then transferred to the 22° Bataillon on 12 October and promoted to Caporal. On 12 August 1915, be became an Aspirant and was later given a temporary promotion to Sous-lieutenant, with effect from 5 December 1914. On 26 November 1915, he was sent to Avord as a student pilot and received Military Pilot's Brevet No.2763 on 23 February 1916. Gigodot was posted to Spa 103 on 21 June. He scored one victory before GC 12 was formed and another afterwards, so his war total became four confirmed.

CHAPTER SEVEN

Bergues, Ier Armée Sector, Flanders

The first day of operations on the new front, 12 July, the flyers had fine weather until a haze set in during the afternoon, but the two Groupes flew four patrols, one covering a Royal Flying Corps bombing raid. A similar day followed and once again cover was given to RFC bombing machines. Also on the 13th, GC 13 under Chef de Bataillon Philippe Féquant, with Escadrilles N 15 (Capitaine Yves Rolland de Chamboudin), N 65 (Capitaine Lamy), N 84 (Lieutenant André d'Humières) and N 124 – Lafayette – (Capitaine Georges Thénault) was assigned to the Ier Armée Sector to augment the other two Groupes. Among Escadrille N 124's Americans was Raoul Lufbery, who would achieve 16 victories before he transferred to the US Air Service, and Bill Thaw who would later command the American Third Pursuit Group.[2]

Louis Risacher arrived to join Spa 3 on 14 July. A Parisien, born in 1894, he was in England studying English when war broke out and he immediately returned home and joined the infantry. Wounded by an exploding grenade in October 1915 he spent almost a year in hospital. Like so many others, being unfit for the army he volunteered for aviation.

He proved such a good pilot that he was asked to be an instructor, which he did not fancy one bit but finally was allowed to go to the Storks for three months as a representative of the Pau training school, which caused some amusement upon his arrival at Bonne-Maison. He quickly found how tight a ship Brocard ran his Groupe. According to an interview the historian Jon Guttman had with Risacher in 1981(see *Cross & Cockade GB Vol.20 No.2*), Brocard took him to one side and pointed to men such as Guynemer and Auger who were nearby, indicating that they were properly dressed and he wasn't. They had their leather puttees on, but Risacher had not, but he did in future.

Risacher also recalled that at one time Brocard arranged with the RFC to have some of their pilots visit the *Storks* in order for his pilots to become familiar with the British types. An experienced Canadian Camel pilot had a mock fight with Guynemer, the Frenchman quickly out-manoeuvring the Camel and no matter how hard he tried he could not shake Guynemer off his tail.

* * *

Mixed weather over the new few days did not preclude operations but the Groupe's pilots did not meet the enemy decisively until 16 July. On this day Sous-lieutenant Rabatel of Spa 3 claimed a probable north of the Forêt d'Houthulst at 16.15, then on the 21st claiming one confirmed kill. Lieutenant Albert Deullin, the CO of Spa 73, claimed an enemy aircraft at 21.40 hours north-east of Dixmuide, for his 17th victory. GC 12 also suffered its first casualty on the new front. Capitaine Jean Eugène Romain Lamon of Spa 73, flying Spad VII No.154, was wounded and shot down in combat at about 18.45 hours and became a prisoner. The most likely victor was Feldwebel-Leutnant Fritz Schubert of Jasta 6, who claimed the only Spad in this sector this date, timed at 20.20 (G), west of Roubaix – his second victory.

Lamon was born on 27 July 1893, at Brive-la-Gaillarde (Corrèze), and entered Military School at Saint Cyr on 1 October 1913. He was commissioned a sous-lieutenant in the 34° Régiment

---

[2] Major Lufbery, later commanding the 94th Pursuit Squadron USAS, was killed in combat with a two-seater on 19 May 1918.

d'Infanterie on 6 August 1914, where he was wounded and evacuated on 13 September. He returned to duty in command of the 4th Compagnie du 19° Bataillon de Chasseurs-à-Pied in January 1915. He was promoted to Lieutenant on 2 July, wounded on 27 September and was made a Chevalier de la Légion d'Honneur on 2 October. Lamon became a student pilot on 5 January 1916. Receiving Military Pilot's Brevet No.3212 on 10 April he was assigned to Escadrille N 3 on 27 December where he was promoted to Capitaine on 31 December. He survived the war and captivity. During WW2 he held the rank of Lieutenant-Colonel but was killed in action on the first day of the German invasion of France on the Western Front, 10 May 1940.

The next day, the 22nd, under clear skies, 32 patrols were flown with numerous combats being reported. A pilot of GC 13 claimed a victory but Lieutenant Pandevant of GC12's Spa 73, flying Spad No.1543, failed to return. Oberleutnant Kurt Döring, the commanding officer of Jasta 4 claimed the only Spad downed in this area, at 10.40 (G) north-east of Bixschoote, for his 4th victory. Louis André Adolphe Pandevant was born 4 October 1890 and entered military service on 1 October 1911 with the 1er Régiment de Dragons. He entered aviation service as an observer with Escadrille N 3 on 21 July 1915, and was promoted to Lieutenant on 1 April 1916. He became a pilot on 14 October and was assigned to N 73 on 11 March 1917. At this time he held the Croix de Guerre with one palme and two étoiles de bronze. Caporal Eduard Moulines of Spa 3 was injured in a landing accident on the 24th at 12.15 hours.

The next action came on 27 July. Cloudy skies during the morning cleared in the afternoon and 29 patrols were flown including an escort to a bomb raid. Capitaine Guynemer was again in his cannon-Spad, flying in company with Lieutenant Deullin of Spa 73. Guynemer blasted an Albatros over Westroosebeke for his 49th victory. He fired eight rounds from his machine-gun followed by one shell from the cannon from a distance of twenty metres. The lone cannon shell blew the German aircraft apart, the wings falling away from the plane's fuselage. The Germans lost Leutnant Fritz Vossen of Jasta 33, killed near Moorslede about 12 kilometres from Guynemer's claim area. Guynemer made it a round fifty on the 28th. Again morning clouds gave way to a clear afternoon and French pilots claimed three destroyed and two probables. Once again Guynemer was up against a DFW two-seater, which he attacked and set on fire above Westroosebeke after 30 rounds and two cannon shells at a distance of 130 down to 20 metres. It is thought that the two-seater pilot was Unteroffizier Friedrich Thasler. Guynemer's Spad was struck five times by return fire but nothing vital was hit.

A blow befell GC12 as Albert Deullin, the CO of Spa 73, was severely wounded during combat at 09.00 hours. He was hit by two bullets in his kidneys, but managed to break off and land in Allied lines from where he was evacuated to hospital.

The second disaster of the day came as Capitaine Alfred Auger, commander of Spa 3, was killed between Woesten and Zuidschoote, at 0730 hours. Auger had attacked five German aircraft single-handed and during the action received a bullet wound in the neck which caused severe bleeding. However, through sheer determination Auger managed to reach his own lines and land successfully, but died almost the moment his Spad rolled to a stop. The only Spad claimed in this northern area was one which was seen to force land after a combat by pilots of Jasta 8 at Bixschoote, just a few kilometres from where Auger went down. The successful pilot was Vizefeldwebel Rudolf Francke but he only had an unconfirmed victory this day. A 19 Squadron RFC Spad was also forced down in this same area this date. However, this was a morning action and the pilot landed back at base so it is unlikely he was the victim.[3] Jasta 8 lost its Staffelführer on this day – Hauptmann Gustav Stenzel – over Rumbeke, and one has to wonder if he was lost due to Auger's engagement before Auger himself was hit.

Auger had been credited with seven confirmed kills and at least this number of probables. He had received the Légion d'Honneur and the Croix de Guerre with ten palmes. With his loss, Guynemer took over temporary command of the Escadrille.

---

[3] The Spad pilot, Lt F B Best RFC, was killed in action the very next day.

* * *

The Third Battle of Ypres commenced on 31 July under low clouds, with rain coming in the evening. The British Fifth Army under General Sir Hubert Gough struck the main blow on a seven and a half mile front, with his right flank being protected by General Sir Herbert Plummer's Second Army, and his left flank by Général François Anthoine's French Ier Armée. The weather was not conducive to good ground operations and August 1917 was to prove to be the wettest ever in over thirty years. The British suffered about 300,000 casualties, and the Germans used mustard gas for the first time – and a new innovation was adopted by the Luftstreitkräfte (German Air Force), strafing troops on the ground. Although the operation was costly (like so many other offensives) it did serve the purpose of taking the pressure off the French Armées down on the French Front for a time, allowing them finally to quell the mutinies and great morale problems in the ranks that arose out of the costly Nivelle offensive. In all the battle was to last until 7 December, including the fighting for Hill 70 during August.

As for the three Groupes in Flanders, inclement weather prevented operations over the first three days of August, and only improved enough for six patrols on the 4th. In l'Ordre de l'Armée No.291 of 5 August 1917, Escadrille Spa 3 was cited for the third time by the Commanding General of the X° Armée:

> A brilliant *escadrille de chasse*. Has fought on all fronts, without respite, for two years, demonstrating the most magnificent spirit and above all an outstanding sense of sacrifice. Under the orders of Capitaine Heurtaux, himself wounded by the enemy, took part in the Champagne and Lorraine operations. During this period it downed 53 German aircraft, which brings the number of its victories to 128 aircraft officially destroyed and 132 others damaged.

The same 5 August, GC12 and GC11 were in action, GC 12 damaging at least six hostile aircraft, one of which was credited to Sous-lieutenant Rabatel at 16.55 between Merckem and the Forêt d'Houthulst, while GC11 scored a probable. Alfred Heurtaux arrived back on the 6th to take command of Spa 3 three months after the wound that put him in hospital and out of action. Also on the 6th by virtue of the 1er Armée Ordre Général No.14 "D.E.", Maréchal-des-Logis Constant Soulier of N 26 was decorated with the Roumanian Croix de la Vertue Militaire de 2nd Classe.

The weather seriously disrupted flying and air actions, and it wasn't until the 9th that two more victories were achieved. Spa 103, led by Capitaine d'Harcourt, escorted bombers but over Dixmuide the two-seaters were attacked by two large groups of German fighters. Most of the Spa 103 pilots went to the bombers' aid and Fonck spotted a two-seater Sopwith which had become separated from the others and was under attack from three German scouts. He attacked and claimed a Fokker in flames on his first diving pass, north-west of Dixmuide for his seventh confirmed victory. A GC13 pilot, Adjudant Borde of N 65, also had a confirmed kill over Clerkem, near Dunkerque.

It is often difficult to assess who was fighting who in these combats. For instance on the 10th, two German aircraft were claimed as probables by GC12. German Kofl 4 Reports show that Leutnant Eberhard Mohnicke of Jasta 11 was lightly wounded in one foot, and Leutnant Oskar Rousselle of Jasta 4 was wounded at 20.00 hours near Artioshoek, and Leutnant Erwin Böhme of Jasta 29 also wounded. The latter had been attacking a two-seater when he was surprised by an attack by a scout that came up beneath him, a bullet hitting his right hand. Lieutenant Lagache of Spa 3 had engaged an enemy aircraft in combat east of Dixmuide, at 15.15 hours and Adjudant Fonck engaged another at 17.15 hours near Ypres.

Groupe de Combat 13 departed for the II° Armée Sector on 11 August, leaving just GC12 and GC11 in the north. Also on this date one flight of six Spads from Spa 3 were fired on by German anti-aircraft positions and four of them were riddled by shrapnel, but the pilots were not harmed. The following morning, Spa 3, Spa 26 and Spa 103 moved to St Pol-sur-Mer, situated in the outskirts of Dunkerque. During the move patrols were still flown and again two probables were claimed. Kofl 4

Reports show that Vizefeldwebel Julius Buckler of Jasta 17 was wounded; Leutnant Erich Schlegelmilch of Jasta 29 was killed over the Forêt d'Houthulst during a fight with Spads. Unteroffizier Friedrich Wassermann of Jasta 27 was killed near Kortenje (but by 7 Squadron RFC) and Gefreiter Willim and Leutnant Faber of KG 4 were missing in action.

Also on the 12th, Guynemer received a citation in l'Ordre de la 1er Armée No.33 in recognition of his 46th, 47th and 48th victories. Capitaines d'Harcourt and Auger, and Lieutenant Deullin were also cited in this ordre. Other news came via the Ier Armée Décision No.364 that Chef de Bataillon Brocard, the CO of GC12, would assume command of the groupes de combat of the Ier Armée upon the departure of Chef d'Escadron Auguste Le Reverend. Furthermore, Adjudant Gustave Naudin of Spa 26 received the Médaille Militaire with the following citation:

> A pilot, who through his spirit, ability, courage and contempt for danger, has won everyone's admiration. On 12 July 1917, he resolutely attacked a group of three enemy aircraft that were flying over their own lines, and downed one of them. Taking off a second time the same day, to carry out aircraft spotting, he was wounded by shrapnel but completed his mission in spite of violent anti-aircraft fire. Already cited in orders.

Further recognition came for Alfred Heurtaux on the 13th, the King of Belgium making him a Chevalier de l'Ordre de Léopold, and the same day making René Fonck a Chevalier de la Couronne. The following day King Albert, in company with Général Henri Philippe Omer Pétain, the hero of Verdun, made Guynemer a Chevalier de l'Ordre de Léopold.

A story of Georges Guynemer, possibly apocryphal, was that he was asked about this time, having received so many awards and decorations, what possible further honour he could expect. His laconic reply was: "the wooden cross." It was a busy time for King Albert for on the 15th, Lieutenant Mathieu Tenant de la Tour was also made a Chevalier de l'Ordre de Léopold.

Maréchal-des-Logis Lemelle of Spa 73 downed his third victim east of the Forêt d'Houthulst with a second claimed as a probable in the same location on 14 August. German Kofl 4 Reports show three losses on this front: Leutnant Kurt Wolff of Jasta 11 wounded at 0920 over Zillebeke Lake; Jasta 4's Leutnant Alfred Hübner, killed over Moorslede at 2035, and Vizefeldwebel Haass of Jasta 29, wounded severely in the neck, time not recorded.

Caporal Oliver Chadwick, an American with the Lafayette Flying Corps[4] who had joined this Escadrille on 28 July 1917, flying Spad No.1429, was killed during combat north of Bixschoote at 09.45. He had been part of a three-man patrol but became separated. Flying alone he noticed a British Sopwith being attacked by an Albatros, with two others hovering above. He immediately went to the Sopwith's aid and was in turn attacked by the two other Germans. His probable victor was Oberleutnant Wilhelm Reinhard of Jasta 11 who claimed a Spad at 1050 (G) near Boesinghe, for his fourth victory. Reinhard had, just minutes earlier, downed his third, a 9 Squadron RFC RE8 observation plane. He would go on to score 20 victories, win the Pour le Mérite and command JGI after Manfred von Richthofen was killed on 21 April 1918, but would himself die in a crash a short time later on 3 July 1918, while testing a new aircraft.

Chadwick came from Lowell, Massachusetts, where he was born on 23 September 1888. He graduated from Harvard College in 1911 and from Harvard Law School three years later. He was also a keen athlete and among other things played goal on the College hockey team and was a coach for the Varsity track teams. Entering a law firm he then tried to enlist when the war in Europe started but was unable to do so in Canada because he was an American. Therefore he joined the US army and in 1916 spent four months at the Mexican Border with the 1st Regiment of the Massachusetts Field Artillery. Later he began flying lessons with Curtiss, and once he had overcome the basics, sailed for France and entered the Foreign Legion on 22 January 1917 and transferred to French Aviation,

---

[4]The Escadrille Lafayette could only take so many pilots, so other US volunteers officially served in the Lafayette Flying Corps, from where they would be assigned to other French units.

gaining his Military Pilot's Brevet on 4 May.

On the fateful day, Chadwick was not down to fly but went to the flying field in the hope of making some sort of flight. A patrol was about to leave and being one man short he took the slot, taking off at 09.00. In July 1919, Chadwick's Croix de Guerre was presented personally to Chadwick's father by Baron d'Estournelles de Constant, Senator of France. He also received the war medal from the Aero Club of America in January 1918, which was inscribed:

> In recognition of the services rendered to France and her Allies for the cause of humanity this certificate has been issued to Serg't Oliver M Chadwick who served during the European war in the capacity of pilot in the Lafayette Escadrille, killed on Aug. 14, 1917: thereby in a measure repaying the great debt which America owes France and contributing to the victory of Liberty and Civilization over military autocracy.

* * *

Twenty-nine patrols were sent out on 16 August despite violent winds in the afternoon. During these two German aircraft were destroyed with two more probables. Lieutenant Raymond of Spa 3 gained his fourth victory at 0832 hours over Houthulst Forest – possibly the machine flown by Vizefeldwebel Walter Hoffmann of Jasta 36, killed near Merckem, about 10 kilometres west of the Forest area. Kofl 4 also noted the loss of Vizefeldwebel Anton Schraeder of Jasta 31, near Ypres, while Leutnant Ehlers of Jasta 17 was wounded on this date.

However, Spa 3 lost two pilots during the day; firstly Sous-lieutenant Henri Rabatel, flying a Spad VII, during an engagement with German Scouts. Wounded and forced down he was taken prisoner at 0920, by Oberflugmeister Kurt Schönfelder of Jasta 7. Caporal Cornet also failed to get home and he too was later reported to be a prisoner. Rabatel's Spad was No.1639 which was taken intact. It carried the number "10" and the inscription *Dick*. The third casualty was that of Maréchal-des-Logis Seigneurie of Spa 103, wounded by anti-aircraft fire during a patrol, and sent to hospital; he returned to duty on 12 September.

Other Spads claimed by the Germans this date and in this sector were by Offizierstellvertreter Johannes Klein of Jasta 18, over Passchendaele; Oberleutnant Bruno Loerzer of Jasta 26 at 0935 (G) over Langemarck, and by Unteroffiziern Emmerich and Brandl a crew of Schutzstaffel 24, east of Bellewaarde. Klein seems certain to have downed Cornet for Loerzer's victim was a British Spad from 19 Squadron RFC. It was Klein's first kill of an eventual 16, scored mostly with Jasta 15 in 1918. For Schönfelder, Rabatel was his second of an eventual 13 victories before his own death on 26 June 1918.

Rabatel had been born on 14 August 1894, (so was just two days past his 23rd birthday), at Monragnirm (Isère) and he received Military Pilot's Brevet No.2929 on 14 June 1915 and prior to becoming a fighter pilot and had flown two-seaters. He had been credited with two official victories and had been awarded the Médaille Militaire on 3 March 1916:

> Maréchal-des-Logis Rabatel, pilot in the 3° groupe de bombardement VC 111: a very good pilot of an avion-canon with excellent control. On 6 February 1916, during the course of a surveillance mission over the lines, he saw a lone balloon which he attacked in spite of violent wind which constrained his return and in an area frequented by enemy aircraft. Having no fear he descended several metres to facilitate his attack and flamed the balloon, after having fired ten projectiles. He came under violent fire which badly damaged a longeron and a control cable. Nevertheless, by grace of his composure and skill, he returned his aircraft to our lines. His machine had been hit fourteen times, and his clothing had holes from shrapnel.

On the 17th of August two victories were scored, both by Guynemer near Dixmuide. His first, a two-seater Albatros, went down at 09.20 and crashed near Wladsloo, thought to be Leutnant Ernst

Schwartz and Oberleutnant Robert Fromm of FA(A) 233. (1 ibid) Five minutes later he shot down a DFW in flames south of Dixmuide, with a shell from his cannon. This was probably crewed by Unteroffizier Johann Neuenhoff and Leutnant Ulrich von Leyser of FA 40, who were both killed near Thourout. (1 ibid) These were Guynemer's 51st and 52nd victories.

Caporal George E Turnure, Jr, an American flying with Spa 103, was injured in an accident on the 17th, and his Spad was badly smashed.

Georges Guynemer rarely rested on his laurels, so it was no surprise that he was out the next day despite generally windy conditions. GC12 claimed one victory on this 18th day of August and another probable. The first went down under the guns of Sergent Hénin of Spa 3, a German machine which crashed in flames near the Forêt d'Houthulst, while the probable was Guynemer's. Kofl 4 Reports show that Leutnant Albrecht Weinschenk of Jasta 18 was slightly wounded this date, and that Vizefeldwebel Otto Gerbig of the same unit was mortally wounded at 20.45 hours over Passchendaele. Caporal Julian Cornell Biddle, another American with GC12, and service with Spa 73, took off on a training flight at 10.20 in the morning near to Dunkerque and did not get home. He was later reported to have crashed into the sea a few kilometres west of the port, but only fragments of his Spad were found floating on the water. Jasta 31 claimed a Spad over Bixschoote, but as this is more than 30 kilometres south-east of the coast and well inland, it is doubtful if they were related in any way. Biddle was born on 13 March 1890, at Andalusea, Pennsylvania. He received French Aéro Club Pilot's Brevet No.6990, and entered French Aviation Service on 25 May 1917, and had joined Spa 73 on 11 August, just one week before he was killed.

Sunday, 19 August 1917, saw Fonck claim his eighth victory, an Albatros two-seater which came down in the front-line area. It may well have been the machine of FA(A) 250 Vizefeldwebel Walter Gabriel and Leutnant Carl Gottlieb Otto Splitgerber who were taken prisoner near Hollebeke. The next day Guynemer gained his 53rd and final victory – another DFW – in flames over Poperinghe. One of the occupants was probably Unteroffizier Martin Ewald who was killed at this location this date. (1 ibid) Guynemer also stated he came across a British DH4 which fired on him and he returned the fire and the 'Four' made off for the German lines. Was this in fact a German or a captured British aeroplane? In any event, his score of 53 was reached flying his normally armed *Vieux Charles* and not his cannon-armed Spad. He had been having trouble with this and had flown it to Paris on a couple of occasions for repair. He had also visited his home. There is little doubt that he was very tired at this stage and no doubt could have done with an extended rest. As it was all he could do was to grab short respites when he flew his Spad to Paris to have it examined, although he did spend the first few days of September at Compiègne with his family. Meantime, the British awarded him the Distinguished Service Cross by order of General Hugh Trenchard, head of the RFC in France.

* * *

On 19 and 20 August Fonck scored victories nine and ten, but on the latter date, Sous-lieutenant André Dezarrois of Spa 26 and Lieutenant Paul Dumas of Spa 103 were both wounded. Fonck made it eleven on the 22nd north-east of Ypres, but this was the final claim by GC 12 for the month. GC 11 put in a couple of claims however.

Sergent Jean Hénin, Adolphe Lemelle, Léon Barés and Pierre Petit of GC 12 were all promoted to Adjudant as the month ended. On the 30th Guynemer was cited for his 49th, 50th and 51st victories in l'Ordre Général No.38 de la 1er Armée. Raymond, Fonck, Hénin and Lemelle were all cited in the same ordre for their recent claims. Then on 1 September, Deullin, who had been wounded on 28 July, returned to take over command of Spa 73.

Almost immediately this was offset by Heurtaux being wounded again, on the evening of 3 September. He took off on a test flight in a new Spad, in order to check-out its motor, guns and new gun sight. He climbed to 6,800 metres and test fired the guns towards the open sea. Later, as he approached Ypres, he saw an enemy aeroplane below him and descended to engage. In his first attack his fire passed below the German, so Heurtaux adjusted the sights and fired again; this time the guns jammed. As he passed over the German the terrified pilot raised his arms as if surrendering, so Heurtaux pulled around and took station behind and to the right of the hostile machine and proceeded to clear his guns, but they jammed again when he tried to fire them and as he broke away to curve down, he was hit in the left thigh by several bullets. Obviously the German pilot had noticed the Frenchman was having trouble and took the opportunity to attack.

Heurtaux was able to elude further fire and went down to make a safe landing, all the while trying desperately to stem the flow of blood with his right hand, controlling the Spad with his left. After he landed inside the British lines near Pervyse, he found his oil line had also been shot through. Later released from hospital, he was pronounced unfit for operational flying so was sent to America to lecture on combat flying and tactics. In addition to having been made a Chevalier de la Légion d'Honneur, he held the Croix de Guerre with 15 palmes and two étoiles de bronze. The German pilot that probably shot him down was Leutnant Otto Kunst of Jasta 7. Kunst ended the war with a single kill, but this was not the one for he was unable to have it confirmed by 'higher authority.'

GQG Ordres des Nominations, Aéronautique, No.1333, 1343, 1351Q, 1364 and 1365, as announced in the 1er Armée Décision No.390, promoted the following GC 12 pilots: Sergents Henin, Barés, Petit, Baron to Adjudants. Chef de Bataillon Brocard, the CO of GC 12, was ordered to Paris by GQG Telegram No.1235 dated 2 September, to assist in a meeting of the Commission on Armament.

The Groupe's next confirmed victory came on 9 September, Sergent Pernell of Spa 103 scoring his first kill north-east of Ypres. However, this was offset the next day as Adjudant Pierre Petit-Dariel of Spa 3, was wounded in combat. GC 11 suffered a grievous loss on the 10th, losing Capitaine Georges Matton, the commanding officer of Spa 48, shot down and killed over Keyem at 19.05 (G). According to Kofl 4 Reports the Frenchman was credited to Leutnant Josef Jacobs of Jasta 7 as his seventh of an eventual 48 victories.

CHAPTER EIGHT

September 1917 – Guynemer Falls

The weather was beautiful on Tuesday, 11 September 1917 and 19 patrols by GC 12 produced 18 combats during which two German aircraft were probably destroyed. A severe blow to the Groupe came with the loss of Capitaine Georges Guynemer, hero and darling of France. Commanding Officer of Escadrille Spa 3, victor in 89 combats, resulting in 53 confirmed kills, he departed on patrol at 08.35 hours accompanied by Sous-lieutenant Benjamin Bozon-Verduraz.

Georges Marie Ludovic Jules Guynemer was born on 24 December 1894, in Paris. He volunteered for the duration of the war on 23 November 1914 and was sent to the aviation school at Pau to train as a mechanic. Although he became a good mechanic he was not satisfied with this, so requested to be trained as a pilot and his application was accepted. His training began on 20 March 1915 and in a little over a month, on 26 April, he received Military Pilot's Brevet No.1832. He was promoted to Caporal on 8 May and assigned to Escadrille MS 3 on 8 June, a unit he remained with until his death. Guynemer scored the second victory achieved by MS 3, which as the designation indicates, was equipped with the Morane-Saulnier machines, the two-seater "L" Parasol, (a single-engined high-wing monoplane), on 19 July in company with Soldat Guerder his observer. He was promoted to Sergent on 20 July and decorated with the Médaille Militaire the following day:

> A pilot of great spirit and daring, willing to carry out the most perilous assignments. After a relentless chase he engaged a German aircraft in combat which ended in its bursting into flames and crashing.

By September 1915 MS 3, having re-equipped with various Nieuport single-seaters, had its designation changed to N 3, and as a fighter pilot Guynemer began to excel. On 24 December – his 21st birthday – after his fourth victory, he was made a Chevalier de la Légion d'Honneur:

> A pilot of great gallantry, a model of devotion to duty and courage. During the course of the past six months he has fulfilled two missions of a special nature requiring the highest spirit of self sacrifice, and has engaged in thirteen combats of which two have terminated in the destruction of the enemy aircraft in flames.

Sergent Guynemer was given a temporary promotion to Sous-lieutenant on 4 March 1916 but was wounded in combat 13 days later. He was soon back with his escadrille and began to score steadily against the Germans. At the time of his death, in addition to the decorations mentioned above, he had received the Croix de Guerre with 25 palmes; the Roumanian Croix de 2 Class de l'Ordre de Michel de Brave; the Serbian Karageorges epee de 4 Classe; the Insigne de l'Ordre Portugais de la Tour 3 Classe; been made an Officer de l'Ordre de Léopold of Belgium; given the Russian Ordre de St.Michel et de Saint Georges; and the British Distinguished Service Order. By 11 September 1917, Guynemer had flown a total of 755 hours in the air, 666 of these over the front lines.

The sequence of events on 11 September is as follows. At 08.35 Guynemer, flying a Spad XIII, departed with Bozon-Verduraz towards the east along the North Sea coast, then turned south-east and approached the German lines over 'No Man's Land', heading for and passing over Bixschoote. They then followed the route Bixschoote to Langemarck and were over the ruins of Poelkapelle, at 4,000 metres height, when Guynemer saw a lone Rumpler CIV below. At 09.25 he attacked. Also in the area was Louis Risacher, who, according to him, had been asked to fly low down with another pilot – to attract the enemy.

As the action began, Bozon-Verduraz noticed a flight of eight Albatros DIIIs to the east and tried to distract them so his leader could finish off the two-seater. His ruse worked and the German fighters engaged him, and after a short time, they peeled off one by one, disappearing from the scene. When Bozon-Verduraz returned to the area where he had last seen Guynemer the sky was empty. He did not give this much thought as Guynemer had always arrived home safely, and he assumed they had merely became separated from each other's sight.

With his fuel running low, Bozon-Verduraz headed for base but at 10.20, flying at about 3,900 metres, he engaged a two-seater himself, but had to break off the attack when he had a gun stoppage. He then flew home, only to discover that his leader had not landed ahead of him. There was still no reason for major concern, but as the minutes ticked by it soon became apparent that Guynemer's fuel would be finished. Everyone expected a call from another airfield to say that he had landed there, but the telephones remained ominously silent. Soon it was the Groupe officers who were telephoning the forward areas for news.

Risacher landed to confirm seeing Guynemer in action and he thought he had been hit while attacking the two-seater as he had seen Guynemer break away and go down. His theory was that Guynemer had mistaken his adversary for a single-seater and been surprised to meet return fire from the observer, but it seems incredulous that a man of Guynemer's standing and experience would make such a mistake. If he did break off the action against the two-seater it was probably because he had seen the scouts closing in.

It was later learned that Guynemer had fallen about 700 metres north-west of a military cemetery near Poelkapelle. German soldiers of Infantry Regiment Nr.413 arrived at the crash site, but upon inspection, found the pilot was dead. On his person they found 800 francs in notes, four identity cards, seven visiting cards, three letters, three note cards and a military geographical map. It was instantly known that before them was the most famous of French aviators. A German doctor made a cursory examination and then he was buried with full military honours by troops of the German Infantry Regiment Nr.204. However, like so many others before and afterwards, his grave site was irrevocably lost in the war-torn landscape. One lasting memorial to Georges Guynemer is the monument in the centre of a cross-roads in Poelkapelle. He is also remembered in the crypt of the Panthéon, Paris, with words written on a marble slab cemented to a wall:

Fallen on the field of honour on September 11, 1917. A legendary hero fallen from the very zenith of victory after three years' hard and continuous fighting. He will be considered the most perfect embodiment of national qualities for his indomitable energy and perseverance and his exalted gallantry. Full of invincible belief in victory, he has bequeathed to the French soldier an imperishable memory which must augment his self-sacrificing spirit and will surely give rise to the finest emulation.

The following list is of the top surviving French aces at the time of Guynemer's death, with their score at that time, and their final score if different.

Sous-lieutenant Charles Nungesser	40 (43)
Capitaine Alfred Heurtaux	21
Lieutenant Albert Deullin	17 (20)
Lieutenant Armand Pinsard	16 (27)
Sous-lieutenant Georges Madon	16 (41)
Sous-lieutenant Jean Chaput	12 (16)
Adjudant Lucien Jailler	12
Sous-lieutenant Jacques Ortoli	11

Sous-lieutenant Paul Tarascon	11 (12)
Adjudant-Chef René Fonck	11 (75)
Sous-lieutenant Raoul Lufbery	10 (16)

Thus Guynemer was head and shoulders above his nearest rival in terms of scoring, and only Fonck would exceed his score of 53 by the war's end.

Several days after his loss became certain, and the only glimmer of hope being that he may yet be reported as a prisoner of war, a communiqué was issued by the French:

> On the morning of 11 September, Capitaine Guynemer departed on a reconnaissance in the area of Flanders. It was found that during the course of pursuing an enemy aircraft he became separated from his patrol comrade and has not returned. All our means of investigation were brought to play but have not given to this date any additional information.

On 26 September, another French communiqué read:

> Certain newspapers have announced that Capitaine Guynemer has died during the course of his mission. This is not true: there is nothing new to lead us to conclude that Capitaine Guynemer is dead. The Official Communiqué concerning the disposition of this brilliant officer remains the only fact.

Finally, proof of what happened was published in the German press on 6 October 1917, in *Die Woche*, which reproduced his identity card with these comments:

> Capitaine Guynemer enjoys a great reputation in the French Army because he has claimed to have downed more than fifty aircraft. It has nevertheless been proven that a great number of these returned to their airfields in a damaged condition. This renders all German verification impossible, and during these last months there is no indication of the place or date of these alleged successes. French pilot prisoners state that his method of combat was as follows: since he flies as commander of his escadrille he lets his pilots attack first and then dives down, picking the easiest adversary. At other times he flies at a great height and dives, surprising isolated German observation planes. If his first attack is not successful he breaks off the combat immediately. He refuses to have individual duels of a long duration or when it is necessary to prove courage.

This, of course, raised a furore in the French press who immediately defended Guynemer's achievements and honour. It is amazing how many of the great aces of WWI were villified in this way even given the intensity of war. Propaganda aside, many people could not understand how a pilot could build up such a high score, and quickly looked for the obvious solution, that it was all lies, or that the pilot had been in some way under-hand. How to explain why fellow or subordinate pilots could stand this method of scoring without a complaint seems always to elude them. In similar fashion, writers always appear to condemn a perfectly legitimate combat tactic of surprise attack, and to break off an action if circumstances dictated that this was better than being shot down oneself. Did these same writers believe that the only true combat victory could be achieved if the attacker announced his presence beforehand. The vast majority of all combat successes were achieved by surprise, the whole idea being to inflict the maximum loss to the enemy with a minimal danger to oneself. If the same tactics were proving successful for an airman of their own side, these same press reporters would praise them for their ingenuity and prowess.

It was finally established by the Germans that Guynemer had been downed by Leutnant Kurt Wissemann of Jasta 3, who claimed a Spad at 10.30 hours (G) near Poelkapelle, his fifth victory. In a letter to his parents, dated 5 September, Wissemann wrote:

By the way, on 11 September I shot down my fifth enemy. ....I was alone on the Front and pretended to be a completely harmless passer-by. My opponent fell into a trap, left the squadron and attacked me from above. At first I calmly let him come close but when he had reached shooting distance, I turned sharply and he, without being able to shoot, flew by me. In the next moment I was behind him and sent him down with relatively few shots. He lies between St. Julien and the south of Langemarck.

In another letter to his parents, Kurt Wissemann wrote later, on 25 September 1917:

I already mentioned my fifth victory; now it has suddenly been discovered that the occupant was the best French flyer, Captain Guynemer, who had shot down about 50 German aeroplanes.

The following account is written by Wissemann concerning the victory, presumably sometime after or about 25 September:

At 0950 I was attacked by a French single-seater east of St. Julien. I was able to frustrate the attack by turning away. My opponent refused combat, but instead dived past me heading towards the front. In the next instant, I moved in directly behind the enemy machine and opened fire. As a result of my shooting, the aircraft turned over sideways several times, then began spinning down in very tight circles. The dive increased with such speed that it was impossible for me to follow, but I continued watching the spinning machine at about 1,500 metres where it became lost in the haze. As to the aircraft, what particularly struck me was its brilliant markings. I distinctly recognized the French insignia, an observation which several men of my staffel also reported soon after landing. The crash site lies in range of enemy fire about two kilometres north of Gravelstafel. There, likewise on the morning 12 September, Unteroffizier Kahmann discovered the shot-down French Spad. It is assumed with reasonable certainty that the occupant of the enemy aircraft is identical with that of the French Capitaine Guynemer. Further enquiries are being conducted by the Flieger-Verfolgunsstafel.[5]

This sounds a little like an account written, or at least edited, by an official, but otherwise seems genuine enough. One has to wonder if Guynemer suffered gun trouble again, which is why he broke off combat so early, or was he going to the aid of Bozon-Verduraz, whom he could see engaged with four or five other German fighters?

Without going into too much detail here, this letter does seem to conflict with Wissemann's earlier report. For one thing he says here he was alone, while in the report he says his staffel mates confirmed seeing the French markings. He also seems pretty cool. Despite his victories, he had only been with the Jasta three and one half months, and it seems pretty certain he would not have acted so calmly had he known it was Guynemer who was attacking him, and in any event, Jasta 3 must have known they had GC12 opposite them, hardly a bunch to let come too close. One might also wonder if Wissemann only attacked Bozon-Verduraz, who simply dived away out of trouble and once in the haze, headed west and climbed back to altitude. Finding the wreck of Guynemer's Spad in the same area later merely seemed to confirm Wissemann's Spad had crashed. Still, the great aces did fall, and often to the guns of lesser experienced men like Wissemann.

It is odd that it took almost two weeks for the Germans to discover the identity of the French pilot, or at least, it had taken this long to attribute his fall to one of their fighter pilots. One might have thought an earlier announcement more in keeping with the status of the man they had brought down.

* * *

---

[5] US *Cross and Cockade Journal, Vol.15, No.1*, ppg 78-79. Article by (the late) A E Ferko *Guynemer's Last Patrol*.

Louis Risacher left us an insight into both Guynemer and Fonck as air fighters. When Guynemer had succeeded in staying on the tail of a Camel pilot during a mock combat, Fonck had also flown, but had asked that three RFC machines be sent up. Whereas Guynemer had out-manoeuvred and then out-fought his opponent, Fonck had flown off then suddenly reappeared, diving through the small formation. 'That was the difference between the two ....' said Risacher. 'Fonck was a very good pilot but he never made a dogfighting manoeuvre in the air, he always flew flat. Not to be seen by anybody .... that was his style.'

Risacher also comments on two other Frenchmen with Spa 3. ' Bozon-Verduraz was a very bad pilot, but he had fantastic courage. When he was attacking a German, he would be shouting, "Pas, encore, pas encore!" He did not manoeuvre at all. He came right up to the huns, shot for a few moments, would not do a half turn, just went straight on, going back with his gloves and flying suit full of holes. He would wait until the last moment, say ten to fifteen metres before he would shoot. Auger was a very good pilot and a very good fighter, and had a high sense of what an aviator had to do. That means, after his patrols he would go low over the German trenches and fire his remaining ammunition into them. Guynemer and most of us [also] did this.'

* * *

As if in mourning for Guynemer, the weather for the next two days was dreadful. However, on the 14th Fonck shot down his twelfth enemy machine north of Langemarck, presumably Leutnant Maximillian von Chelus of Jasta *Boelcke* who went down in flames over Dixmuide.

GC11 transferred to the VI° Armée Sector on the 15th, leaving GC12 to cover this Flanders area in the north. This same day Fonck scored again, this time his victim going down in flames over Zonnebeke. On 18 September, another American pilot with Spa 103, Sergent Leonard M Reno, was hit by AA fire and had to crash-land. Following a period in the hospital he was sent to Escadrille Br 134 (Bréguet two-seaters), serving with this unit in June and July 1918, before being made an Ensign in the US Navy on 18 July. For his service with the French he received the Croix de Guerre with one Palme.

With the vacancy as CO of Spa 3 created with Guynemer's loss, Lieutenant Gustave Lagache assumed temporary command until Lieutenant Georges Raymond took over in accordance with Général Commandant-en-Chef message No.16.595 of 16 September (1er Armée Décision No.399 of the same date). Raymond was born 19 June 1889, at Lyon, and entered military service on 20 November 1905, assigned to the 7° Régiment de Cuirassiers as a Soldat de 2 Classe. He was promoted to Brigadier on 26 September 1906, and to Maréchal-des-Logis on 13 July 1907. After the war started he was named an Aspirant on 7 August and promoted to Sous-lieutenant (TT) on 16 November. He entered the Aviation Service on 23 July 1915, and served as an observer until 25 November when he was sent to flight school. Raymond received a Military Pilot's Brevet on 14 January 1916, and was assigned to Escadrille N 3 on 25 April where he was promoted to Lieutenant on 16 November. He was transferred to N 73 on 2 August 1917, where he was when assigned this command.

On 19 September, Chef de Bataillon Félix Brocard was transferred to assume duties as the Chef-de-Cabinet du Sous-secrétaire d'État à l'Aéronautique in Paris. He was temporarily replaced at the head of GC12 by Capitaine Jean d'Harcourt, the CO of Spa 103, until command went to Capitaine Henri Horment, a former CO of N 62.

Capitaine Henri Jacques Jean Horment was born on 3 March 1883, in Féan (Basses Pyrénées). He entered military service on 29 October 1904, and was sent to the Special Military School at Saint Cyr. He was promoted to Brigadier on 1 May 1905, and to Maréchal-des-Logis on 1 November. Commissioned a Sous-lieutenant on 1 October 1906, he was assigned to the 6° Régiment de Chasseurs d'Afrique, then on 10 August the following year he was re-assigned to the 7° Régiment de Hussards, where he was promoted to full Lieutenant on 1 October 1908, and still serving with this unit when the war came. He was wounded on 12 August 1914 and after becoming a Chevalier de la Légion d'Honneur on 30 December, Horment was designated as a student pilot on 25 January 1915. Breveted as a Military Pilot he was given command of the newly forming Escadrille MF 62 during August. Promoted to Capitaine on 26 December, his escadrille became N 62 with the arrival of Nieuport machines on 25 May 1916. Horment received his second war wound during a combat on 16 July 1916.

Escadrille N 62 was cited under his leadership in l'Ordre de la VI° Armée No.437 of 13 January 1917. This stated that N 62 had been credited with carrying out 52 long-distance photographic reconnaissances during which it had downed 15 enemy aircraft and six balloons. On 20 February 1917, Capitaine Horment was replaced at the head of N 62 by Capitaine François Coli. It is not known what Horment's postings were prior to his assumption of command of GC12.

Lieutenant Georges Raymond, Spa 3, was decorated with the British Military Cross on 22 September.

* * *

The late summer skies proved an obstacle to operations in mid-to-late September, and on the 23rd during a Spa 103 patrol, five Spads met up with a flight of six Albatros Scouts. Fonck gained his 14th victory east of Langemarck, a two-seater he had engaged over Houthulst Forest. This may have been a crew from FA(A) 6, Unteroffizier Rudolf Franke and Leutnant Gustav Rudolf. During this combat Sergent Haegelen's aircraft had been hit in the radiator by two bullets, and he was forced to land at the Belgian airfield at Moeres.

There was a staff change on 25 September, Lieutenant Pierre Barbey of Spa 103 being assigned by GQG to assume command of Parc 112, replacing Capitaine Joseph Peralda who was transferred to the command of Parc 8. Barbey came from Nancy, where he was born on 23 March 1888. He entered military service in October 1909, and was assigned to the 8° Régiment d'Artillerie. After the war began he transferred to aviation and after being breveted a military pilot he was assigned to GB 1 on 10 January 1916, later serving with N 103 where he remained until 20 August 1917 when he was transferred to Parc 4 prior to this assignment. Also on the 25th, Adjudant Pierre Petit of Spa 3, and Sergent André Pernelle of Spa 103 were cited for flying skills and downing enemy aircraft, in l'Ordre Général No.45 de la 1er Armée.

Groupe de Combat 12 moved to Bierne on the 26th. The following day Deullin shot down his 18th opponent near Dixmuide, Fonck claiming a probable near Zonnebeke.

Pilots were not immune from disciplinary action, and on 27 September Sergent Roger Tassou of N 73 was given 30 days house arrest for having flown very low over a beach, without necessity, and causing a severe accident.

Then on the 28th, Spa 26 had two pilots wounded in combat; Maréchal-des-Logis Noël Fontaine, flying a Spad VII, was hit in both legs, and Maréchal-des-Logis Mortureux, in another Spad VII had his machine catch fire at about 200 metres above the airfield. He put his Spad down as quickly as possible but overturned and he was slightly burned, while his aircraft was burnt out on the ground.

More success came on the 30th, starting with Sergent Prou of Spa 26 claiming a two-seater over Poperinghe, while Fonck, assisted by Adjudant Dupré of Spa 102, sent down another C-type in the same vicinity. Contrary to what has been written in the past Fonck did NOT down Leutnant Wissemann on this day, thereby extracting revenge for Guynemer. Wissemann in point of fact was killed in action over Westroosebeke two days earlier, the 28th, by a member of 56 Squadron RFC.

Pursuant to GQG Aéronautique No.32.360 of 30 September 1917 (E/1569) Capitaine Horment, the Commandant of the 11° Corps d'Armée Air Service, was named temporary commander of GC 12 in replacement of Chef de Bataillon Brocard designated as the sous-Secrétariat de l'Aéronautique.

CHAPTER NINE

October – December 1917

The month of October began with hazy skies and low clouds which meant only a few patrols were flown. Caporaux Gilbert Loup and George Turnure of Spa 103 were promoted to Sergent while Sergent Guerin of Spa 26 made Adjudant. The Groupe lost Lieutenant Jean Richard, an Assistant to the Commandant, who was transferred to SFA on the 4th, in accordance with GQG Aéronautique Telegram No.4770 (E/1606). He was replaced by Lieutenant André Rouget from Escadrille N 152 as ordered by GQG Aéronautique No.8123 (E/1628) of 5 October.

The weather had not improved over much on the 5th, high winds adding to the difficulties. Sergent Gaillard of Spa 3 was killed colliding with a British RFC machine. Gaillard fell into a spin which ended in a fatal crash. With no apparent fatal RFC losses this day it seems the British pilot survived the encounter.

So bad was the weather during the first week of October, that finally six aircraft from Spa 73 and Spa 103 went out low and strafed German trenches and gun emplacements on the 9th, followed two days later by further strafing raids by Spa 26 and Spa 103. The latter were against the village of Merckem, and also the batteries in action with troops, in the Forêt d'Houthulst area, again from low level.

While the weather hadn't improved by the 14th, patrols were flown in the afternoon as it did begin to clear. Successful engagement with enemy aircraft resulted, Brigadier Andras de Marcy of Spa 3 sending down an Albatros two-seater to crash near Bixschoote at 14.00 hours for his confirmed victory, which was the 136th for Spa 3. He had been on patrol with Adjudant Ambroise-Thomas and Brigadier Dubonnet and came across the recce machine, attacking it from about 100 metres, firing 20 rounds. As the other two pilots were about to attack, just as the German observer was trying to aim his gun at them, the machine suddenly erupted in flames. The luckless crew plummeted into the ground on fire near the forested area.

Caporal Collins, an American with Spa 103, who was on patrol with Sergent Haegelen, the patrol leader, and Sergents Lecomte, Barault, Pietri and Seigneurie (from 15.20 to 17.05 hours), claimed his first victory also. He attacked a flight of five Albatros Scouts from out of the sun and began firing from 300 metres, down to 100 metres. One German fell into a spin and crashed near Langemarck. Collins was then set upon by the other four Albatri, but then a strong British patrol arrived and they quickly broke off the action and headed east.

Four other victories were scored by GC 12 this day but cannot be documented as due to the conditions of the combats nobody for certain could make a definite claim, so they were added to the Groupe's total. However, the Groupe did not get off without a loss. Sergent Gaston Drou, Spa 73, flying a Spad VII, was killed during another combat at 16.25 hours, probably falling victim to either Leutnant Xavier Dannhuber of Jasta 26, or Leutnant Franz Ray of Jasta 28w, who both claimed Spads in this sector at 17.35 hours (G) respectively, their tenth and seventh victories. Also on this day Lieutenant Deullin, CO of Spa 73, was promoted to Capitaine while Adjudant-Chef François Bergot of Spa 73 was given a temporary promotion to Sous-lieutenant pursuant to GQG Décision No.13.267 (E/I.751) of 14 October 1917. Bergot had served with the 2° Régiment de Chasseurs before becoming a pilot. He first served with Escadrille N 49 from 29 May to 17 June 1916, he then was assigned to N 73 from July to 6 January 1917, when he was reassigned to N 38. His stay here was only a few weeks and on 30 January he was transferred back to N 73 where he received the Médaille

Militaire on 10 July.

The next day, the 15th, Sergent Pietri of Spa 103 claimed his first victory over Houthulst, the Groupe also claiming a probable. Also on this date Lieutenant André Rouget arrived for service on the staff of GC 12 as the Technical Assistant, relieving Lieutenant Jean Richard who was transferred to the Service des Fabrications de l'Aéronautique (SFA) as mentioned earlier. Rouget had been born on 20 August 1888 at Troyes (Aube) and entered military service on 12 October 1909 as a Soldat de 2° Classe with the 21° Régiment d'Artillerie. He was promoted to Brigadier on 9 June 1910, and to Sous-lieutenant (Reserve) on 10 August 1913, assigned to the 5° Régiment d'Artillerie. He was promoted to Lieutenant on 10 August 1915, and reassigned to the 47° Régiment d'Artillerie Lourde. He transferred to aviation as an observer on 14 August 1916, assigned to Escadrille MF 386 in the Orient. He returned to France on 16 January 1917 as a student pilot receiving Military Pilot's Brevet No.3997 on 4 May. After additional training he was assigned to Escadrille N 152 on 10 July from where he came to take this appointment.

The following day, in the 1er Armée Ordre Général No.50 the late Capitaine Georges Guynemer received his last citation, the words of which are recorded earlier, written on a marble slab in the Panthéon.

After much exhortation, and influenced by letters written to members of the Chambre, it was voted that these words should indeed be inscribed on the wall of the Panthéon, following the motion to do so of Monsieur Lasies made on 19 October 1917. Two of the letters written to M. Lasies came from Guynemer's own flying companions. The first from Lieutenant Georges Raymond, who was temporarily in command of Spa 3 at the time.

> Having the honour to command Spa 3 in the absence of Capitaine Heurtaux, still wounded and in hospital, I am anxious to thank you, in the name of the few surviving Storks, for what you are doing in the memory of Guynemer. He was our friend as well as our chief and teacher, our pride and our flag, and his loss will be felt more than any that has thinned our ranks so far. Please be assured that our courage has not been laid low with him; our revenge will be merciless and victorious. May Guynemer's noble soul remember us fighting our aerial battles that we may keep alight the flame that he bequeathed to us.

Chef de Bataillon Félix Brocard also wrote:

> My Dear Comrade, I am profoundly moved to hear of the thought you have of giving the highest consecration to Guynemer's memory at the Panthéon. It had occurred to all of us that only the dome of the Panthéon was large enough for such wings. The poor boy fell in the fullness of triumph with his face towards the enemy. A few days earlier he had sworn to me that the Germans would never take him alive. His heroic death is not more glorious than that of a gunner defending his gun, the infantryman rushing out of his trench, or even that of the poor soldier perishing in the mud.
>
> But Guynemer was known to all. There were few that had not seen him in the sky, whether blue or cloudy, bearing on his frail linen wings some of their own faith, their own dreams, and all that their souls could hold of trust and hope. It was for them all, whether infantrymen or gunners or pioneers, that he fought with the bitter hatred he felt for the invader, with his youthful daring and the joys of his triumphs. He knew that the battle would end fatally for him, no doubt, but knowing also that his war-bird was an instrument of saving thousands of lives, and seeing that his example called forth the noblest imitation, he remained true to his idea of self-sacrifice which he had formed a long time before, and which he saw develop with perfect calm. Full of modesty as a soldier, but fully conscious of the greatness of his duties, he possessed the national qualities of endurance, perseverance, indifference to danger, and to these he added the most generous heart. During his short life he had not time enough to learn bitterness or suffering or disillusionment. He passed straight from school where he was learning the history of France, to where he himself could add

another page to it. He went to the war driven by a mysterious power which I respect as death of genius ought to be respected. He was a powerful thought, living in a body so delicate that I, who lived so close beside him, knew it would some day be slain by the thought. The poor boy!

Other boys from every French school wrote him every day. He was their legendary ideal, and they felt all their emotions, sharing his joys as well as his dangers. To them he was a living copy of the heroes whose exploits they read in their books. His name is constantly on their lips, for they loved him as they had been taught to love the purest glories of France. Monsieur le député, gain admittance for him in the Panthéon, where he has already been placed by the mothers of the children of France. There his protecting wings will not be out of place, for under that dome where sleep those who gave us our France, they will be the symbol of those who have defended her for us.

Brocard
Chef de Bataillon

* * *

With some further better weather on the morning of the 17th, patrols and combats took place and Adjudant-Chef René Fonck of Spa 103 gained his 16th and 17th victories (believed to be two-seaters). Sergents Lecomte and Turnure of the same unit collaborated in the destruction of a German machine over Ypres, for their first victories.

Further combats took place the next day despite morning mist and low clouds starting the day off slowly. But in the afternoon Fonck claimed a probable at Houthulst, but during one fight, Maréchal-des-Logis Pierre Marcel Jolivet of Spa 73, flying Spad VII No. 1118, was killed in combat. He was probably the victim of Leutnant Walter von Bülow of Jasta 36, who claimed his 24th victory, a Spad, east of Passchendaele – the only Spad claimed by the Germans over this sector.

Jolivet was born 19 March 1893, at Doingt (Haute Savoie). He began military service with the 4° Régiment de Dragons but took up flying and received his French Aero Club Pilot's Brevet No. 5336 on 16 February 1917.

On this day, Lieutenant Mathieu Tenant de la Tour, commanding officer of Spa 26, was given a temporary promotion to Capitaine in accordance with GQG Cavalerie Décision No.21.204 (E/1843) of 18 October 1917. Fonck was cited in l'Ordre de 1er l'Armée No.52, in recognition of having been credited with his 12th, 13th and 14th victories. Adjudant Joseph Baron, Spa 103, and Sergent Louis Risacher, Spa 3, were cited in l'Ordre de l'Aéronautique de la Ier Armée No.1.397 for their flying skill and combats. The next combats occurred on 21 October. Fonck claimed his 18th victory by downing a German in flames over Passchendaele, possibly Vizefeldwebel Fritz Bachmann of Jasta 6, who was killed at Ypres at 1120 hours (G). This proved a great day for Fonck as he was made a Chevalier de la Légion d'Honneur by Ordre No. 5837 "D" issued by GQG with the following citation:

Adjudant-Chef pilot, Mle 3713, Escadrille Spa 103. A fighter pilot of great value combining bravery with exceptional qualities of skill and composure. He came to this chasse escadrille with 500 hours of flight time in a G IV aircraft, he became in a short time one of the greatest French combat pilots. On 19, 20 and 21 August 1917, he downed his 8th, 9th and 10th enemy aircraft. Already cited in ordres seven times and awarded the Médaille Militaire for feats of combat.

Hazy skies turned clear on the afternoon of 22 October and seven patrols were sent out. Two aircraft of Spa 103 strafed German trenches and batteries, plus a road convoy north of Westroosebeke. Capitaine Albert Heurtaux, the recent commander of Escadrille Spa 3, was made an Officier de la Légion d'Honneur by Ordre No. 5850 "D" with this citation:

Capitaine of the 9° Régiment de Hussards, an elite officer, initially in the cavalry he showed brilliant bravery, then he became a pursuit pilot of incomparable skill and composure, and has fought for three years with the same joy and respect of duty. Keeping in the midst of the most perilous attacks, a most astonishing calm and splendid audacity, and gives a magnificent example of devotion to his country. Wounded on 5 May 1917, while attacking nine enemy scouts alone he was again gravely wounded on 3 September 1917, during the course of a difficult combat. He has downed 21 German aircraft. Cited in orders 15 times, Chevalier de la Légion d'Honneur.

* * *

On 24 October, during very limited activity, Sergent Robert Brière of Spa 103 was wounded by anti-aircraft fire, forcing him to make a crash-landing in the French lines. The following day, the 25th, Fonck was again cited in orders of the French 1er Armée (No. 54) for downing his 15th, 16th and 17th enemy aircraft. Capitaine Kiyotake Shigeno of Spa 26, Adjudant François Barra, Spa 103, Maréchaux-des-Logis Xavier Andras de Marcy, Spa 3, and Noël Fontaine Spa 26, Sergent Camille Pietri, Spa 103 and Caporal Phelps Collins, an American in Spa 103, were also cited in the same order for their general good work and flying abilities. It was noted by Décision No.438 of 25 October that Lieutenant Paul Emile Henri Dumas of Spa 103 had been made a Chevalier de la Légion d'Honneur.

> Lieutenant pilot, Escadrille Spa 103. A chasse pilot of exceptional courage and energy, giving under all circumstances the greatest example of devotion and spirit of sacrifice. He downed two enemy aircraft on 28 and 30 April 1917. On 21 August 1917, having resolutely attacked two German two-seaters alone, he received a serious wound during the combat. Two citations.

Lieutenant Georges Raymond, acting CO of Spa 3, got his fourth victory on the 27th by shooting down a German machine over Houthulst Forest. Raymond would be given full command of the escadrille on 2 November. Adjudant Fonck raised his score to 19 with a victory over Westroosebeke, while claiming two others as probables.

More unconfirmed victories were claimed on the 28th. Also on this date a Caudron GIV machine, No. 5057, was assigned to GC 12 from RGAé Calais, to assist in training in air-to-air gunnery. During the month Escadrille N 73 was officially designated as Spa 73. (In order for it to be less confusing to the reader, we have been recording all of GC 12's escadrilles by Spa over the last chapter or so, but it must still be borne in mind that while units were flying Spad fighters, they were still officially an escadrille prefixed by 'N' until designated Spa in orders.)

November 1917

The month of November began just as October had with poor weather and little active flying. On 3 November Adjudant Léon Barés, Spa 26, and Sergents Pierre Prou, of the same unit, and Pierre Schmitter, Spa 103 were cited in l'Ordre de l'Aéronautique de la Ier Armée No.4629 for their general good work and flying ability.

Promotions came on 5 November for Spa 103 pilots, Sergents Marcel Haegelen, Lucien Barault and Seigneurie who were promoted to Adjudant, while Caporal Phelps Collins made Sergent. Lieutenant Paul Dumas of this escadrille was wounded, however. Another day of low clouds and rain restricted flying on the 6th, but the Commanding General of the 1er Armée cited the following listed personnel in l'Ordre Général No.57: Fonck had his 18th and 19th victories acknowledged. The others were Georges Raymond, now confirmed as CO of Spa 3, Lieutenant Daniel Dumêmes, Spa 26, Sous-lieutenants Jean Bozon-Verduraz and Emile Letourneau of Spa 3 and Spa 26 respectively, Adjudant Marcel Paris, Spa 73, Sergents Jean Dedieu, Spa 26, René Lecomte, Spa 103, Roger Tassou, Spa 73, George Turnure, Spa 103 and Pierre Prou, Spa 26 and Maréchal-des-Logis Pierre Jolivet, Spa 73 who were all cited for their flying abilities and bravery and general good work.

On the 7th, Sergent Charles Biddle, an American serving with Spa 73, was promoted to

Captain in the US Air Service, but remained with the Escadrille. This 27-year-old Philadelphian, a graduate of Princeton University in 1911, and then Harvard three years later, was a lawyer. However, he volunteered to join the French Air Service in the spring of 1917 and had trained at Pau and Avord. He had been with Spa 73 since 28 July. He would gain one official victory with this unit before going to another French escadrille, and would eventually transfer to the USAS. He was to end the war an ace, and his book, *The Way of an Eagle*, is very well known even today.

Capitaine Deullin, CO of Biddle's Spa 3, claimed a Pfalz Scout over Hollebeke on the 8th for his 19th victory, the same date that Barés of Spa 26 was promoted to Adjudant-Chef. On 11 November, detachments from Spa 3, Spa 26, and Spa 103 of GC 12, departed for Maisonneuve, situated near Villers-Cotterêts, in the VI° Armée Sector, commanded by Général Paul Maistre. The next day 36 sorties were flown during eight patrols. Sous-lieutenant Battesti of Spa 73 claimed his third victory by downing an aircraft west of the Forêt d'Houthulst. Possibly one of his victims was Leutnant Georg Behnisch of FAA211, who was killed over Houthulsterwald on this date. Capitaine Duval, who had reported to Spa 73 on 30 October, was killed attempting to land returning from a patrol. Two days later Adjudant Guiguet returned to Spa 3 following recovery from his wound received back on 23 May.

The Groupe had a more unusual loss on 18 November. More low clouds and mist didn't help the situation for Maréchal-des-Logis Louis Paoli, who had reported to Spa 73 on 23 October. Flying Spad No. 1832, he became disoriented in the air and landed in neutral Holland where he was interned at Bergen-op-Zoom. However, he later effected an escape and returned to Spa 73 on 7 March 1918.

On 28 November Capitaine Jean Varenard de Billy, the Officier de Renseignements of GC 12, was assigned as temporary commanding officer of Escadrille N 313 while Capitaine Langevin was hospitalized.

For the next few days the weather remained bad. Then on the 29th a serious accident occurred. Sergent Jean Dedieu of Spa 26 was severely injured in a collision with an aircraft of Escadrille V 116, which shared the same airfield, on take-off. The two-man crew from V 116 were killed and one of their mechanics, going along for the ride, badly injured. The Voisin, normally a night bomber, was making a day practice sortie just as the Spad was taking off from across the airfield. Captain Biddle, in his book, gives the dramatic description of the event, but does not name the Voisin crew, but they were Maréchal-des-Logis Aurmaitre, pilot, Soldat Chopping, gunner, and the mechanic was Soldat Crouillère.

Adjudant Guiguet of Spa 3 was given a temporary promotion to Sous-lieutenant on 30 November.

December 1917

The up-and-coming René Fonck was commissioned a Sous-lieutenant on 2 December, and three days later, Charles Biddle claimed his first success. While Biddle had been made a Captain in the USAS on 7 November, this same 5 December only saw him promoted to Sergent in the French Air Force. His claim was over an Albatros C-type which went down over Langemarck. Another American, Phelps Collins of Spa 103, probably downed a German aircraft too, over Houthulst, while a third American, Caporal Charles Jones, with Spa 73, was promoted this day to Sergent. Two Sergents with GC 12, Pierre Prou and Camille Pietri, Spa 103, were both promoted to Adjudant.

On the 8th, Lieutenant Paul Tourtel, of Spa 103, was killed in an accident in a Spad XIII near Verrines. He had been born on 4 March 1896, at Nancy, and had received his Pilot's Brevet No. 2309, on 15 September 1915.

1er Armée Ordre Général No.69 dated 10 December cited the following GC 12 personnel: Capitaine Albert Deullin, CO Spa 73, for downing his 18th and 19th enemy aircraft; S/Lt François Battesti, Spa 73, for downing an enemy aircraft; S/Lt Louis Bucquet, Spa 3, for participating in 130 combats and having flown almost 600 hours over the lines; and Adj François Barra, Spa 26, for general good work.

Escadrille Spa 73 departed to Maisonneuve on 11 December, the date Général Paul Maistre, the commander of the VI° Armée, was replaced by Général Denis Duchène. Général Maistre would assume command of the Groupe d'Armées du Centre during 1918.

Sergent George Turnure, Jr., the American flying with Spa 103, was transferred on 17 December. He was commissioned a 1st Lieutenant in the USAS on 2 January 1918, and served with N 124 prior to it being broken up into two units, Spa 124, the French unit and the 103rd Pursuit Squadron, USAS. He was assigned to the 103rd until sent to the 28th Pursuit Squadron as a flight commander on 28 August. He was made a Chevalier de la Légion d'Honneur after the war and held the Croix de Guerre with two palmes and one étoile. Turnure was credited with three combat victories during the war, two being balloons with the Americans and one kill with Spa 103.

The Groupe suffered a serious loss on 17 December. Capitaine Mathieu Tenant de la Tour, commanding officer of Spa 26, was killed in an accident in a Spad VII at Auchel. He had celebrated his 34th birthday on 5 December. Lieutenant Daniel Dumêmes assumed temporary command.

Dumêmes was born on 12 August 1890, and enlisted for four years military service on 10 October 1911, assigned to the 8° Régiment de Chasseurs. Promoted to Brigadier on 6 March 1912, he was posted to the Special Military School at St. Cyr on 10 October. He graduated as a Sous-lieutenant on 1 October 1913, and assigned to the aviation service as an observer on 27 September 1915, going to Escadrille N 26. Dumêmes was promoted to full Lieutenant on 1 October 1915, and transferred to Buc as a student pilot on 7 May 1916. He received Military Pilot's Brevet No. 4885 on 10 November, and was then sent to GDE before returning to N 26 which was now flying single-seaters.

The next day, 18 December, Maréchal-des-Logis de Tascher, who had been shot down and taken prisoner on 12 April, rejoined Escadrille Spa 26. He had escaped from the prison camp at Dilligen on 10 September and managed to get into Switzerland. He was quickly named *The Fugitive*.

Lieutenant Joseph Marie Xavier de Sevin, an ace with six victories, from Escadrille N 12, assumed command of Spa 26 on Christmas Day, the date of his promotion to full Lieutenant. De Sevin was born on 10 March 1894, in Toulouse (Haute Garonne). He volunteered for military service on 2 September 1914, and was sent to the 14° Régiment d'Infanterie. At the time he volunteered he had been a student at the Special Military School and St. Cyr. He was promoted to Caporal on 5 November and Sergent on the 30th. Then on 5 December he was given a temporary promotion to Sous-lieutenant, probably due to his schooling at St. Cyr. Wounded in action, he transferred to aviation on 15 July 1915 at Pau, and received Military Pilot's Brevet No. 1804 on 18 October. De Sevin was assigned to Escadrille N 12 on 11 November where he was made a Chevalier de la Légion d'Honneur on 19 April 1917 with the following citation:

> A brilliant *pilot de chasse* with a high conception of devotion to duty. He is always prepared for the most difficult missions. Wounded in the infantry at the beginning of the war, he transferred to aviation and downed his second enemy aircraft on 4 March 1917. Already cited three times in orders.

On 29 December Adjudant Naudin, Spa 26, claimed his second victory. On the same day, Sous-lieutenant François Battesti of Spa 73 became a Chevalier de la Légion d'Honneur. His citation read:

> A magnificent officer with audacity and initiative. He distinguished himself as a pilot for an Army Corps, executing over the German lines numerous spotting of long-range guns, and by missions at low altitude despite the presence of enemy planes. He transferred to pursuit aviation at his request, and has had daily difficult combats and has given proof of the most offensive spirit. He has downed several enemy aircraft which have crashed in their lines, especially on 4 July and 12 November 1917. Three wounds, three citations.

* * *

left: Chef de Escadron Charles de Tricornet de
_e_, the commander of fighting forces
_e_rdun, part of which was Escadrille N 3.

right: de Rose in his Nieuport Scout. Note the rose
nia on the fuselage.

Bottom: Capitaine Félix Brocard, commander of
N 3 in 1916 and later commander of GC12; note the
Stork insignia on his Nieuport Scout, and its
rear-view mirror.

Top left: Among the pilots of N 3 at Verdun were Jules Verdrines....

Top right: André Chainat......

Bottom left: Albert Deullin........

Bottom right: Jean Peretti (died 28 April 1916) ....

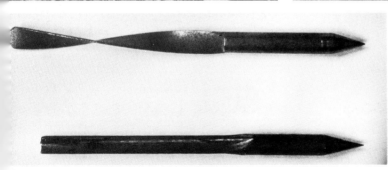

and Georges Guynemer (Brocard with his
to camera)

dle left: Guynemer with one of his early Nieuports
ving the name *Le Vieux Charles.*

dle right: Jean Navarre airborne in his Nieuport 11
76) in April 1916.

Bottom left: Fletchets; darts dropped by aviators,
generally on cavalry, or horse-drawn transport.

Bottom right: Sergent André Steuer of N 103, missing
24 September 1916.

Top left: Pilots at Cachy in 1916 were René Dorme of N 3.......

Top right: Alfred Heurtaux of N 3.....

Above: Lt Gustave Lagache, N 3 ....

Right: and Paul Tarascon of N 62.

left: Major Brocard was named commander of GC
n October 1916.

right: When GC 12 was formed, Guynemer had
eved 18 victories....

Bottom left: ..... René Dorme, 15 kills.

Bottom right: Victor Ménard CO of N 26, later became
a Groupe Commander.

Top left: Another of the early aces was Armand Pinsard, who flew with N 26.

Top right: Spad in German hands, used by GC12 but still carrying the star marking of VB 103, forerunner of N 103.

Above: Adjudant Charles-Achille Jeronnez of N 26.

Right: Adjudant W 'Bert' Hall, an American with N 103 in 1916.

Top left: Heurtaux (left) with two N 67 aces, Georges Flachaire and Marcel Pierre Viallet.

Top right: Deullin and Tarascon – note N 3's Stork-marked Nieuport.

Middle: Nieuport No.7, usually flown by Alfred Auger, at Villers Bretonneux, October 1916.

(SHAA)

Left: Nieuport No.9 with lighter paintwork (N1538). Note petrol cans below the wing.

(SHAA)

Top: Nieuport Scouts of the Stork Group.

Middle: An N 3 Nieuport – No.12 – usually flown by Père Dorme.

Bottom: Another view of No.12 (N1428), Dorme in cockpit with Maréchal Joseph Joffe (in black) talking with him.

Top left: Nieuport Scout N 1135 of N 26. Capitaine J de Sieyes de Veynes, the CO, was brought down and captured in this machine on 3 July 1916.

Top right: André Chainat achieved 11 victories with N 3 before being wounded on 7 September 1916. Note the Stork emblem above his Médaille Militaire.

Middle: Four aces of GC12, Tenant de la Tour, Alfred Heurtaux, Albert Deullin and Georges Guynemer. Note that like their RFC compatriots, their uniforms differ greatly, depending on previous units.

Bottom: Chainat's Spad VII "L'Oiseau Bleu 6" (The Blue Bird).

(SHAA)

Top: MdL Constant Soulier's Nieuport XVII
(Esc N 26) following an accident on 14 January 1917.
(SHAA)

Middle left: Another Nieuport accident, this time by
N 73, the pilot explaining 'how it happened'.
(SHAA)

Middle right: The Russian pilot, Lt Ivan Orlov, flew
with N3 late 1916 to early 1917. He gained four kills in
Russia, and one in France.

Right: Brig. Edmond Thomassin, Spa 26, wounded in
action 16 April 1917. *(Vacher via R Feuilloy)*

p left: Joseph Henri Guiguet of N 3 (centre); Pilot
med as de Bois de Connei at right.

p right: Heurtaux and Duellin with Stork-marked
euport.

iddle: Heurtaux, Guynemer and de la Tour. The officer
r right is Le Prieur, the inventor of the Le Prieur
ckets used in balloon attacks.

Bottom left: Line up of Spa 3's Spad fighters. Individual
recognition was by a number at the rear of the fuselage.

Bottom right: Félix Brocard's Spad with (presumably) a
'6' marked by the tail, and a red, white and blue stripe
around the fuselage.

Top left: Guynemer and one of his Spads. Several were marked *Vieux Charles* although at least one had the name of *Dorme* on it after Père Dorme was killed.

Top right: Capitaine Alfred Auger of N 3; note Stork insignia on left breast, and the '31' on his hat referring to his former infantry regiment.

Middle left: Albert Deullin had flown with N 3 but by February 1917 commanded N 73.

Middle right: Lieutenant Georges Raymond with his Spad VII '9'.

Right: René Fonck's Spad VII (S1461) with the Spa 103 'Stork' and the Roman IX number. Force landing in May 1917 – note crumpled fin indicating the Spad had turned right over. Note the torn fabric dangling from the far side of the fuselage, and that the machine had previously been numbered XV.

(via Jon Guttman)

left: Sgt Georges Lutzius, Spa 103, left to go to N
on 30 June 1917.

right: Lieutenant Mathieu Tenant de la Tour flew
N3 and then commanded N 26.

Bottom: Georges Flachaire in front of a Spad VII of
Spa 67, with what appears to be an early 'shark mouth'
marking on the cowling.

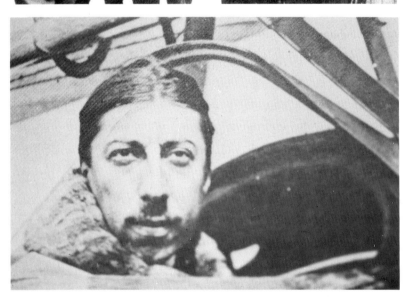

Top left: Another view of a 'shark mouth' marking on this crunched Spad VII of Spa 67, perhaps even the same machine as above. Note the 'eyes' painted on the cowling. *(SHAA)*

Top right: Capitaine Kiyotake Shigeno, from Japan, flew with N 26 in 1917. He achieved two confirmed and six probable victories, and flew Spad No.'II'. He died of pneumonia in 1924 aged 42.

Middle: Kiyotake Shigeno with French Navy Pilots . St Pol, August 1917. *(Vacher via R Feu*

Bottom left: Lieutenant Pierre (Henri) Hervet, N 10

Bottom right: Lieutenant Didier Lecour-Grandmais commanded C 46 within the Groupe.

left: Grandmaison being decorated on the airfield.

right: A well known picture of Guynemer, it is ever, one of the few of him with a smile.

Middle: Alfred Heurtaux in his Spad Mes Rénee.

Bottom: Spad VII of Spa 103. Note the Le Prieur rocket tubes on the wing struts.

(SHAA)

Top left: René Fonck arrived in the Groupe in April 1917, assigned to N 103.

Top right: The great Père Dorme fell in combat on 23 May 1917 having achieved 23 confirmed victories.

Bottom left: Joseph Guiguet of N 3 was commission[ed] in May 1917 but wounded the same day.

Bottom right: Adj Céléstin Sanglier, N 3, killed in ac[tion] 10 May 1917.

Top left: MdL Moulines and '14', N 3.

(Risacher via Jon Guttman)

Top right: MdL Moulines - wounded in action
24 July 1917.   *(Risacher via Jon Guttman)*

Left: Oliver Chadwick, an American with Spa 73, was
killed in action on 14 August 1917.

Middle right: Capitaine Alfred Auger, CO of N 3 in
1917 but was killed in action on 27 July.

Above: Other Americans who flew with GC12, Sgt
Phelps Collins, Spa 103 ....   *(Jon Guttman)*

Top left: ... and Sgt Charles Evans Turnure, also of Spa 103. Note the earlier version of 103's stork insignia. *(Jon Guttman)*

Top right: Sous-lieutenant Henri Rabatel, Spa 3, shot down and taken prisoner on 16 August 1917. Pictured in his prison camp.

Middle: Spa 3 lost two pilots on 16 August, Rabatel and Cpl Cornet. One of them was flying No.1639 '10', seen here behind German lines.

Right: Guynemer in one of his Spads about to take off.

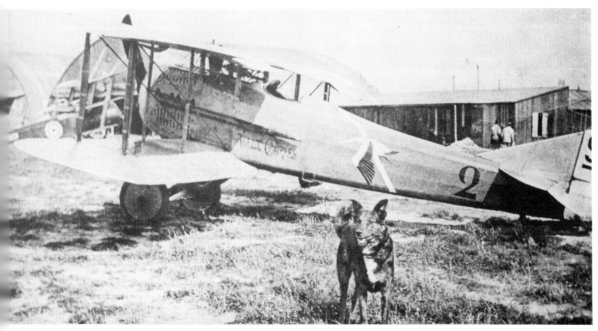

op left: Guynemer being presented with a new Spad, t Pol, August 1917. Albert Deullin stands in front of he machine talking to Louis Béchereau, designer and ngineer for the S.P.A.D. company. Guynemer stands entre. *(Risacher via Jon Guttman)*

op right: Sous-lieutenant André Dezarrois, Spa 26, in is Spad *Annette*. Wounded in combat 20 August 1917.

Middle: Inspection line-up of GC12 – Guynemer centre in dark uniform. *(Risacher via Guttman)*

Bottom: Guynemer's Spad '2' – with 'friend'. Note Triplane in the background indicating the picture was taken at St Pol.

Top: Guynemer in front of his badly damaged Spad XIII on the day it was hit by an artillery shell.

Bottom left: Fonck gained his tenth victory on 20 August 1917. Here he walks away from one of his Spads which is having its guns and sights tested.

Bottom right: Alfred Heurtaux was badly wounded on 3 September 1917.

Top left: Adjutant Roger Guillamet, N 3, killed in action.

Top right: Guillamet and Bozon-Verduraz by '13'.

Middle left: Louis Risacher's Spad VII after a crash-landing on the beach at Dunkirk.

(Risacher via Guttman)

Above: One of the last photographs of a much-bemedalled Georges Guynemer, hero of France. His decorations include the Légion d'Honneur, Ordre de Léopold, British DSO, Médaille Militaire, and Croix de Guerre with 26 palmes.

Left: Guynemer's medals.

Top left: Lieutenant Benjamin Bozon-Verduraz, of Spa 3 was on the same flight as Guynemer when the latter fell over Poelcapelle. He later rose to become an 11-victory ace and later commanded Spa 94.

Top right: Guynemer's personal identity card found on his body and returned to France by Germany in 1938.

Bottom left: After his death, postcards of one of Guynemer's Spads, which was exhibited in Paris, we sold in their hundreds.

Bottom right: Lieutenant Georges Raymond becam the next permanent CO of Spa 3, a position he held July 1918.

left: Chef de Bataillon Brocard left GC 12 on 19 [Nov]ember 1917 but under his command the Groupe [had] become an élite unit.

[Top] right: American Charles Biddle scored his first [victo]ry with Spa 73 with which unit he served during [the s]econd half of 1917. He later became an ace with [the] USAS.

Bottom left: Joseph Guiguet, Spa 3, commissioned at the end of November 1917.

Bottom right: Lieutenant Joseph Xavier de Sevin arrived from N 12 to command Spa 26 on Christmas Day 1917. Note Spa 26's Stork insignia.

Top left: Sergent Louis Risacher, Spa 3.

(Risacher via Jon Guttman)

Top right: Another American to serve with Spa 3 was Caporal E David Judd.

Bottom left: American William T Ponder served brie with Spa 103 in early 1918. He later became an ace the 103 US Aero Squadron.

Bottom right: Ed Parsons, yet another American, fle with the Lafayette and Spa 3.

left: Among the Americans with GC 12, Frank
lies saw much combat during his six months with
3.

right: Commander of Spa 103 from 26 March 1918

was Capitaine Joseph Battle (right) seen here with one
of his ace pilots, Lieutenant Louis Coudouret.

Bottom: On 9 May René Fonck claimed six victories,
seen here with his Spa 103-marked Spad.

Top left: Sgt Jean Laffray of Spa
103 with Spad XIII No. XVI.
(Jon Guttman)

Top right: Sgt Pierre Schmitter,
Spa 103, with No.III.
(SHAA)

Middle: Spad VII No.8 – Spa 73.
(SHAA)

Right: Spad XIII No.14 – Spa 67.
(SHAA)

*: A group of Spa 3 pilots. In the dark uniform is
L André Dubonnet, who gained his second victory
0 May 1918. Sergent Risacher in on the far right.*

*dle left: Lieutenant Louis Coudouret of Spa 3
ame a Chevalier de la Légion d'Honneur in May
3, having also fought in Russia. Note the Le Prieur
et rails on the wing struts.*

*Bottom left: Bozon-Verduraz and Louis Risacher, Spa 3.
Note unusual cowling cooling holes.*

(Risacher via Jon Guttman)

*Bottom right: Frank Baylies fell in combat on 17 June
having gained 12 victories.*

Top left: Edmond Pillon (right) left Spa 67 on 18 June, and later served with Spa 98. Adjudant Marchal, (left).

Top right: Fonck brought his score to 50 on 16 July 1918. In addition he had more than 40 unconfirmed claims.

Bottom left: The business end of a Spad XIII.

Bottom right: Sous-lieutenant Pierre Pendaries of Spa 67. The word is assumed to be *Moustique* – Mosquito.

left: Lieutenant Bernard Barny de Romanet came
~e Groupe to command Spa 167 in August 1918 and
~d eight victories to his previous score of ten. Note
~pa 167 Stork badge.

right: Spa 3 Spad – No.7.

Bottom left: Edwin Parsons brought his score to eight
on 1 October 1918.

Bottom right: Barny de Romanet and René Fonck, late
1918.

Top: Spa 103 group, with Barny de Romanet and Fonck standing third and fourth from the left centre row.

Bottom left: Louis Risacher, Spa 3, went on to Spa 159, and added three victories to become an ace.

Bottom right: Lieutenant Francois Dumas flew with 167 during the last two months of the war.

left: Lieutenant Zebau, by a Spa 103 Spad.

right: Groupe de Combat 12 and France's ace-of-, René Fonck, ended the war with 75 confirmed ories.

Middle left: One of Fonck's victories was this Rumpler, on the French side of the lines.

Bottom: Blériot-built Spad XIII of Spa 67. Picture believed taken at the war's end. *(SHAA)*

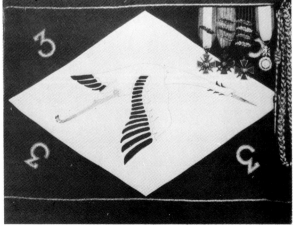

Top left: Another Blériot-built Spad XIII (No.IX), th
time serving with Spa 103. The inscription is dated
September 1919.

Top right: Three brothers who each served with GC
in WW1. René (Pierre), Max (not a pilot) and Jacqu
de Linière were with Spa 103, Spa 67 and Spa 26
respectively.   *(Peter Kil*

Middle left: Spa 3's battle honours, also showing the
Croix de Guerre and palmes (top R/H corner of
top flag.)

Middle right: Spa 103's battle honours, also showing
Croix de Guerre awards.

Left: Spa 3's flag with the unit's decorations top righ

By the end of 1917, the following pilots were known to have been on the strength of Groupe de Combat 12:

Spa 3

Lt Georges Raymond – CO
S/Lt Benjamin Bozon-Verduraz
S/Lt Louis Bucquet
S/Lt Guy de la Rochefordière
S/Lt Dutreul
Adj Charles Albanel
Adj Roger Guillaumoit
Adj Louis Risacher
Adj Ambriose Thomas
Sgt Frank Baylies (US)
Sgt Edouard Moulines
MdL Xavier Andras de Marcy
Cpl Maurice Chevannes
Cpl David Judd (US)
Cpl Francois Macari
Cpl Marius Ribardière

Spa 26

Lt Xavier de Sevin – CO
Lt Daniel Dumêmes
S/Lt Jean Dombray
S/Lt Emile Letourneau
S/Lt Jacques Puget
Adj Léon Barés
Adj Adrien Fétu
Adj Gustave Naudin
Sgt Jean Dedieu
Sgt Pierre Prou
MdL Julius Antoine
MdL Benjamin de Tascher
MdL Le Quellec
MdL Mortureux
MdL Emile Picard
MdL Auguste Pouchelle
Cpl Aimé Vincent

Spa 73

Capt Albert Deullin – CO
Capt Duval
Lt François Battesti
Lt Bernard de Girval
Lt Robert Gerdes
S/Lt François Bergot
Adj André Lamande
Adj Marcel Paris
MdL Gaston Claude-Fontaine
Sgt Charles J Biddle (US)
Sgt Charles Jones (US)
Sgt Georges Mauger
Sgt Roger Tassou
Cpl Georges Gobé

Spa 103

Capt Jean d'Harcourt – CO
S/Lt René Fonck
S/Lt Fontaine
Adj Joseph Baron
Adj Marcel Haegelen
Adj Camille Pietri
Adj Seigneurie
MdL Butruille
Sgt Phelps Collins (US)
Sgt René Lecomte
Sgt Gilbert Loup
Sgt Pierre Schmitter
Cpl Henry Batchelor (US)
Cpl Henri Drouillh
Cpl Robert Hoeber (US)

CHAPTER TEN

1918

Groupe de Combat 12 started the New Year with eight patrols involving 22 aircraft but the Germans remained on the ground. The next day it snowed so the French pilots too remained indoors and around their fires.

The first claims of 1918 occurred on the 3rd – two probables. The first was by a patrol of Spa 73 at 13.15 hours near the Réservoir, and the second by a Spa 3 patrol at 1510 between Corbeny and Craonne. Patrols on the 4th produced two unsuccessful combats but saw the promotion of Auguste Pouchelle of Spa 26 to Adjudant.

The serviceability of the Groupe during these winter days can be judged by the fact that out of 70 aeroplanes assigned to it, only around 40-45 were available for operations towards the end of the first week of January. This was not helped on the 9th by one pilot returning from a protection patrol smashing up Spad XIII No.2.034, but then severe bad weather ended flying until the 12th.

During this period, Sergent Phelps Collins, one of the Americans in Spa 103, was transferred to the Lafayette Escadrille, N 124, in preparation for the transformation of the unit into the 103rd Pursuit Squadron of the United States Aero Service planned for 18 February. At that time, N 124 *Lafayette* would become Spa 124 *Jeanne d'Arc* of the French Air Service under the command of Lieutenant André d'Humières, while Major Bill Thaw, a veteran of N 124, would take command of the 103rd Aero. Collins would be promoted to Captain in the US Air Service (quite a jump from sergent), two days after he left Spa 103 (the 9th) and serve as a flight commander with the 103rd until he was killed in action on 12 March near Château-Thierry. He had by then received the Croix de Guerre with two palmes.

Another American with the Groupe, Captain Charles Biddle, serving with Spa 73, was also transferred to N 124 on the 10th, in order to be assigned to the 103rd as a flight commander. Biddle would later command the 13th Pursuit Squadron and finally the 4th Pursuit Group in the USAS. He would be promoted to Major on 1 November 1918, by which time he had received the Distinguished Service Cross, been made a Chevalier de la Légion d'Honneur in addition to holding the Croix de Guerre with three palmes and the Belgian Ordre de Léopold. In all he would receive credit for a total of seven aerial victories. As mentioned earlier, he has left us his worthy book *The Way of the Eagle*, first published in 1919.

The 12th of January saw Spa 103 begin a move of airfield to a new base at Beauzée-sur-Aire, situated about ten kilometres south-west of Souilly, in the II Armée Sector, which was commanded by Général Auguste Edouard Hirschauer. This brought them again to the old Verdun area, Souilly being about 17 kilometres south-south-west of the city opposite the Vallée de la Meuse. The next day Spa 3 too began to move its base.

In accordance with GQG Ordre No. 2115M of 5 January 1918, an Ordre de Movement was issued by the État-Major, Aéronautique de la VI° Armée No.23081 on 13 January 1918, Escadrilles Spa 26 and Spa 73 were put at the disposition of the II Armée and were directed to proceed to Beauzée-sur-Aire on the 15th. Escadrille Spa 67, commanded by Capitaine Marie Jacques d'Indy, was assigned to Groupe de Combat 12 pursuant to an Ordre de Movement issued by the VI° Armée État-Major, Aéronautique No.23097 on 16 January. Parc 112 was moved from Evres and Spa 67 was directed to report to Beauzée-sur-Aire as well.

Escadrille Spa 67, which was to replace Spa 73, had been formed on 17 September 1915, at

Lyon-Bron, under Sous-lieutenant Mathieu Tenant de la Tour, who was in charge until 21 September, at which time Capitaine M M O Galouzeau de Villepin arrived to take over. The unit was assigned to the IV° Armée and reported to La Cheppe on the 24th. Then on 29 October the unit was assigned to the Région Fortifée de Verdun (RFV). On 15 January 1916, N 67 was cited for the first time as a part of a groupe of escadrilles in l'Ordre de l'Armée No.48. On 22 February command of N 67 passed to Lieutenant Henri de Saint Sauveur under whom the unit was based at several airfields in the RFV which evolved into the II° Armée until it had been sent to Cachy in August 1916.

N 67 was cited for the second time during July in l'Ordre de l'Armée No.278 which gave the escadrille the right to display the fourragère of the Croix de Guerre on its standard by Ordre No.4 'F' dated 30 July. On 1 November N 67 went to Groupe de Combat 13, commanded by Chef de Bataillon Philippe Féquant, along with Escadrilles N 65, N 112, and N 124. N 67 was detached from GC 13 on 1 June 1917, and assigned to the Groupe Provisoire de Bonneuil, in the III° Armée Sector. On 1 August Capitaine Marie Jacques d'Indy replaced Capitaine Henri de Saint Sauveur as commanding officer. By the time Spa 67 joined GC 12 it had been credited with 28 confirmed victories, credited to the following pilots:

MdL Georges Flachaire	8 including one shared with two pilots of other escadrilles	
S/Lt Jean Navarre	7	
S/Lt Marcel Viallet	6	
Lt Jean Derode	2	
S/Lt Jean Peretti	1	
Sgt Marie Joseph Goux	1	
Sgt Henri Massot	1	
Capt Bernon	1 shared	⎫
Adj Georges Toulze	1 shared	⎬
Sgt Robert de Marolles	1 pilot	⎫
Cpl Gaston Vitalis	1 observer	⎬

It had suffered the loss of five men missing, seven wounded and one injured in an accident.

* * *

Capitaine Marie Jacques d'Indy was born 20 May 1888, at Villain, and entered military service on 8 October 1908, joining the 18° Régiment de Chasseurs. He was promoted to Brigadier on 12 February the following year and to Maréchal-des-Logis on 16 September. He was named an Aspirant and sent to a Special Military School on 16 May 1910, graduating as a Sous-lieutenant on 1 October 1911, and assigned to the 14° Régiment de Hussards. Exactly one year later he became a full Lieutenant and transferred to the 3° Régiment de Chasseurs d'Afrique. Then on 10 July 1914, he was reassigned to the 1er Régiment de Spahis until 29 August when he was sent to the 5° Régiment de Chasseurs d'Afrique, but within days he returned to the 3° Régiment. He entered aviation on 21 July 1915, was promoted to Capitaine (TT) on 18 June 1916, which was made permanent on 6 July 1917.

The make up of GC 12 as of 16 January 1918, was as follows:

Commanding Officer	Capitaine Henri Horment
Technical Assistant	Lieutenant André Rouget
Intelligence Officer	Capitaine Jean Vernard de Billy
Armament Officer	Lieutenant Joseph Point-Dumont
CO Spa 3	Lieutenant Georges Raymond
CO Spa 26	Lieutenant Xavier de Sevin

CO Spa 67   Capitaine Marie Jacques d'Indy
CO Spa 73   Capitaine Albert Deullin
CO Spa 103   Capitaine Jean d'Harcourt
CO Parc 112   Capitaine Pierre Barbey

* * *

René Fonck of Spa 103 opened his 1918 account on 19 January in fine style by gaining his 20th and 21st confirmed kills. The first he achieved over Beaumont, the second at 14.15 hours over Samogneux, the latter confirmed by the 17° Auto-Canon DCA (artillery) 56, from the 3rd Sector. In addition Fonck had twenty unconfirmed claims at this time.

The next day de Sevin and MdL Fontaine, Spa 26, combined efforts and crashed a German aircraft between Magenta and Samogneux at 10.40 hours. Caporal Henry A. Batchelor, an American who had joined Spa 103 on 26 December, was injured in an accident which put him in hospital for over a month. While he was waiting his return to active duty he received a commission as an Ensign in the US Naval Air Service, thereby ending his service with the French.

Poor weather reduced activity over the next few days, but on 25 January, despite a hazy morning it cleared in the afternoon allowing 14 patrols to be flown during which eight combats were fought. At 14.50 five Albatros Scouts attacked a patrol of Spa 67 during which Adjudant Duret claimed one of them shot down at 15.15 over Bértincourt. Unfortunately, Brigadier Phillip Benney, another American, was wounded in the right hand and forced to put down about 500 metres west of Fort Choisel, but not before he had seriously damaged another of the Albatros formation. Benney came from Pittsburgh, Pennsylvania, and had joined the French Military on 31 May 1917, receiving a Military Pilot's Brevet on 16 October 1917. He joined Spa 67 on 12 December. His wound proved to be more serious than was first thought and he died the next day, the 26th, in the hospital at Glorieux. He was awarded the Croix de Guerre with palme.

Also on the 25th, Marcel Haegelen of Spa 103, was given a temporary promotion to Sous-lieutenant by Ordre No.28.293. Sergent Roger Tassou of Spa 73 was promoted to Adjudant. More promotions were announced the next day. Sous-lieutenant Jean Dombray, Spa 26, was made a temporary full lieutenant. MdL Benjamin de Tascher, the ex-POW from Spa 26, and Adjudant Seigneurie, Spa 103, were both commissioned Sous-lieutenants. Then on the 27th Adjudant Charles Albanel of Spa 3, was given a temporary promotion to Sous-lieutenant.

The serviceability rate improved through the month, so that on the 29th 51 aircraft were available, while 49 were on line the last day of the month. This was increased to 56 as February began, although this fell to 45 by the 4th. Bad weather continued to prevent any real action until the 5th.

At 12.05 hours, Lieutenant Fonck attacked a German two-seater over the Argonne and shot it down between Clermont-en-Argonne and Varennes-en-Argonne. Other pilots in this patrol confirmed seeing it break up in the air and fall in pieces. At the same time Marcel Haegelen engaged another C-type in the same locality and forced it to dive for its lines, the observer evidently killed or wounded as no return fire was experienced.

At 12.45 a patrol of Spa 67 attacked four hostile aircraft. Lieutenant Willemin went after a two-seater from close range with other members of the patrol each taking turns to engage it. The two-seater appeared badly hit and it dived steeply for its lines. Caporal William Hallet Tailer, yet another American in Spa 67, having arrived on 14 December, was killed in the area of Montzéville, at 13.30, possibly hit by anti-aircraft fire. Tailer was born at Roslyn, New York, and had joined the French Military Service on 21 May 1917, becoming a pilot on 10 October.

Low clouds prevented further operations until the 11th, but the Germans failed to turn up, then the weather clamped again. Meantime on the 7th, Marcel Haegelen left the Groupe upon transfer to Spa 100 (part of GC 17). Already the holder of the Médaille Militaire but with only two victories, he would go on to score 20 more combat successes, including 12 balloons and be made a Chevalier de la Légion d'Honneur on 19 July 1918. He ended the war with 15 palmes and three étoiles de vermeil to his Croix de Guerre. Another to leave the Groupe was Lieutenant Jean Thobie, having been made commanding officer of Spa 48 (GC 11) from 10 February. Thobie was born 27 June 1894, at Châlons-sur-Saone (Saone et Loire) and had attended St. Cyr, commissioned a Sous-lieutenant on 6 August 1914, assigned to the 7° Régiment de Hussards. He served on the Staff of the 35th Brigade d'Infanterie from 15 August 1915, until he entered aviation as an observer on 5 December. He was attached to both Escadrille N 3 and N 62, and was promoted to Lieutenant on 4 April 1916. He went into pilot training and received Military Pilot's Brevet No.9727 on 15 May 1917. After additional training he was assigned to N 95 on 10 August transferring to Spa 67 on 19 November. He commanded Spa 48 until 23 July when he was reassigned as commanding officer of Spa 156. Thobie ended the war with the Croix de Guerre and two palmes and two étoiles de bronze, and would be made a Chevalier de la Légion d'Honneur for his war services on 16 November 1920. Three days later Spa 73 was detached from the Groupe and assigned to GC 19, moving to Villeseneux.

Further disruption came on the 14th, Capitaine Albert Deullin, Spa 73, being given command of the forming Groupe de Combat 19, handing over the Escadrille to Capitaine Pierre Cahuzac, who moved from Spa 67 to take up this appointment. GC 12 was now made up of just Spa 3, 26, 67, and 103.

Groupe de Combat 19 was assigned to the newly created Escadre de Combat No. 1, which was authorized by Grand Quartier Général des Armées du Nord et du Nord-Est, Service Aéronautique Ordre No.4553. Its commander was Chef de Bataillon Victor Ménard, an old Stork and the former commander of N 26 and GC 15. The Escadre was made up of GC 15 (Spa 37, Spa 81, Spa 93, and Spa 97); GC 18 (Spa 48, Spa 94, Spa 153 and Spa 155); GC 19 (Spa 73, Spa 85, Spa 95, and Spa 96). This organization was created as a tactical formation to be moved to any sector where it would be needed and would function under one unified command. This was the first time during the war that twelve escadrilles de chasse had been placed under the command of just one man.

* * *

Lieutenants Bozon-Verduraz and de la Rochefordière of Spa 3 engaged and claimed a two-seater shot down at 11.35 hours on 17 February, which crashed at Damloup. The next day, in good weather, Bozon-Verduraz claimed his second victim, another two-seater which fell at 12.15 between Montfaucon and Malancourt.

Caporal William T Ponder, an American in Spa 67, was transferred on the 17th and promoted to commissioned rank in the USAS ten days later. He would be assigned to Spa 163, then the 103rd Pursuit, and be credited with six victories. He would receive the French Croix de Guerre with four palmes and the American Distinguished Service Cross for his war service.

Fonck scored again on the 18th, shooting down an Albatros in flames at 13.06 hours between Cauières and Bezonvaux for his 23rd victory. To this he added his 24th the next day, an Albatros two-seater at 12.05 above Montfaucon, while Caporal Baylies, yet another American with Spa 3, was credited with the destruction of his first enemy aircraft – a two-seater – north of Forges.

Frank Leaman Baylies came from New Bedford, Massachusetts, born there on 23 September 1895. Yet another keen athlete and swimmer, he had also learned to drive, something which helped in the early days of the war when he volunteered for the US Ambulance Service in May 1916. Once in France he saw active duty on the Somme in 1916, then at Verdun, the Argonne before moving to Serbia for three months. Here he received the French Croix de Guerre, on 25 March 1917, for evacuating wounded while under fire. He then volunteered to become a pilot with the French. By the beginning of November 1917 he was a Stork with Spa 73 at Dunkirk then moved to Spa 3 on 18 December. With all the recent changes in personnel, men moving to the USAS, NCOs being commissioned and so on, Baylies was one of the few who decided to continue with the French, refusing a captaincy with the Americans, remaining a sergent. However, he was eventually persuaded and took an American commission but still stayed with the Storks until his untimely death in action.

Bozon-Verduraz and de la Rochefordière were back in the news on the 20th, again combining efforts against a two-seater at 11.20 hours near the trenches of Calonne. Then at 16.40, Lieutenant Raymond, the CO of Spa 3, claimed his sixth victory over Vauquois. The following day Adjudant Baron of Spa 103 was promoted to Adjudant-Chef, while Caporal Brugère of the same unit became Sergent Brugère.

Fonck scored another double on the 26th, in good weather, a two-seater at 10.10 south of Montfaucon, and another C-type fifteen minutes later near Dieppe, about 10 kilometres north-east of Verdun. These brought his total to 26.

Bad weather again forced a reduction in front-line work, but Xavier de Sevin was promoted to Capitaine on 2 March, a rank commensurate with his job of leading Spa 26. However, while the weather persisted, the Groupe completed the move from Beauzée-sur-Aire to Lhéry, about 20 kilometres west-south-west of Reims, in the 1er Armée Sector (commanded by Général Marie Eugène Debeney) – the Champagne Front.

Meantime Caporal Baylies downed his second victim, by crashing a scout north-east of Courtecon. Another American in the Groupe, Caporal Robert B Hoeber, Spa 103, made Sergent on 10 March, the same day Brigadier Drouillh was promoted to Maréchal-des-Logis.

Things had become so quiet in the air, what with the poor weather, that Sergent Schmitter, Spa 103, dived to 50 metres and shot up German trenches in front of Loivre on the 12th. Then Adjudant Naudin, Spa 26, experienced problems with his Spad XIII No.4360 and was almost back at the airfield where he had to crash-land, but he escaped without injury. On the 13th – it had to be the 13th – two more crashes occurred luckily without injury to the pilots. One was Lieutenant Dombray, Spa 26, who overturned his Spad XIII No.685, and Sergent Ribardière, Spa 3, did the same thing with No.4654. During a patrol Lieutenants Puget and Dombray had strafed trenches too from about 150 metres north of the Fort de la Pompelle, and south-east of the village of Cernay-les-Reims. Sergents Schmitter and Baux, Spa 3, also shot up troop columns in the same village.

March 15th saw Fonck's 27th kill – another two-seater. This one crashed east of the village of Bremiercourt at 10.15, confirmed by Lieutenants Letourneau and Thouzellier, and Sergent Schmitter. Then at 17.25 Fonck made it 28 with another two-seater about one kilometre north of Courtecon. This machine was seen on the ground by Capitaine de Sevin and Lieutenants Thouzellier and Fontaine. At 17.30 Sergent Schmitter who was having a busy and productive few days, downed his first victim, a two-seater, which crashed between Vorges and Lierval. This was confirmed by the artillery of the VI° Armée.

On 16 March, under cloudy skies, the Groupe had two successive air actions during 13 patrols. Fonck attacked a two-seater between Reims and the Fort de la Pompelle at 11.50 and sent it down in flames through the clouds, confirmed by the observers at the station at Pusieux, for victory number 29. At 14.20 Adjudant Pendaries, Spa 67, attacked one of two two-seaters he found at 2,500 metres which had been under attack from French AA fire. He chased his chosen victim towards Tahure, causing it to go down near the woods south of Challerange, but due to lack of witnesses it could only be noted as a probable. At 17.35 Caporal Baylies, Spa 3 attacked a flight of three German scouts, firing into one of them at close range. It went into a long glide then fell into a spiral in the area of Chevregny – his third confirmed victory.

Ten minutes later, Sergent Baux of Spa 103 attacked a scout, out of a formation of seven, from close range and it turned sharply and was attacked in turn by Adjudant Gustave Douchy of Spa 38, finally falling in flames near Witry-les-Reims, Douchy receiving credit for his fifth victory. Sous-lieutenant Letourneau, also of Spa 103, attacked a two-seater at 16.45 but the observer's return fire hit his motor and he was compelled to make a forced landing north of Fismes.

Two more successful combats were achieved the following day, the 17th. At 11.40 Adjudant Mion of Spa 67 engaged a two-seater at 2,800 metres between Marchais and Montaigu. He certainly disabled it but being unable to follow it down it was left to the personnel of the 51st Infantry Division to confirm its fall – his second victory. Fonck went after another C-type at 4,200 metres with another close-range attack over Nogent l'Abbesse. It fell away in a spin and was lost to sight, so he only gained a probable.

At 18.20 Fonck attacked a Pfalz DIII he found between Guignicourt and Neufchâtel- sur-Aisne, and again while his fire sent it down he could not watch his kill, but this time people on the ground confirmed its fall – which brought him victory number 30. At the same time Sergent Loup, Spa 103, attacked a couple of scouts in the vicinity of Laval, firing 20 rounds at one that dived vertically but it could only be claimed as a probable. The last fight of the day came at 18.40, Lieutenant Bozon-Verduraz, Spa 3, attacking two fighters at 4,000 metres above Guignicourt. However, he then spotted a third scout above him and he broke off the action, although none of the three attempted to engage him.

* * *

The great German Spring Offensive, known as the Second Battle of the Somme – or Operation Michael by the Germans – and the Kaiser's Battle by later historians – began on 21 March 1918. With von Marwitz's Second Army flanked on the right by von Below's Seventeenth Army, and on the left by von Hutier's Eighteenth Army, the assault against General Hubert Gough's British 5th Army along a 44-mile front, consisted of 74 divisions. These were supported by 6,473 guns and howitzers as well as 3,532 trench mortars. The Luftstreitkeräfte consisted of 51 Flieger Abteilungen, 35 Jagdstaffeln, 27 Schlachstaffeln and four Bombengeschwadern assigned as follows:

> 2nd Army – 17 FAs, 10 Jastas, 11 SSs, one BG.
> 17th Army – 17 FAs, 13 Jastas, 7 SSs, one BG.
> 18th Army – 17 FAs, 12 Jastas, 9 SSs, two BGs.

The British 5th Army consisted of just 12 infantry and five cavalry divisions and was flanked to the north by the 3rd Army (General Julian Byng) and to the south by the French VI° Armée (Général Denis Duchène). The Germans had advanced far enough towards Montdidier, that on 23 March 'Big Bertha' (a huge long-range gun) was able to lob shells into the suburbs of Paris, causing a disastrous effect on French civilian morale. By the time the advance was stopped on 31 March, the British had lost about 150,000 men of whom 90,000 had been taken prisoner. They had also lost a great many guns, ammunition and other material and had used up all their reserves; about half the French Army had been sent to the front.

Allied troop morale was very low at this time, although the Germans had failed to reach their objectives. However, one good thing did come out of the battle, the unified command concept on the Western Front with Maréchal Ferdinand Foch in overall command.

* * *

On the first day of the offensive, under misty skies and limited visibility, Adjudants Baron, Baux and Tasqué, Spa 103, attacked a Rumpler two-seater at 13.40 hours over the Montagne de Reims, and forced it to land inside French lines near Rilly-le-Montagne. Both crew members had been wounded and were taken prisoner. Their machine had been hit several times and the fuel tank punctured.

Due to the German breakthrough the 1er Armée was moved quickly to the Picardy area. Spa 26 started their move to Mesnil-St.Georges, about three kilometres south-west of Montdidier, on the 22nd. In spite of mediocre visibility ten patrols were flown during the day. Sergents Schmitter and Hoeber, Spa 103, attacked one of a pair of scouts near Berry-au-Bac at 15.15, firing at close range. It dived steeply but could only be claimed as a probable. At 17.15, while Adjudant Naudin of Spa 26 engaged a two-seater over Nogent l'Abbesse, he was in turn attacked by eight scouts. In disengaging himself he fired about 40 rounds into one of them that fell away in a glide but once more only a probable was allowed. Fonck had the next action, against a two-seater in the same area but he was experiencing carburetor trouble and had to break off the fight.

The next day Adjudant Gaston Tasqué, Spa 103, was killed in an accident and on the 24th, Spa 3 and Spa 103 began their move to Mesnil-St.Georges. Spa 67 arrived at the same location on the 25th.

On the 26th, the 1er Armée (Général Marie Eugène Debeney) entered the lines to the left of the III° Armée (Général Georges Louis Humbert) with the dividing line situated along from Nesle, through Roye to Montdidier. Spa 3, Spa 26 and Spa 67 were moved from Mesnil to Raray, about 15 kilometres north-east of Senlis. Some patrols were flown on this day, Adjudant Lecomte of Spa 3 smashing up his Spad trying to land while coming back from one of them. The Groupe lost a pilot on the 27th – Sous-lieutenant André Willemin of Spa 67 failing to return from a 16.30 patrol. At this time Capitaine Jean d'Harcourt, CO of Spa 103, was designated as commander of Groupe de Combat 13, and was replaced at the head of his Escadrille by Lieutenant Joseph Battle.

Battle was born 16 December 1894, at Rhodés. He had entered military service on 16 December 1912, assigned to the 26° Bataillon de Chasseurs-à-Pied. Promoted to Caporal on 19 April 1913, then to Sergent Fourrier on 1 October he became an Adjudant after the war began, on 4 September 1914, and was decorated with the Médaille Militaire eight days later. On 11 May 1915 he was commissioned and reassigned to the 25° Bataillon de Chasseurs. He was promoted to full lieutenant (TT) on 6 January 1916 but wishing to join the Aviation Service, he was sent to Pau as a student pilot on 15 November. Once qualifying he served with Spa 77 from 6 April 1917, until taking command of Spa 103, at which time he had been credited with one confirmed victory.

Fonck scored again on the 28th, a hostile machine down in flames east of Montdidier at 10.30 that morning. Lieutenant Battle, having hardly unpacked, was hit and wounded in the foot by a bullet fired from the ground, which was not a good start. Frank Baylies failed to come back from a patrol but he returned the next day, having been forced down into no-man's-land between the trenches. Two promotions occurred on the 28th, Adjudants Marcel Duret and Pierre Pendaries becoming temporary Sous-lieutenants.

Fonck gained another double on the 29th – his 32nd and 33rd victories – by downing scouts at 18.30 and 18.35 east of Montdidier. Also on the 29th, Caporal Jasper Brown, an American with Spa 67, was commissioned a Second Lieutenant in the US Air Service, but he remained with his French unit. Brown hailed from New York City and had entered French aviation on 19 June 1917, receiving a Military Pilot's Brevet on 6 November. After additional training he was assigned to Spa 67 on 3 February.

By the last day of the month the ground crews were able to have 65 Spads on the line, but the month ended with strong winds and a German aircraft damaged by Sergent Schmitter of Spa 103 at 08.35 over Montdidier. Pilots known to have been assigned to GC 12 as of 31 March 1918 were:

Spa 3

Lt Georges Raymond – CO	Sgt Auguste Mourey
Lt Benjamin Bozon-Verduraz	Sgt Edwin Parsons (US)
S/Lt Guy de la Rochefordière	Sgt Louis Risacher
Lt Tadia Sondermayer	Cpl Maurice Chevannes
S/Lt Louis Bucquet	Cpl Georges Clémont
S/Lt Charles Albanel	Cpl Gustave Decatoire
Adj Joseph Barouillet	Cpl David Judd (US)
Sgt Frank Baylies (US)	Cpl Robert Martin
Sgt Francois Marari	Cpl Marius Ribardière
Sgt Edouard Moulines	Brig Jules Denneulin

Spa 26

Capt Xavier de Sevin – CO
S/Lt Benjamin de Tascher
S/Lt Jean Dombray
S/Lt Emile Letourneau
S/Lt Jacques Puget
S/Lt Jacques Puget
Adj-Chef Léon Barés
Adj Jean Dedieu

Adj Gustave Naudin
Adj Auguste Pouchelle
MdL Julius Antoine
MdL Noël Fontaine
Sgt Pierre Devaulx
Sgt Aimé Vincent
Cpl Lester Brady
Cpl Désiré Mabereau

Spa 67

Capt Jacques d'Indy – CO
Lt Alfred Rougevin-Baville
Adj Marcel Duret
Adj Henri Prétre
MdL-Chef Fernand Quinchez
MdL Emile Fumat
Cpl Joseph Bouillet
Cpl Jasper Brown
Cpl Edward Kalvelage
Cpl René Ménard

Spa 103

Lt Joseph Battle – CO
Lt Fontaine
S/Lt René Fonck
S/Lt Seigneurie
S/Lt Léon Thouzellier
Adj Joseph Baron
Adj René Lecomte
Adj Camille Pietri
MdL Henri Drouillh
Sgt Auguste Baux
Sgt Gilbert Loup
Sgt Pierre Schmitter
Cpl Romanel

* * *

April began with the eighth victory of Capitaine de Sevin of Spa 26. Under light cloud cover GC 12 flew eight patrols, de Sevin downing an opponent east of Montdidier at 14.15. Half an hour later Caporal Mabereau and Sergent Loup of Spa 26 and Spa 103 respectively probably shot down a German machine over the Bois de Tilloloy, about 10 kilometres east of Montdidier. Next day Caporal Mabereau was promoted to Sergent.

Another probable was scored on the 3rd, a patrol of Spa 3 attacking a two-seater over the front at 07.15. The observer appeared to be killed and the pilot put down inside German lines between Faverolles and Peinnes. At 10.30, Sergent Vincent, Spa 26, attacked one scout out of a flight of five and scored a probable over Fignières, but was unable to watch its fall being too heavily engaged by the other four. Unfortunately, the Groupe lost a good pilot this day. Sergent Pierre Devaulx, Spa 26, flew a patrol at 10.00 hours and did not return.

Rain curtailed operations over the next two days but Sous-lieutenant Benjamin (his full forenames being Jean Seraphin Benjamin Emmanuel) Bozon-Verduraz was made a Chevalier de la Légion d'Honneur. It will be recalled that he had been with Guynemer on his last flight.

A remarkable officer pilot, during two years he has gained the admiration of the Army Corps Escadrille with which he serves, while carrying out the most arduous missions, never ceasing to seek battle with joyous zeal. He downed one after the other three enemy aircraft in the space of four days. One wound – three citations.

De Sevin claimed a probable at 1135 over Fignières on the 6th, but the weather at this time was still proving bad. Then on the 8th, Spa 67 and Spa 103 moved to Hétomesnil, about 30 kilometres north-

north-west of Beauvais, in the III Armée Sector (Général Georges Louis Humbert), followed by the other two escadrilles on the 9th. On the 11th Frank Baylies brought his score to four with a German two-seater machine in flames at 13.30 between Mesnil-St.Georges and Courtemanche.

Baylies became an ace on the 12th. Fifty-seven sorties were flown this day in 12 patrols and the American crashed a two-seater at 06.50 south of Moreuil. A Spa 26 patrol led by de Sevin attacked a two-seater in the late afternoon, 17.45, which became a probable, while Fonck set a German scout on fire between Piennes and Romagne at 18.25, followed 15 minutes later by a two-seater south of Moreuil, making his score up to 35.

Frank Baylies had by this time received two citations, one on 27 March 1917, the second on the 9 March 1918. They read:

> Frank Baylies, an American volunteer in the Automobile Sanitary Section No.3, twice volunteered duty at the Front and then for the Army of the Orient. He showed to wounded men perfect devotion and fearlessness, being daily tested under bombardment. From Dec.19, 1916 to March 28, 1917, during the evacuation of wounded from the Monistir sector, he showed no fear under the bombardment of cities, roads, and encampments.
>
> Frank Baylies, an American citizen, enlisted in the French Army before the United States declared war. He passed at his own request into fighter aviation, in which he displayed the very finest enthusiasm. On Feb. 18 he shot down single-handed an enemy aeroplane which crashed within our lines.

More poor weather restricted activity over the next few April days, there were even snow flurries, so it was not until 20 April that the next claims came. Sous-lieutenant Rougevin-Baville and Adjudant Pillon, Spa 67, brought down a German between Moreuil and Souvillier, while Bozon-Verduraz, Spa 3, brought his own score to four at 10.05 between Hangard and Thennes. He made acedom on the 21st – the day that Baron Manfred von Richthofen was killed on the British Front, atop the Morlancourt Ridge.

At 08.15 a patrol from Spa 67 attacked an enemy aircraft between Thory and Rouvel, and Bozon-Verduraz joined in, and it was his fire which caused the machine to burst into flames and fall. However, he had to share it with Spa 67's Sous-lieutenant Duret (second victory) and Adjudant Mion (third victory) and Brigadier Ouvrard de Linière (first victory). Sous-lieutenant Bucquet of Spa 3 raised his personal score to three by downing a two-seater in the vicinity of Roye. René Fonck raised his score to 36 the next day, a German shot down over Assainvillers-le-Monchel, at 18.05 hours.

Again weather interrupted flying but on the 24th MdL Noël Fontaine of Spa 26 was commissioned, while Fernand Quinchez, Spa 67, and Pierre Schmitter, Spa 103, were both made Adjudants. On the last day of April, Lieutenant Guy Gonzague de la Rochefordière, Spa 3, took command of Spa 94 (GC 18) but he was destined to fall in combat on 11 June, which would affect the promotion of another Stork.

CHAPTER ELEVEN

May 1918

The poor weather of late April continued into May, but it cleared a little on the 2nd to allow GC 12 to mount several patrols, serviceability being maintained at about 44 Spads. There were 15 combats of varying degrees but only one produced a positive result. Frank Baylies, Spa 3, claimed his sixth kill by shooting down a German two-seater Rumpler at 13.20 hours between Ayencourt and Assainvillers. Three other German machines were claimed as probably destroyed during the late afternoon.

Baylies was on form the next day, this time attacking a German photo-reconnaissance machine. However, he only got off eight or nine rounds before his guns jammed, but to his surprise and delight, he watched the German head down for a forced landing only about five kilometres inside the German lines. While he was unable to claim a kill, an afternoon patrol paid better dividends. He and MdL Dubonnet went after another two-seater at 17.25 hours between Montdidier and Faverolles. The machine fell and was confirmed, probably being that crewed by Leutnants Willi Karbe and Erich Meuche of FA(A)245 who were both killed over this locality on this date. Unfortunately, the Groupe lost Sergent Désiré Mabereau of Spa 26 this day. Flying Spad VII No.3802, he took off on patrol at noon and failed to return. He fell victim to either Leutnant Moritz-Waldemer Bretschneider-Bodener of Jasta 6 who claimed a Spad at 12.20 east of Cayeux, or possibly Leutnant Hans Kirschstein of the same unit, his Spad going down west of Rosières at 12.50. Another loss occurred on the 4th, Sergent Marcel Dupont, Spa 26, being wounded in the foot during combat.

This same day saw command of Groupe de Combat 12 change hands. Capitaine Henri Horment handed over to Capitaine Charles Dupuy, one of the staff team of GC 12. Dupuy had been born on 21 July 1881, in Paris, and when the war began he was a reserve officer. He was assigned to a staff post with a cavalry unit but requested pilot training and was sent to Pau on 7 September 1915. Receiving Military Pilot's Brevet No.2106 on 19 December he was then sent to the Réserve Générale de l'Aviation at Bourget until 15 May 1916, at which time he was posted to Escadrille N 48. He had hardly started combat flying before he was wounded in the neck on 24 May and rushed to hospital where he remained until 28 June. He was made a Chevalier de la Légion d'Honneur which was to rank from the same 24 May:

> Excellent pilot officer, very seriously wounded during the course of a combat which he had with an
> enemy aircraft. He had, nevertheless, the strength to return his aircraft to his airfield and land.

On 19 November, Lieutenant Dupuy was transferred to N 351 and promoted to Capitaine on 1 May 1917. He was reassigned to Escadrille N 31 on 18 May and took command of this unit on 17 July. He remained here until transferred to the staff of GC 12 on 2 May 1918, with orders to assume command two days later.

* * *

Adjudant Edwin Parsons of Spa 3 downed his second official victory on 6 May, a two-seater at 17.15 hours between Mesnil-St.Georges and Montdidier. Ed Parsons, an American from Holyoke, Massachusetts was no new-boy to aviation. After leaving Phillips Exeter Academy, he had served with the Mexican Army Aviation Corps between 1913 and 1915 having learned to fly in Los Angeles,

California before he was 21. Sailing to France in December 1915 he joined the US Ambulance Service in the New Year and after seeing action at the Front, transferred to the French Foreign Legion in order to enlist in French Aviation. He ended up with the Escadrille *Lafayette* – N 124 – and downed his first German aircraft – a Rumpler – on 4 September 1917. He moved to Spa 3 on 26 February 1918.

Parsons came from Springfield, although born in Holyoke on 24 September 1892. He had joined N 124 on 24 January 1917 and promoted to Sergent in February. He was cited in orders for his fighting in the air, and won his Croix de Guerre for his first confirmed victory. He returned to the US on leave in January 1918, went back to join the Storks in April, where he remained an NCO till late 1918.

No fewer than 64 aircraft took part in ten patrols on 9 May. Fonck really added to his laurels and those of the Groupe by claiming six German two-seaters destroyed. The first three went down within five minutes of each other between 16.00 and 16.05 hours – the first two in ten seconds – and a third five minutes later. The first two crashed south of Moreuil, the third falling in flames over the same locality. During a second patrol which began at 17.30 that afternoon, Fonck, leading Sergent Brugère and Sous-lieutenant Thouzellier, attacked a two-seater at 18.20 which broke up in the air over Montdidier, but he lost sight of the other Spads. In Fonck's own words: *"I had lost sight of my companions, but was not too angry with myself over this. I prefer to fly alone in the middle of my adversaries anyway, without having the additional responsibility of protecting my comrades. Comraderie imposes on us the duty of rescuing a compatriot who is in a bad spot. I never try to let a comrade down; but above all, I like my freedom of action, for it is indispensable to the success of my undertakings."* [6] Proving this theory Fonck attacked a flight of four Fokkers and five Albatros two-seaters at 18.55, two of which fell in flames between Hargicourt and Braches, bringing his total to 42.

At 19.30 Sergent Baylies claimed a Halberstadt two-seater between Braches and Gratibus for his eighth victory. Earlier at 14.55, Spa 3's patrol probably downed an enemy aircraft over Ayencourt. Also on this day, Lieutenant Georges Raymond, the commanding officer of Spa 3, was promoted to Capitaine.

More victories came on the 10th. Spa 3 engaged two C-types between Faverolles and Montdidier, one shot down by MdL Dubonnet, his second, the other by the unstoppable Baylies, this one shared with MdL Clément for his first victory. Two days of bad weather was only relieved by the announcement of an award to Sous-lieutenant Fonck, this time making him an Officier de la Légion d'Honneur, by GQG Ordre No.12927. The award was made by Général Debeney, the commander of the 1er Armée:

> A remarkable officer from every point of view, of an admirable fighting spirit. First-rate pilot, for reconnaissance missions and artillery-range intelligence as well as for the surveillance service that he has undertaken many times despite unfavorable atmospheric conditions. He demonstrated, in the course of an uninterrupted series of aerial duels, exceptional energy and a will to win which set an example for the French fighter pilots of today. He has shot down 36 enemy aircraft, received 15 citations, the Médaille Militaire, and the Chevalier de la Légion d'Honneur for feats of combat. On 15 May he was made a full Lieutenant, by decree of the President of the Republic, Monsieur Raymond Poincairé.

* * *

The next actions occurred on 15 May under clear skies. In all there were five successful combats. At 08.25, Capitaine Sabattier de Vignolle, CO of GC 18, together with Brigadier Ouvrard de Linière of Spa 67, sent a scout down in flames between Montdidier and Dompierre. Then at 11.35 Lieutenant Bozon-Verduraz and MdL Moulines of Spa 3, crashed a two-seater near Assainvillers. Two enemy

---

[6] *Mes Combats* by René Fonck.

planes went down at 12.25, the first to Capitaine de Sevin, Sous-lieutenant de Tascher and Adjudant Antoine of Spa 26, between Assainvillers and Rubescourt, the second by Lieutenants Dombray and Letourneau, Spa 26, in the same area. Sergent Pietri, Spa 103, gained his second victory by downing a German at 19.55 near Moreuil.

On 16 May there were clear skies which produced more fighting. Three confirmed and three unconfirmed kills were achieved, the former by the 'on form' Bozon-Verduraz, with Sergent Risacher and Sergent Moulines of Spa 3, who attacked a two-seater which crashed between Montdidier and Faverolles. Adjudant Ed Parsons gained his third victory, a two-seater at 09.45 between Mesnil-St.Georges and Montdidier (he also claimed one of the probables this day); while the third went down under the guns of de Sevin – his 10th victory – which he shared with Lieutenant Puget, the latter's first success.

Sous-lieutenant Charles Albanel of Spa 3, on patrol at 08.00, failed to make it home flying a Spad XIII, possibly falling victim to Leutnant Max Näther of Jasta 62, his first of an eventual 26 victories. It was later learned that he had become a prisoner of war. Albanel was born 14 January 1888, at St.Just and entered military service on 3 October 1910, as a Soldat de 2nd Classe assigned to the 2° Régiment d'Artillerie de Campagne. He entered aviation on 22 September 1915, and received a Military Pilot's Brevet 15 January 1916. Then came promotion to Brigadier on 23 January, and assignment to Escadrille N 62 on 27 April but he left for MF 24 on 15 June where he was promoted to Maréchal-des-Logis on 15 July, and was awarded the Médaille Militaire on 8 November. Albanel was promoted to Adjudant on 25 April 1917, and joined Spa 3 on 22 October.

Two confirmed and three probables fell on the 17th, the confirmed going to Sous-lieutenant Pendaries – a two-seater at 11.40 north-east of Moreuil – for his fourth victory, while in the afternoon, at 13.30 Sergents Loup and Drouillh, Spa 103, crashed a Pfalz DIII near Montdidier, thereby gaining their respective first victories. Adjudant Pillon, Spa 67, made the only confirmed claim the next day, a two-seater crashed east of Montdidier for victory number seven.

Fonck was back in the hunt on the 18th, scoring victories 43 and 44, with an Albatros Scout at 09.40 over Faverolles, followed by a two-seater five minutes later between Montdidier and Grivesnes. In contrast, Adjudant Brugère, Spa 103, gained his first victory, a scout down north-east of Montdidier at 09.50. These successes were followed up at 12.20 by Ed Parsons, MdL Denneulin and Sergent Chevannes, Spa 3, crashing a German machine near Gratibus. Then at 15.45, Lieutenant Courdouret, Spa 103, took part in a combat involving several Spads and an Albatros Scout, the latter being forced to put down into French lines near Rouvel, where the pilot was taken prisoner.

Ed Parsons became an ace on the 20th. At 09.15 he crashed a two-seater at Gratibus, while at 11.10, Adjudant Naudin of Spa 26, downed another near Onvillers. French units, not the least of which GC 12, had a variety of nationalities amongst their pilots, French, including men from some of the far reaches of its colonies, as well as Americans, Russians, Chinese, and so on. Another nationality with Spa 3 was a Serbian, Lieutenant Tadia Sondermayer, and he scored his first victory over a two-seater near Assainvillers on the 21st. This day also saw another two-seater fall, this time a probable, at 13.50 between three pilots of Spa 3 near Gratibus. Adjudant-Chef Baron and Adjudant Pietri were two of the pilots involved.

Indifferent weather again hampered operations, but in the final weeks of May there were several promotions. Brigadier Max Ouvrard de Linière of Spa 67 became a Maréchal-des-Logis. Max was born 26 September 1894, at Amiens, and entered military service, after the war began, on 21 August 1914 as a Soldat de 2nd Classe assigned to the 24° Régiment de Dragons. He was promoted to Brigadier on 25 April 1915, and emulated his brother Jacques, who was flying with Spa 26, and entered aviation on 1 July 1917. Max received Military Pilot's Brevet No.7300 on 21 September 1917, and was assigned to Spa 67 in early 1918. Brigadier Joseph Bouillet, Spa 67, was also promoted to Maréchal-des-Logis, while Sergents Auguste Baux and Gilbert Loup became Adjudants.

Baylies continued to make a name for himself on 28 May, attacking a scout whose pilot was harassing a French artillery machine, and shot it down near Courtemanch at 08.15 for his tenth victory. He followed the next day with victory number eleven, a German machine downed close to Etelfay at 18.15. At the same time, Bozon-Verduraz got another, for his eighth in the same area. During the final days of May GC 12 were flying what patrols the weather allowed until nightfall, in order to support to the best of their ability the 1918 Battle of the Aisne (3rd Battle of the Aisne) which began on 27 May and was to last until 6 June.

Frank Baylies had by this time been cited again, the first dated 6 May:

> An excellent pursuit pilot; refused to enter American Aviation as an officer, not wishing to leave his French squadron; delivers daily combats; has destroyed alone his second enemy aeroplane.

Then on the 29th:

> Frank Baylies is a brilliant high-class pursuit pilot. On May 9 and 20 he destroyed his seventh and eighth German aeroplanes.

At this time Lieutenant Louis Fernand Coudouret, who had joined Spa 3 on 18 May, and who for the last year or more had been fighting as part of the Military Mission to Russia, was made a Chevalier de la Légion d'Honneur:

> A pursuit pilot and a model of skill and courage, who had downed five enemy aircraft, all of which were on the Russian Front.

Coudouret hailed from Marseille, and his award came the day before his 22nd birthday. He had become a pilot back in 1915 and despite the wording of his citation, had in fact scored two victories flying with N 57 and N 102 in 1916, prior to his departure for Russia, where he added three kills between October and December 1917. From the Russians he received the Officier's Ordre de Saint-Georges, Sabre d'Ordre Saint Georges and the Ordre de Saint Vladimir.

* * *

Baylies, together with MdL Dubonnet, crashed another German machine on 31 May at 10.45 near Montdidier during a Spa 3 patrol fight with two-seaters. This was followed on 1 June with the second victory of Adjudant Baux over Moreuil. Coudouret destroyed a scout on the 2nd, for his first victory with Spa 3 – his sixth overall. He shared it with Sergent Hoeber in the region of Carlepont.

Promotions at this time were commissions for Adjudants René Lecomte and Pierre Schmitter of Spa 3; Schmitter was born 7 May 1897, at Nancy, and entered military service on 14 December 1915, as a Soldat de 2nd Classe assigned to the 1er Groupe d'Aviation. He became a student pilot on 1 April 1916 and received Military Pilot's Brevet No.4277 on 21 August. Promoted to Caporal on 6 September, he was sent to Br 311 in the course of formation at Villacoublay, on 9 January 1917 but transferred to N 103 on 12 April. Lieutenant Joseph Battle, the CO of Spa 103, was made a Capitaine, while in Spa 26 Brigadier Albert Beroulle was made a Maréchal-des-Logis, and Caporal Armand Lebroussard became a Sergent, as did Caporal Romanel of Spa 103. There was also a move of base. Spa 26 went to Sacy-le-Grand, situated about 20 kilometres west of Compiègne on 3 June, coming under Général Charles Mangin's X Armée Sector. Spa 3, Spa 67 and Spa 103 completed the move on the 5th. However, this was short lived for all GC 12 units moved back to Hétomesnil, two days later.

On 4 June Lieutenant Alfred Rougevin-Baville of Spa 3 was nominated for command of Escadrille Spa 99. He had been born 30 November 1892, at Versailles (Seine et Oise) and volunteered for military service on 9 October 1911 being assigned to the 21° Régiment de Dragons as a Cavalier de 2nd Classe. He was promoted to Brigadier on 7 February 1912, and to Maréchal-des-Logis on 12 October 1912. After the war began he was named an Aspirant on 5 August 1914, and was commissioned on 6 September 1915. Then on 21 September he was assigned as a student pilot to Dijon, and received Military Pilot's Brevet No.8775. During 1916 he was posted to Escadrille N 67, and his rank made permanent on 9 February 1917. Then on 27 November he was made full Lieutenant and transferred to Spa 3 on 3 May 1918. He would be promoted to Capitaine on 12 September 1918.

On 7 June GC 12 moved back to Hétomesnil, now in the 1er Armée Sector (Général Marie Eugène Debeney). At 16.45 hours on the 11th, Adjudant Naudin of Spa 26 gained his third victory, shot down between Mortemer and Rollot, while Capitaine d'Indy, the CO of Spa 67, achieved his first confirmed claim, between Fécamp and Reims at 18.30. Two days later, Sergent Chevannes and MdL André Dubonnet, Spa 3, teamed up and sent an observation balloon down in flames, which was Dubonnet's fourth victory.

GC 12, and Spa 3, suffered a great blow on 17 June. The mercurial Frank Baylies failed to return from patrol and later reports came in of his Spad XIII seen going down in flames at 17.00 hours between Rollot and Orvillers. This was an area about 18 kilometres south-south-west of Roye, and he probably fell victim to a pilot of JGII – either Leutnant Rudolf Rienau of Jasta 19 or Leutnant Ulrich Neckel of Jasta 12, both men claiming Spads around Roye this day. Baylies' Médaille Militaire, Croix de Guerre with six palmes and one étoile stood testimony to his prowess in combat.[7] André Dubonnet also came down this day but inside French lines and was not harmed. He may have been downed by Leutnant Wilhelm Leusch of Jasta 19, in the same fight as Baylies was lost, but Leusch's victim fell in French lines so was more than likely Dubonnet.

Sergent Prêtre of Spa 67 gained his first victory at 05.45 on the morning of 25 June, a German machine downed near Frétoy. In contrast, Fonck gained his 45th, 46th and 47th victories. Two days later came his 48th and 49th. His triple had been on an evening patrol, a two-seater and then two Fokkers. First to go on the 27th was a Halberstadt two-seater in flames after just five rounds found the petrol tank at 08.10 over Morisel. Five minutes later a Pfalz DIII went down over Moreuil. Fonck had just returned to his Escadrille having been assigned to attend a presentation at Dijon of his Officer's Cross of the Legion of Honour. He was to write:

> Back at the squadron, I left on patrol on 25 June. At six o'clock that evening I had the pleasure of shooting down a superb two-seater artillery spotting plane near the village of Coutoire. Continuing on because the weather was excellent, I met a second plane at 6.15 pm near Villers-aux-Érables. With a burst of 25 rounds I put an end to his mission. It was the same with the third I brought down near Montdidier.
>
> On 27 June, having taken to the air early, I had the opportunity at 8.10 am to get one of them in range over Morisel. It did not take long. I had hardly fired five cartridges before I saw him burst into flame. He crashed into a house, setting it on fire, it was a reconnaissance plane.
>
> At 8.15 I brought down another one which was coming back from the direction of Amiens. His mission must have been very important, for he held his own for ten kilometres. Despite the fact that during the course of the battle I had problems because of the jamming of my machine-gun, I did not want to let him off. Opening the throttle a little more, I succeeded in approaching within 100 metres of him and fired another volley. He fell near the city of Moreuil.

Adjudant Naudin and Lieutenant Dombray of Spa 26 blasted another German machine over the Bois de Faye on the 28th, this would bring Naudin into the ranks of the aces. Unfortunately the following day Caporal Jean Mandray of Spa 103 was shot down in flames and killed flying a Spad VII, probably the victim of Vizefeldwebel Josef Schwendemann of Jasta 41, the German's eighth victory of an eventual 17.

---

[7] (See *Cross and Cockade US*, *Vol.20*, No.3 ppg 193-216).

Capitaine Jacques d'Indy was made a Chevalier de la Légion d'Honneur on 30 June, with this citation:

> An excellent officer pilot, combining with audacity and courage the great qualities of spirit and energy. Detached for more than 30 months in aviation he commanded with success for one year an escadrille de corps d'armée where he obtained the highest recognition. Appointed the commander of an escadrille de chasse, he leads the pilots of his unit into combat each day with a zeal and spirit deserving the highest praise. Recently he attacked and downed in its lines an enemy aircraft. Two citations.

Pilots known to be on the roster of GC 12 as of 30 June 1918:

Spa 3

Capt Georges Raymond – CO
Capt Henry Ferguson (USAS)
Lt Benjamin Bozon-Verduraz
S/Lt Jean Caël
S/Lt René Cornemont
S/Lt Louis Bucquet
S/Lt Edouard Moulines
S/Lt Roger Roy
Adj Jean Laulhé
Adj Edwin Parsons (US)
Sgt Robert Brière
Sgt Maurice Chevannes
Sgt Gustave Decatoire
Sgt François Macari
Sgt Louis Risacher
MdL Georges Clémont
Mdl Jules Denneulin
MdL André Dubonnet
MdL Robert Martin
Cpl David Judd (US)

Spa 26

Capt Xavier de Sevin – CO
Lt Jean Dombray
S/Lt Benjamin de Tascher
S/Lt Noël Fontaine
S/Lt Emile Letourneau
S/Lt Jacques Puget
Adj-Chef Léon Barés
Adj Jean Dedieu
Adj Gustave Naudin
MdL Julius Antoine
MdL Marcel Plessis
MdL Albert Beroulle
Sgt Aimé Vincent
Sgt Armand Lebroussard
Brig Hubert Lambotte
Cpl René Dard
Cpl François Hugues
Cpl Jean Pelletier
Cpl Jean Poublan

Spa 67

Capt Jacques d'Indy – CO
S/Lt Marcel Durat
S/Lt Pierre Pendaries
S/Lt René Schurck
S/Lt Auguste Pouchelle
2/Lt Jasper Brown (USAS)
Adj Adrien Mion
Adj Henri Prétre
MdL-Chef Fernand Quinchez
MdL Emile Fumat
MdL René Ménard
MdL Max Ouvrard de Linière
Sgt Maurice Deschamps
Sgt Marcel Jaubert

Spa 103

Capt Joseph Battle – CO
S/Lt Louis Coudouret
S/Lt René Fonck
S/Lt Fontaine
S/Lt Léon Thouzellier
S/Lt Pierre Schmitter
Adj-Chef Joseph Baron
Adj Auguste Baux
Adj Jean Brugère
Adj Gilbert Loup
Adj Camille Pietri
MdL Henri Drouillh
Sgt Lenoir
Sgt Romanel

Brig Henri Alibert   Brig Laffray
Brig Edouard Kalvelage   Cpl Sansom

* * *

On 3 July 1918, Sous-lieutenant Benjamin Bozon-Verduraz, Spa 3, was transferred to assume command of Escadrille Spa 94, following the death of another former Stork, Lieutenant Guy de la Rochefordière. Bozon-Verduraz was born on 29 May 1889, at Saint Etienne de Cuines (Savoie) and entered military service on 1 October 1910, being sent to the 4° Régiment de Dragons. He was promoted to Brigadier on 3 April 1911, and Maréchal-des-Logis on 25 September the following year, the day of his release from active duty. When war came he returned to the colours assigned to the 9° Régiment de Hussards. He then requested aviation training and transferred on 8 October 1915, earning Military Pilot's Brevet No.2437 on 19 January 1916, then posted to Escadrille C 11 on 10 March, where he was injured on 12 May.

Bozon-Verduraz was promoted to Adjudant on 21 November and sent to 'Chasse School' on 28 May 1917, then on 15 June he joined N 3. He departed this unit with eight victories, adding three more while in command of Spa 94, and received a temporary promotion to Lieutenant on 18 July. As well as his Légion d'Honneur, he ended the war with the Croix de Guerre with eight palmes, two étoiles de vermeil and one étoile de bronze, as well as the Cross de Saint Georges, 4th Classe. He had flown a total of 683 hours, 13 minutes during his time at the front.

Also at this time, Capitaine Georges Raymond, CO of Spa 3, was slightly injured in a Spad XIII crash upon returning to land from a patrol, although he was hospitalized for several weeks. Four promotions were announced, that of Sergent for Caporal Sansom of Spa 103, Adjudants Adrien Mion and Henri Prétre of Spa 26 were both commissioned, while Brigadier René Dard of the same Escadrille became a Sergent.

The Groupe received urgent orders to return to the Champagne Front on the morning of 15 July. The 4th Battle of the Champagne had just commenced, and by mid-month this would blend into the start of the 1918 Battle of the Marne. The object was to push back the German army to Château-Thierry. With this in mind Spa 103 moved from Hétomesnil to Trécon, about seven kilometres west of Vertus, which is about 39 kilometres south-west of Châlons-sur-Marne (V° Armée, Général Henri Mathais Berthelot) on the 16th. Word was that the German flying service had amassed a large portion of their air effort opposite this sector and the Storks understood they were in for a busy period of active duty.

It had already seemed a busy time for Caporal Honoré Millot on the 15th. On a Spa 73 patrol he was forced to land between Aussons and La Neuville-en-Tournafuy, about ten kilometres north of Moronvillers, his Spad having been damaged in combat. He managed to replace a magneto wire that had been damaged by bullets and re-started his machine, took off before any Germans arrived and landed back at Givry-en-Argonne a very relieved man.

Fonck took off alone on the morning of the 16th to head for the new area, landing in Paris to collect some personal items and take lunch with some comrades. In the afternoon he took off again for Champagne and was following the Marne River, his cockpit full of packages and luggage. Approaching Château-Thierry in order to have a quick glimpse of the area before heading for the new airfield, he saw several German aircraft above Dormans. Faced with the prospect of breaking away because of all the clutter in the cockpit he observed two two-seaters operating over the French lines protected by six Fokker biplanes above. Fonck recorded:

> The single-seaters were watching the rear of the observation planes, which were flying parallel to the front. It was therefore to be a frontal attack against the two-seaters. A single pass and 'goodbye'.
> If the single-seaters were to lose only a second in hesitating, they would no longer be able to get me.
> I made a big detour and came full speed at the first two-seater, whom I fired at from a distance of

100 metres. Without waiting for the result, I kept on going like a rocket toward the second one who was behind him. From 25 metres I triggered my burst. The single-seaters began to dive at me. I was a little worried because of the luggage but while keeping an eye on my packages I made a little banking dive at full speed. Nothing budged in the cockpit. The Germans behind me were still 500 metres away but they did not gain an inch and I was heading in the direction of our lines. While turning around I spotted, down below Dormans, two big black trails of smoke which told me that my bullets had hit home and that my two-seaters had gone down in flames.

These were his 50th and 51st victories. He was only the second Frenchman to reach a score of 50 after the great Guynemer, and nobody else would reach this figure during the war on the French side.

Spa 3 and Spa 26 moved to Trécon on 17 July, where the sky was cloudy but it cleared considerably in the afternoon. GC 11 and GC 12 were now in the battle area and these two Groupes flew 102 sorties during 15 patrols, resulting in nine combats, and six attacks on balloons. Spa 103 claimed a probable but Adjudant Auguste Baux was seen to crash inside the German lines near Cuchery, possibly shot down by Leutnant Georg von Hengl and Gefreiter Johann Baur, a two-seater crew with FA295. They claimed two Spads this date, the first of a total of seven for Hengl and six for Baur. They flew the Hannover CLIII machine and in later life, Baur gained fame when he became Adolf Hitler's personal pilot, rising to the rank of Generaloberst in the German SS.

It has been reported that Auguste Baux had five victories but evidence to this effect cannot be established at this time. He had joined Spa 103 on 16 January 1918, and had been the recipient of the Médaille Militaire and Croix de Guerre with four palmes. Baux entered military service three days after the war was declared and served with the infantry. Taken prisoner on 3 September 1914, he managed to escape and returned to the front, this time in the aviation service, on 4 May 1917.

* * *

The new offensive got underway on 18 July with the Allies having a force of 45 infantry divisions, which were supported by an equal number of chasse escadrilles, 34 bombardement escadrilles, 71 observation and attack escadrilles, along with 1,206 artillery batteries (made up of four guns each, of all calibres and types) and 683 tanks, mostly medium sized.

Against this array of strength the Germans reportedly had 31 divisions in the line and eight in reserve, plus an additional 40 divisions in general reserve, with plenty of artillery in support. The French X° Armée (Général Charles Mangin) was to make the main assault, flanked on the right by the VI° Armée (Général Jean-Marie Degoutte). The V° Armée (Général Henri Berthelot) on the left of the VI° Armée, was to make an attack designed to meet the X° Armée in the area of Fère-en-Tardenois. The IX° Armée (Général Marie Antoine Henri de Mitry) was held in reserve until 20 July, at which time it entered the line between the V° and VI° Armées. The operation lasted until 4 August, closing the salient. It was the beginning of the end for the German Army. With American forces now arriving in France and supporting and cooperating with the French along their sectors of the front, the war, although no one knew it, was entering its last crucial phases.

Fonck scored another double on the 18th within ten minutes – 11.20-11.30 – two Fokkers between Cuchery and Villers-sous-Châtillon. He made it three later that afternoon, at 15.35 over Dormans, which brought his score to 56 and overtook Guynemer's total of 53.

Both GC 11 and GC 12 flew numerous sorties during the offensive and several unconfirmed victories were claimed. Adjudant Loup and Sergent Drouillh of Spa 103 gained a confirmed victory over a Fokker on the 21st – both men's second – near Cambrecy, but in this combat Sergent Lenoir was wounded in the foot. During another patrol, Caporal François Hugues of Spa 26 failed to return in his Spad XIII.

On the 22nd, with beautiful weather with high clouds, both French Groupes were heavily involved in operations including balloon attacks. At 05.45 Sous-lieutenant Pendaries, with Adjudant

Jaubert, Spa 67, crashed a German machine near Ville-en-Tardenois. It put Pendaries into the ranks of the aces and gave Jaubert his first victory. At 07.00 Capitaine Battle, Spa 103's CO, flamed a balloon north of Epoye for his second victory. Fonck failed to have a victory confirmed at 18.10 hours between Cuisles and Baslieux-sur-Châtillon – it was his 43rd **unconfirmed** claim.

After the good weather of the 22nd, the next three days were poor but flying continued as and when possible. On the 24th Spa 26, Spa 67 and Spa 103 moved from Trécon to Herbisse, about 25 kilometres south of their former base, in the IV Armée Sector, commanded by Général Henri Gouraud. Spa 3 made the move on the 25th, but then on the 28th, Spa 67 and Spa 103 returned to Hétomesnil, followed the next day by Spa 3 and Spa 26. This was in preparation for the battle to reduce the area of the Amiens Salient, which took place from 8 to 15 August.

This operation was in conjunction with General Henry Rawlinson's British 4th Army which was to make the main attack on the 8th, with the French 1er Armée under Général Marie Eugène Debeney, to launch its attack the same day on its right.

In the meantime, Brigadier Henri Alibert of Spa 67 was promoted to Maréchal-des-Logis on 29 July, and on 3 August Caporal Jean Pelletier of Spa 26 was made Sergent. On 31 July, Adjudants Naudin, Usse, and Vincent of Spa 26, combined their efforts to destroy an enemy aircraft at 19.40 hours over Gratibus. It was Naudin's sixth but his companions' first.

CHAPTER TWELVE

August – September 1918

August 1918 was to see the beginning of the final offensives against the Germans in France. On the British Front, Rawlinson's seven divisions began the push forward on 9 August. In the air the British Royal Air Force were heavily engaged in ground-attack sorties with its fighters and day-bombing missions with their two-seater bombers – DH4s and DH9s. All the while the British Corps squadrons kept up a similar high tempo of operations, not only in pure observations and contact patrols, but also ranging artillery and ground support, bombing and strafing in company with the single-seat Camels, Dolphins and SE5s.

Just prior to this offensive Lieutenant Fonck of Spa 103 gained his 57th victory on 1 August by sending down a two-seater east of the Bois d'Hangard, at 11.00. Also GC 12 had some of its pilots cited and promoted. Caporal Jean Pelletier of Spa 26 was made a Sergent on the 3rd, while Sous-lieutenant Pendaires of Spa 67, Capitaine Battle, René Fonck and Adjudant Loup were all cited in orders. Fonck for his feat of scoring seven victories over a three-day period. Also on 1 August Capitaine Georges Raymond returned to reassume command of Spa 3, his wounds healed.

Sous-lieutenant Risacher of Spa 3 gained his second victory over Bouchoir, and Capitaine Battle of Spa 103 claimed his third over Etelfay, on the 9th. Sous-lieutenant Puget, and Sergent Pelletier and Sergent Lebroussard of Spa 26 each claimed one victory on 11 August.

With the concentration of air effort by the Germans directed towards the Amiens Front from the 9th, activity on the French Front naturally declined a little, although the French were keen to keep up the pressure in order to support their British comrades further to the north. However, the first successful combat by the *Cigognes* was not forthcoming until 14 August. On this date Fonck succeeded in downing three German aircraft in the space of ten seconds. All fell in the vicinity of Roye-Gruny-Crémery, and brought his score to a round 60. He was now far and away the most successful living fighter pilot of any nation in terms of combat victories. In fact only the dead Manfred von Richthofen had scored more, and presumably the fallen Major Mick Mannock of the RAF, a probable 61 or so. (Billy Bishop's score of 72 remains in doubt by most historians.)

Two days later, on the 16th, GC 12 claimed three German aircraft destroyed. Capitaine Battle, CO of Spa 103, with MdL Dubonnet of Spa 3 downed one at Carrépuis; it was Battle's fourth and made Dubonnet an ace. Then at 11.30 Dubonnet teamed with Capitaine de Sevin, CO Spa 26, and gained his sixth victory, and de Sevin his 11th east of Roye. S/Lt Schmitter and Adjudant Baron combined forces and downed another west of Roye; it was the second victory for both. Unfortunately, Sous-lieutenant Caël was shot down and taken prisoner by Ernst Udet, leader of Jasta 4. It was the German's 56th victory, which he claimed south of Foucaucourt at 10.40.

Jean Edouard Caël was born 9 July 1895 in Paris (Seine) and had entered military service on 23 April 1915, as a Soldat de 2nd Classe. After various short assignments he was sent to Escadrille MF 25 on 6 August, and on 14 September he entered pilot training receiving a Military Pilot's Brevet on 9 November. He then passed to RGAé on 12 November and was promoted to Caporal on 21 November. Caël was sent to MF 16 on 15 January 1916, but returned to RGAé to be reassigned to MF 2 on 23 January. Here he was promoted to Sergent on 29 April and returned to GDE on 9 May. He was then sent to C 56 on 10 July where he remained until 28 July before returning to GDE. After a few weeks training on fighters he joined N 102 on 20 September 1916. Promoted to Adjudant the following 6 February, he must have caused some upset as he was demoted back to Caporal on 27 June

– two ranks down, not just one! However, he climbed back to Sergent on 20 July then to Adjudant again before he was commissioned (TT) on 25 January 1918. Credited with three victories with N 102 before joining Spa 3 on 15 June, he had not added to his score before falling to Udet. At this time Caël held the Croix de Guerre with four palmes and the Belgian Croix de Guerre. He was made a Chevalier de la Légion d'Honneur after the war on 24 January 1919.

> An officer pilot of great value and remarkable courage, he has had numerous combats during the course of which he downed three enemy planes. On 16 August 1918, after having disengaged a British aircraft being attacked by several Fokkers, he fell in enemy lines, his aircraft having been greatly damaged by the fire of a German plane. He was repatriated soon after the Armistice. One wound – five citations.

Maréchal-des-Logis Patay of Spa 26, flying a Spad VII failed to return from a patrol on 17 August. Three days later Capitaine d'Indy, the CO of Spa 67, collaborated with MdL Lambotte of Spa 26, and crashed an adversary near Amancoeur at 17.55. Also, more promotions at this stage were Maréchal-des-Logis Fumat of Spa 67, Sergents Brugère and Drouillh of Spa 103, all becoming Adjudants on the 20th, while Adjudant Naudin of Spa 26 became an Adjudant-Chef.

* * *

Escadrille Spa 167 was created on 22 August, by Grand Quartier Général, Aéronautique Ordre No.33.912. Its designated commander was Lieutenant Bernard Barny de Romanet from Escadrille Spa 37, who had been credited with his tenth confirmed victory this very day.

Bernard Barny de Romanet was born on 28 January 1894, at Saint Maurice de Sathonay (Saone et Loire). He entered military service during October 1913 and was assigned to the 16° Régiment de Chassseurs à Pied. He was promoted to Maréchal-des-Logis within six months and shortly after the war started he received his first citation, dated 20 August – within a week of hostilities beginning.

He was then transferred to the 56° Régiment d'Infanterie where he remained until his request for transfer to aviation was approved during July 1915. His first assignment was as an observer with C 51 (Caudron). His appetite whetted, he requested pilot training, and was sent to Pau as a student in October, receiving Military Pilot's Brevet No.2248 on 5 January 1916. He returned to C 51 two days later. Now in action as a pilot he was twice cited in orders before being sent to train as a fighter pilot during February. Duly converted he was posted to N 37 where he received the Médaille Militaire on 23 May 1917. The citation read:

> An élite pilot, as brilliant in pursuit aviation as he was in reconnaissance. He has had numerous combats giving proof of the highest military qualities under all circumstances. On 3 May 1917, he attacked two enemy scouts over their lines and downed one of them. Already cited three times in orders.

Barny de Romanet was promoted to Adjudant but did not score any victories during the remainder of 1917, but by the time he scored his second kill he had been promoted to Sous-lieutenant; by June he was a full lieutenant and had three victories.

Eighteen pilots were assigned to the new Spa 167, one lieutenant, four sous-lieutenants, one aspirant, one MdL, three sergents and eight caporaux. Other personnel comprised one sergent-chef pay clerk, four sergent mechanics, one sergent armourer, one caporal pay clerk, three caporal mechanics, and 94 soldats for general duties. Aircraft assigned were 12 Spad XIIIs and six Spad VIIs. Spa 167 did not actually report for duty with GC 12 until September, the times in between used for what the British called 'working up'.

Also on the 22nd Caporal Gaston Sachet, Spa 67, was killed when he crash-landed his Spad VII. Adjutant Usse of Spa 26 gained his second victory on 25 August south- west of Meharicourt, at 11.25, and on the 29th Adjutant Parsons, Spa 3, downed his sixth adversary, a Fokker, near Morchain.

* * *

With the British offensive going well, despite heavy resistance by the German land forces, plans were now underway for the follow-up punch from the French and American Sectors. With the massive support brought up by the Americans, who had steadily built up their forces since the spring of 1918, a major offensive was planned along the Meuse-Argonne, which was to commence with the Saint Mihiel Battle on 12 September.

The build-up was well under way by the 8th, with American Colonel Billy Mitchell being in overall command of the air units, both French and American. For this offensive, GC 12 moved from Hétomesnil to Quinquempoix, about 20 kilometres south-west of Montdidier, in the 1er Armée Sector, on 3 September. Also on this date Capitaine Georges Raymond, the CO of Spa 3, was admitted to hospital with 'Spanish' flu where he died on 4 October from the disease which was to cause many deaths over the next few months. In fact more deaths than from all the fighting in WW1. Temporary command of Spa 3 was assumed by Lieutenant Aimé Grasset, who came from Spa 150; and two promotions were announced. Caporal Papineau and Brigadier Gui, both of Spa 103, became a Sergent and MdL respectively.

Lieutenant Grasset had been born on 20 December 1888, at Bonnefoi (Orne), and had entered military service on 10 October 1909, as a lowly Soldat with the 86° Régiment d'Infanterie. Two years later he applied and received permission to train as a pilot, eventually receiving Military Pilot's Brevet No.236, on 22 March 1913. When war came he was a Sergent with MF 22 (Maurice Farmans). Promoted to Adjutant on 3 September 1914, he left the Escadrille on the 20th. His next operational posting was to MF 14 on 1 January 1915.

He was awarded the Médaille Militaire on 10 April and commissioned in the reserve during September. He served with N 48 for a few days in April 1916, but on the 20th of that month he was sent to Russia for service with the Russian 6th Aviation Division. After being made a Chevalier de la Légion d'Honneur on 1 October he was made a full lieutenant the same day. Returning to France, he was assigned to Escadrille Spa 150 on 1 July 1918. In addition to his French decorations he also had been awarded the Russian Officier de la Croix de Saint-Georges, the Ordre de Vladimir de 3rd Classe; the Ordre de Stanislas de 3rd Classe and the Ordre de Sainte Anne de 4th Classe. Evidently he was given this acting command by rank and experience rather than combat success.

Spa 67 moved to Lisle-en-Barrois, about 25 kilometres south-west of Souilly, in the II° Armée Sector (Général Auguste Edouard Hirschauer in command) on 8 September. The following day, Sergent André Dubonnet of Spa 3 was awarded the Médaille Militaire:

> After distinguishing himself in the artillery, he transferred to aviation where he was rapidly classed among the best pursuit pilots. A very good non-commissioned officer, excellent patrol leader, cheerfully leading into combat pilots who have confidence in him. On 16 August 1918, he reported his fifth victory. Four citations.

On the 9th, Spa 3 and Spa 26 moved to Lisle-en-Barrois followed the next day by Spa 103. Escadrille Spa 3 received its third citation in l'Ordre de la 1er Armée No.107, of 9 September 1918, by Général Debeney. The unit citation read:

> Under the orders of Capitaine d'Harcourt through Capitaine Battle, and brilliantly led by Lieutenant Fonck, became a unit of great value. It has unceasingly, for twenty months, waged battle on all fronts. Attacking the enemy very deep in his own territory, was able to inflict heavy losses on him. 85 official victories and 69 aircraft disabled.

Two other events followed in September. Adjudant Aimé Vincent of Spa 26 was wounded in combat on the 14th, and Caporal André Nugues of Spa 103 was made a Sergent a few days later.

* * *

Following receipt of a telegram – No.7052/B, from GAC – Escadrilles Spa 3 and Spa 26 departed for la Noblette, on the 18th, a base situated north-east of Châlons-sur-Marne, between St Etienne-au-Temple and la Cheppe, in the IV° Armée Sector (Général Henri Gouraud); Spa 67 and Spa 103 followed the next day. Poor weather restricted any form of offensive actions until the 20th, although even on this day there were no combats, but they were now anticipating the start of the Meuse-Argonne Offensive with some relish, although intelligence indicated some very experienced German air units coming into the area opposite them.

Lieutenant Joseph Point-Dumont, the Armament officer of GC 12, was promoted to Capitaine on 24 September, and the next day Lieutenant André Rouget, the Technical Assistant to the commander of GC 12 was also promoted to Capitaine.

As if to herald this major offensive, the sky remained cloudy and rain soaked over the next couple of days. Indecisive skirmishes over the period only resulted in two probables – both Fokker biplanes. On the first day of the offensive, the 26th, aerial activity intensified as expected. In the morning the weather was hazy but it cleared for the rest of the day. During the period from 07.30 to 13.00 hours, 36 aircraft of the *Groupe de Cigognes* were used for five patrols that produced five combats in which four German aircraft were claimed.

At 1015, Adjudant Naudin, Spa 26, probably crashed a two-seater over Ripont; between around noon-time, Lieutenant Fonck gained his 61st, 62nd and 63rd victories, shooting down two Fokker DVIIs in flames and a Halberstadt two-seater, at Ste-Marie-à-Py, Saint Souplet and Perthes-les-Hurlus respectively. During the afternoon, seven patrols were flown, commencing 13.30 hours and involving 39 Spads. They engaged in 15 combats and scored seven victories. The first two were probables by Barny de Romanet, CO of Spa 167 and a Spa 3 patrol. At 18.00 the American Ed Parsons and MdL Denneulin, Spa 3, assisting Spa 67's Sous-lieutenant Pendaries, shot down a two-seater south of Tahure. Five minutes later, Fonck spotted a Fokker DVII about to attack a Spad two-seater between St Souplet and Ste Marie-à-Py, shooting it down for his 64th victory.

Continuing with his patrol ten minutes later, Fonck attacked and shot down two two-seaters (one being a Halberstadt) east of Souain, bringing his score to 66 – making this his second 'six in one day' achievement. Adjudant Brière, Spa 103, also claimed a scout as a probable north of Souain, at 18.20.

On day two of the offensive, GC 12 carried out nine patrols with 59 aircraft despite low clouds and intermittent rain. During the afternoon the rain let up and seven more patrols went out, with Sous-lieutenant Coudouret, Spa 103, claiming a Rumpler north-east of Somme-Py, as a probable. Records also noted a very difficult combat with several Fokkers which carried black and white checkered markings whose pilots were better than normally encountered. (JGII)

The next day saw several German artillery planes engaged over the Front, Fonck attacking and claiming one which was being protected by three scouts east of Somme-Py at 10.30. Sergent Chauffaux, Spa 3, also probably downed a two-seater over Ste Geneviève at 11.30, but bad weather later in the afternoon restricted further patrols and combats.

As well as patrols, ground-attack sorties were also flown. During one such operation on the 29th, again in bad weather, Adjudant-Chef Gustave Naudin of Spa 26 was seriously wounded in one foot by ground fire, but he got home and landed safely. In the same action MdL Robert Brillaut had his Spad severely shot-up, forcing him to make a forced landing near the front-line trenches but he scrambled out unharmed. One enemy aircraft was claimed as a probable by a Spa 67 patrol over Somme-Py, at 11.35. Inclement weather restricted patrols even further on the 30th, just six uneventful patrols being flown this last day of the month. Pilots known to be on the strength of GC 12 on 30 September were:

Spa 3

Capt Georges Raymond – CO
Lt Aimé Grasset
S/Lt Louis Bucquet
S/Lt Edouard Moulines
S/Lt Roger Roy
Adj Louis Bourgeois
Adj Jean Laulhé
Adj Emile Legros
Adj Edwin Parsons (US)
Sgt Robert Brière
Sgt Maurice Chevannes
Sgt Gustave Decatoire
Sgt Georges Chauffour
Sgt François Macari
Sgt Edouard Monet
Sgt Marcel Perrotey
MdL Georges Clémont
MdL Jules Denneulin
MdL André Dubonnet
MdL Robert Martin

Spa 167

Lt Bernard Barny de Romanet – CO
S/Lt François Dumas
S/Lt Victor Esperon du Tremblay
S/Lt Joseph Guiguet
S/Lt Marcel Lechevallier
Asp Emile Villard
Sgt Jean de Lombardon
Sgt Roger Gérard
Sgt Victor Nugues
Sgt Robert Soudin
Sgt Paul Trouillet
Cpl René Colomies
Cpl Jean Ferraz
Cpl André Henon
Cpl Joseph Thèze

Spa 67

Capt Jacques d'Indy – CO
Lt Robert Le Petit
S/Lt Marcel Duret
S/Lt Adrien Mion
S/Lt Pierre Pendaries
S/Lt Auguste Pouchelle
2/Lt Jasper Brown, USAS
Adj-Chef Fernand Quinchez
Adj Pierre Prou
MdL Henri Alibert
MdL Joseph Bouillet
MdL Emile Fumat
MdL René Ménard
Sgt Maurice Deschamps
Sgt Marcel Jaubert
Sgt Max Ouvard de Linière
Brig Jean Louseau
Cpl Joseph Neveu
Cpl Etienne Maragrit

Spa 26

Capt Xavier de Sevin – CO
Lt Jean Dombray
Lt Emile Letourneau
S/Lt Benjamin de Tascher
S/Lt Roland Garros
S/Lt Noël Fontaine
S/Lt Jacques Puget
Adj Julius Antoine
Adj Gustave Naudin
Adj Justin Usse
MdL Albert Beroulle
MdL Hubert Lambotte
MdL Marcel Plessis
Sgt Armand Leboussant
Sgt Marius Montels
Sgt Aimé Vincent
Brig Jean Dard
Brig Jean Dard
Cpl Robert Brillaut
Cpl Jean Pelletier

Spa 103

Capt Joseph Battle – CO
Lt René Fonck
Lt Fontaine
S/Lt Louis Coudouret
S/Lt Pierre Schmitter
S/Lt Léon Thouzellier
Adj-Chef Joseph Baron
Adj Jean Brugère
Adj Henri Drouillh
Adj Gilbert Loup

MdL Gui
MdL Laffay
Sgt Debaud
Sgt Guers
Sgt Robert Hoeber
Sgt Lenoir
Sgt Papineau
Sgt Romanel
Sgt Sansom

CHAPTER THIRTEEN

The Final Weeks

The first day of October the skies were hazy in the morning but clearer during the latter part of the day. During the morning patrols between 06.30 and 09.30, covering the area between Aubérive and Somme-Py, 21 aircraft took part in two patrols, resulting in three non-productive combats. 40 Spads were activated for the afternoon sorties, flying seven patrols during which four German aircraft were claimed.

At 10.45 Caporal de Lombardon, Spa 167, crashed a German reconnaissance two-seater north of Bétheniville, while at 12.45 two German fighters were claimed by Spa 103, Sergent Sansom and Adjudant Drouillh destroying one north-east of Somme-Py, and a probable in the same area. Then at 15.10 Edwin Parsons of Spa 3, claimed his eighth victory, an artillery observation two-seater, north of Somme-Py; this was possibly the crew Leutnant Hermann Kottwitz and Ltn Victor Neumann of FAA239.

Two promotions this day for two Spa 67 pilots, were Sergent Marcel Jaubert to Adjudant, and Caporal Etienne Maragrit to Sergent.

* * *

The autumn of 1918 had seen the return to active duty of one of the early heroes of French aviation, the renowned Roland Garros. Eugène Adrian Roland Georges Garros had been born on 6 October 1888, at Saint Denis (Ilse de la Réunion) and had received his pilot's brevet No.117 on 19 July 1910. When war came he volunteered his services for the duration, and as a Soldat de 2nd Classe, assigned to the 2° Groupe d'Aviation and Escadrille MS 23 after he received Military Pilot's Brevet No.494.

Promoted to Caporal on 4 September and to Sergent one day later, he then received a commission to Sous-lieutenant on 28 December 1914. Flying with MS 23, he scored three victories in April 1915, on the 1st, 15th and 18th. Garros quickly found that the best way of attacking successfully a German aircraft was to aim the aircraft at the opponent and fire, but at this stage there were no machine-gun interrupter gears in operations in order for bullets to pass through the whirling blades of the propeller. To overcome this, Garros and other early fighter pilots had metal deflector plates fitted on to the propeller blades, then mounted a single machine-gun atop the fuselage in front of the cockpit. By aiming the aircraft and firing the gun, the majority of the bullets would pass harmlessly through the blades at the enemy. Those few that might have hit and damaged the blades were now deflected away. He was by no means the only pilot to use this method, but he was the first to gain fame with it.

However, soon after gaining his third victory he was forced down behind enemy lines during an attack on a train on the Ingelmünster-Courtrai Line. Some say ground fire, others that he damaged the alignment of his propeller with his machine-gun fire which forced him down. The story goes that having captured his aeroplane intact, the device was shown to Anthony Fokker who was designing aircraft for the Germans, who asked him to duplicate it. Fokker could see that the real answer was to design a proper interrupter gear, whereby the gun stopped firing momentarily when the propeller blade was in front of the gun muzzle. Thus the first such gear was developed and used to good effect on Fokker's famous Eindekker monoplane fighter that was about to make such a dramatic change in air fighting over France.

While in captivity, Garros was promoted to full lieutenant on 25 December 1916. After several unsuccessful attempts at escape, he finally got away from his captors at 'Kavalier Schärnhorst', disguised as a German soldier, on 14 February 1918. After rehabilitation and retraining on aircraft that must have seemed tremendously advanced from his 1914-1915 days, he requested front-line duty and was assigned to Spa 103 on 20 August, and then transferred to Spa 26 three days later.

Pre-war he had been made a Chevalier de la Légion d'Honneur (civil) during October 1913, evidently for his flying prowess in the pioneering days of flight; he was made an Officier de la Légion d'Honneur on 7 March 1918, with this citation:

A great aviator before the war, whose name is a symbol of bravery and modesty. He was in the service of his country from the start of hostilities, displaying admirable qualities of intelligence, audacity and professional competency. Having fallen into the hands of the enemy he kept his confidence, energy and his indefatigable will intact. He escaped from the Germans in circumstances that made him even more famous.

His return to active duty must have been a great challenge for him, but undoubtedly quite a boost for GC 12. He could, of course, have remained in the comparative safety of a training post or even with some headquarter unit. He was still only 29, coming up 30, but the majority of active pilots were much younger.

Garros was in combat on 2 October. It was a hazy morning and it remained cloudy all day. However, patrols were flown during the morning and at 09.00 Capitaine de Sevin and Garros attacked three Fokker DVIIs which had flown about two kilometres inside French lines, no doubt looking for balloons. Garros, who seemed to have lost none of his aggressiveness or ability, swooped on the tail of one of them and shot it down between Ste Marie-à-Py and Somme-Py. He also claimed a probable in the same locality – almost becoming an ace, but with a probable his score remained at four.

More patrols were flown on the 3rd, covering the front of two Army Corps while they attacked along their sectors. At 10.10 Capitaine Barny de Romanet and Caporal de Lombardon of Spa 167, crashed a Fokker which burst into flames on the ground between St Pierre-à-Arnes and Mont Blanc. This was de Romanet's 11th victory.

During the afternoon, an estimated 14 Fokkers, in two groups, were seen to assault the balloon lines and one 'gas-bag' went up in flames. A Spa 26 patrol intercepted them and one Fokker went down to crash near Somme-Py, claimed by Sergent Robert Brillaut, although he himself was wounded by a bullet which struck him in the thigh and another that caused a flesh wound to his back. At 14.50 Spa 67 engaged a patrol of Fokkers and Lieutenant Le Petit gained his first confirmed victory by destroying one between Moronvillers and Dontrien. It is believed that Leutnant Fritz Höhn, Staffelführer of Jasta 41, an ace with 21 victories, was the victim of one of these GC 12 pilots falling at Saint Martin l'Heureux, which is about 10 kilometres west of Somme-Py.

During several patrols on 4 October, in hazy weather with poor visibility, the Groupe suffered a great loss. Capitaine Georges Raymond, the commander of Spa 3, succumbed to the influenza epidemic, which in his weakened condition from injuries he suffered back on 13 July he was just unable to fight off. He had achieved five victories and nine probables, was a Chevalier de la Légion d'Honneur and had the Croix de Guerre with seven palmes; from the British he had received the Military Cross. He was one of the great leaders.

The second great loss of the week came on the 5th. Roland Garros fell in combat flying a patrol with Spa 26 in Spad XIII No.15.409, last seen in action with seven enemy fighters south-west of Vouziers. Lieutenant Hermann Habich of Jasta 49 claimed a Spad over Somme-Py at 11.06 German time for his fifth victory, and Vizefeldwebel Alfons Nagler of Jasta 81 also claimed a Spad on the 3° Armée front near Sechault at an unknown time.

During the afternoon of the 5th, a two-seater was attacked at 16.00 hours by a Spa 26 patrol over Suippes, the observer being hit as well as the motor which forced the pilot to land inside the French lines near Bétheniville. Just over an hour later Spa 26 claimed another two-seater but only as a probable. Fonck of Spa 103, made it three two-seaters at 17.30 between Liry and Marvaux, followed by a fighter between Hauvine and Clément, which brought his confirmed score to 69. Fonck then engaged two scouts at 18.00 between St Etienne and Orefeuil to make it four for the day. Two promotions came on the 6th, Spa 26's Sergent Aimé Vincent being made Adjudant, Caporal Jean de Lombardon, Spa 167, to Sergent.

Two days of poor weather were followed by a better day on the 9th but no real success was achieved until the afternoon of the 10th. Barny de Romanet, Spa 167's CO, crashed a two-seater south of Bignicourt at 07.00, for his 12th victory, confirmed by the 21st and 55th Balloon Companies. Then a fighter which tried to attack the balloon north of Somme-Py at 15.35 was possibly shot down by a Stork pilot. Caporal Joseph Neveau of Spa 67 became a Sergent on this date and Caporal Paul Trouillet of Spa 167 also made Sergent.

Also on the 11th, Capitaine Joseph Battle, the commanding officer of Spa 103, was decorated with the British Distinguished Conduct Medal – at least this is what seems to be stated on Battle's abstract of service, noting the award of the Médaille de la Conduit Distinguée. This may be a mistaken entry for the DSO – Distinguished Service Order, as the DCM is an award strictly for non-commissioned personnel and a DSO would be more in keeping with Battle's position.

The winter weather seemed to be settling in now, rain and clouds continuing to prevent combats and patrols. However, at 13.15 hours on 14 October, Barny de Romanet brought down a two-seater between Arleux and the Bois de Voncq, assisted by Sous-lieutenant Dumas. This was their 13th and first victories respectively.

*   *   *

Groupe de Combat 12 had another new unit assigned to it on the 16th, following the formation of Spa 173 under the command of Lieutenant Jacques Allez at la Noblette. GC 12 now comprised Spa 3, Spa 26, Spa 67, Spa 103, Spa 167 and Spa 173, under the overall command of Capitaine Charles Dupuy.

Lieutenant Jacques Allez was born on 10 October 1894, in Paris. Entering military service on 1 September 1914, he went to the 3° Régiment de Cuirassiers. Just one year later he became a student pilot and following training received a Military Pilot's Brevet on 30 January 1916. His first posting was to Escadrille N 65, where he remained until 6 November 1917, at which time he was commissioned and transferred to CIACB as an instructor until given command of Spa 173. He held the Croix de Guerre with one palme and one étoile de bronze.

Patrols and protection flights were flown on the 18th. At 14.20 hours Sergent de Lombardon, Spa 167, probably destroyed a two-seater over Allen'Huy. At the same time Barny de Romanet and Sous-lieutenant Dumas claimed two Fokker DVIIs over Civry-sur-Meuse, one of which was confirmed by the 88° Cie d'Aérostières and the 7° and 73° Régiments d'Infanterie to give de Romanet his 14th confirmed victory and a third for Dumas.

At 16.25, Adjudant Drouillh and Sergent Sansom, Spa 103, shot down a Fokker DVII which crashed north-west of Rethel; this was Drouillh's fourth and Sansom's second victories. It was confirmed by an observer with the 264° Régiment d'Artillerie, and DCA Batterie 55. On 22 October Second Lieutenant Jasper C Brown, USAS, of Spa 67 was promoted to First Lieutenant.

Bad weather again restricted operations until the 23rd although some flights had been made during the interim. At this time Brigadier Loisseau, Spa 67, made Maréchal-des-Logis. On the 23rd no fewer than 60 aircraft took part in ten patrols which resulted in six combats and three successes. At 08.25 hours, Adjudant Brière of Spa 3 claimed a probable artillery machine, seen to lose part of its wing over Novy. Lieutenant Barny de Romanet had his two-seater confirmed at 12.10 near le Chesne, in company with Sous-lieutenant Lechavellier, confirmed by Lieutenant Decurgis of the 136° Régiment d'Artillerie and observers with the 69° Division d'Infanterie.

Five minutes later, de Romanet probably downed another south of le Chesne, but was more successful at 16.25, crashing a Fokker biplane near Attigny. This his 16th victory was confirmed by Lieutenant-Colonel Garden of the 22° RCTS and the 69° Division d'Infanterie.

Capitaine de Sevin, the CO of Spa 26, had not scored a confirmed success since August, but on 24 October he gained his 12th and final victory of the war by shooting down a German aircraft north-east of Vouziers at 14.00 hours, confirmed by the 313th Heavy Artillery Battery. At 15.00 Barny de Romanet and Sous-lieutenant Guiguet of Spa 167, combined their efforts to send a recce two-seater down for their 17th and fifth victories respectively, witnessed again by Colonel Garden of the 22 RCTS and a gun crew of the 55th DCA.

The next combats occurred on 28 October. At 15.30, Adjudant Usse of Spa 26 claimed a fighter for his third confirmed victory, north of Rethel, while 15 minutes later Lieutenant Letourneau and Sergent Dard of Spa 26 each claimed a fighter between Méry and Cogny, and between Attigny and Vouziers.

Lieutenant Aimé Grasset, commander of Spa 3, was re-assigned to CIACB on the 28th, for further transfer to Spa 173, command of the Escadrille passing to Lieutenant Jean Dombray from Spa 26. Jean Marie Auguste Dombray had been born on 30 January 1890, at Charleville in the Ardennes. He entered military service on 8 October 1912 as a lowly Soldat de 2nd Classe with the 8° Régiment d'Infanterie. He transferred to the 69° Régiment on 8 May 1913 and became a Caporal on 8 November.

After the war began he was promoted to Sergent on 2 November and then commissioned a Sous-lieutenant in the Reserve on 25 May the following year. Wounded in action on 5 July 1915, he returned to the front on 13 November. He now applied for pilot training which commenced on 1 July, receiving Military Pilot's Brevet No.4445 on 9 September. He was assigned to Groupe de Bombardement No.5 on 12 March 1917, and to Escadrille BM 121 three days later, where he was wounded in combat on 4 September. When he was fit again for front-line service he went to Spa 26 on 5 October where he remained until given command of the élite Spa 3.

The Groupe's pilots were very successful against two-seaters on 29 October. At 10.30 hours, Sergent de Lombardon and Aspirant Villard of Spa 167 crashed one north of Attigny. At 13.17 Sous-lieutenant Pendaries, Spa 67, sent down his seventh adversary – a two-seater near Lametz, followed on the half hour by another by Spa 26's Sergent Lebroussard – a probable near Longwy. Before the hour was out, Sergent Sansom and Brigadier Ouvrard de Linière of Spa 103 probably downed another, the wings of which were seen to break during the action. At 15.00 hours Barny de Romanet scored his 18th and final confirmed victory, another two-seater south of the Bois de Loges near Grand Pré.

On 30 October the weather was beautiful and 76 Groupe aircraft participated in ten patrols, resulting in 18 combats and nine successes. A patrol of Spa 103 opened the account during a balloon raid north-east of Vouziers at 08.10. The balloon ignited and the observer took to his parachute. A probable two-seater kill 15 minutes later by Spa 3 was followed at 10.20 by a confirmed two-seater between Vouziers and Chestre by Adjudant Brière – his second victory.

At 11.45 Sous-lieutenant de Tascher and MdL Plessis of Spa 26 crashed a two-seater between Vouziers and le Chesne, Spa 167 gaining a probable north of Rethel at 13.00 in the afternoon. Fonck was back in action this afternoon, with a two-seater in flames at 15.25 near Falaise and 15 minutes later this was followed by two fighters crashed between Semay and Terron, bringing his score to 72. Fonck made it 73 on the 31st – a two-seater crashed after losing its wings north of Vouziers at 1120. He secured his 74th at 11.35 between Vouziers and Attigny.

November 1918

The final month of the Great War to end all wars, saw GC 12 flying patrols and having five combats the first day. René Fonck brought his WWI score to 75 by downing a Halberstadt C-type at 14.20 east of Vouziers. Thus he became the French and the Allied ace of aces, for this was his last confirmed success.

Another victory was claimed by Sous-Lieutenant Schmitter and MdL Gui of Spa 103, a crashed machine at Croix-aux-Bois. Fonck also attacked another but it was not confirmed. This day also saw the promotions of Adjudant Loup to Adjudant-Chef, and then Spa 3, 26 and 103 moved bases to Hauvine which is about 25 kilometres east-north-east of Reims, but still within the IV° Armée's area of operations. They were followed by Spa 67 and Spa 173 the next day, despite mist and rain.

Four probables were achieved on the 3rd and two more on the 4th. This latter date saw Spa 167's Emile Villard commissioned, and Capitaine Joseph Battle transferred out, command of Spa 103 being taken over by Charles Dupuy, although he also retained command of the whole Groupe. Spa 26 suffered the loss of Sergent Albert Beroulle this day on a morning patrol.

On the 6th, Adjudant-Chef Joseph Baron of Spa 103 was promoted to commissioned rank. Léonard Joseph Baron was born 10 April 1890 at Saint Léonard (Seine Inferieur), and entered military service on 10 October 1911, being assigned to the 1er Régiment du Génie. He was promoted to Sergent in September 1913, and on 5 August 1915 he was transferred to aviation but did not take pilot training until later. After receiving a Military Pilot's Brevet he was assigned to Escadrille N 103 on 29 September 1916, one of the few pilots to serve with GC 12 throughout its entire existence.

The next day Adjudant-Chef Gustave Naudin, Spa 26, was made a Chevalier de la Légion d'Honneur. The 9th saw Brigadier René Ouvrard de Linière of Spa 103 promoted to Maréchal-des-Logis. René Marie Guillaume Ouvrard de Linière was born 6 August 1897, at La Fontaine. He volunteered for military service on 8 February 1915, and was assigned to the 322° Régiment de Dragons as a Soldat de 2nd Classe on 28 July. He was promoted to Soldat de 1er Classe on 29 June and to Brigadier on 16 May 1916. He transferred to aviation on 24 October 1917, and received Military Pilot's Brevet No.11.669 on 19 February 1918, then assigned to Spa 103.

The successful combats on 1 November proved to be the last achieved by GC 12. Over the final few days of WWI, poor weather did not favour too many sorties and with peace in the offing, no flights at all took place on the 10th or 11th. Finally at 11.00 hours on the 11th day of the 11th month of 1918, the guns fell silent. The war which began in August 1914 and which many thought would run its course by Christmas of that year was finally over.

From the time GC 12 commenced operations on 1 November 1916, until the Armistice, the Groupe was credited with a total of 286 aircraft and five balloons destroyed, distributed as shown below:

Spa 3	106 aircraft and 1 balloon	107
Spa 26	31 aircraft	31
Spa 67	14 aircraft	14
Spa 73	20 aircraft and 1 balloon	21
Spa 103	103 aircraft and 3 balloons	106
Spa 167	10 aircraft	10
Spa 173	nil	0
C 46	2 aircraft	2
Totals	286 aircraft and 5 balloons	291

The Escadrilles of GC 12 also suffered the following casualties:

	KIA	MIA	POW	WIA	KIAcc	Inj	Total
Spa 3	5	3	3	7	2	3	23
Spa 26	–	6	1#	12	1	1*	21
Spa 67	1	1	–	2*	1	–	5
Spa 73	3	4	2#	2	1	2	14
Spa 103	3	2	–	5	3	4	17

Spa 167	–	–	–	–	–	–	–
Spa 173	–	–	–	–	–	–	–
C 46	5	–	-	1	–	–	6
Totals	17	16	6	29	8	10	86

* Died of wounds.
\# One interned in Holland and later escaped.

Pilots known to have been assigned to GC 12 on 11 November 1918 were:

Groupe Commander   Capitaine Charles Dupuy
Technical Assistant   Capitaine André Rouget
Intelligence Officer   Capitaine Jean Varenard de Billy
Armament Officer   Lieutenant Joseph Point-Dumont

Spa 3
Lt Jean Dombray – CO
S/Lt Louis Bucquet
S/Lt Demarzé
S/Lt Edouard Moulines
S/Lt Roger Roy
Adj Louis Bourgeois
Adj Jean Laulhé
Adj Edwin Parsons (US)
Sgt Robert Brière
Sgt Maurice Chevannes
Sgt Gustave Decatoire
Sgt Georges Chauffour
Sgt François Macari
Sgt Edouard Monet
Sgt Frédéric Papineau
Sgt Marcel Perrotey
MdL Georges Clémont
MdL Jules Denneulin
MdL André Dubonnet
MdL Robert Martin

Spa 67
Capt Jacques d'Indy – CO
Lt Robert Le Petit
S/Lt Marcel Duret
S/Lt Adrien Mion
S/Lt Pierre Pendaries
S/Lt Auguste Pouchelle
Adj Emile Fumat
Adj Pierre Prou
MdL Henri Alibert
MdL Joseph Bouillet
MdL René Ménard

Sgt Maurice Deschamps
Sgt Marcel Jaubert
Sgt Max Ouvrard de Linière
Brig René Loiseau
Cpl Etienne Margarit
Cpl Joseph Neveu

Spa 26
Capt Xavier de Sevin – CO
Lt Emile Letourneau
S/Lt Benjamin de Tascher
S/Lt Noël Fontaine
S/Lt Jacques Puget
Adj Julius Antoine
Adj Aimé Vincent
MdL Robert Brillaut
MdL Hubert Lambotte
MdL Maurice Maréchal
MdL Maurice Montels
MdL Jacques Ouvrard de Linière
MdL Marcel Plessis
Sgt René Dard
Sgt Armand Lebroussant
Sgt Jean Pelletier
Cpl Jean Eldon
Cpl Léon Gaucher
Cpl Joseph Plessier

Spa 103
Capt Charles Dupuy – CO
Lt René Fonck
S/Lt Joseph Baron
S/Lt Louis Coudouret
S/Lt Pierre Schmitter

S/Lt Léon Thouzellier
Adj Jean Brugère
Adj Henri Drouillh
Adj Gilbert Loup
MdL Gui
MdL René Ouvrard de Linière

Sgt Debaud
Sgt Robert Hoeber (US)
Sgt Lenoir
Sgt George McCall (US)
Sgt Romanel
Sgt Sansom

Spa 167
Lt Bernard Barny de Romanet – CO
S/Lt François Dumas
S/Lt Victor Esperon du Tremblay
S/Lt Joseph Guiguet
S/Lt Emile Villard
MdL Louis Boscher
Sgt Jean de Lombardon
Sgt Roger Gérard
Sgt Victor Girard
Sgt André Nugues
Sgt Robert Soudin
Sgt Paul Thouillet
Cpl René Colomies
Cpl Jean Ferraz
Cpl André Henon
Cpl Raymond Marcon
Cpl Joseph Thèze

Spa 173
Lt Jacques Allez – CO
Lt Aimé Grasset
S/Lt Bailly
S/Lt Bourgeot
Adj-Chef Fernand Quinchez
Adj Chambrelan
MdL Laffay
MdL Tournarie
Sgt Bloyart
Sgt Brenier
Brig Schmitt
Brig Smits
Cpl Filaine
Cpl Granger
Cpl Huc
Cpl Meunier

After the war, on 5 December 1918, Spa 3 was cited for the fourth time by the Commanding General of the IV° Armée, allowing the unit to display the fourragère of the Médaille Militaire on their colours.

> Conscious of a sublime heritage of abnegation and of sacrifice which was left to you by Capitaine Guynemer who gloriously fell on the field of honour, in spite of the losses you have sustained during the course of operations during 1917, the unit has maintained with the highest spirit and ardour its reputation as an élite escadrille.
>
> Under the orders of Capitaine Raymond the unit continued to assert its overwhelming superiority over the enemy, initiating combats daily with remarkable audacity and determination and brought the number of its victories to 175 aircraft officially destroyed and 160 more disabled.

Post-WW1 to the Present Day

After a period served in the Army of Occupation at various bases in Germany, several escadrilles were formed into the 2° Régiment de Chasse *Strassbourg*, on 31 December 1919, commanded by Commandant Félix Brocard. There were three Groupes which comprised the unit:

1er Groupe: Spa 3, Spa 26, Spa 103, and Spa 15.
2° Groupe: Spa 65, Spa 84, Spa 57, Spa 77.
3° Groupe: Spa 124 and Spa 174.

Capitaine Erhard replaced Brocard as temporary commander of the Regiment during January 1920 until the arrival of Capitaine Garde in July. Later Escadrilles Spa 15 and Spa 77 were dissolved leaving the Regiment with eight escadrilles.

On 25 September 1931, the constitution of the 1er Groupe de Chasse du 2° Régiment d'Aviation de Chasse was:

1er Groupe de Chasse		Capitaine Barancy
Spa 3	Spa 26	Spa 103
Lt Daru	Lt Pelissier	Capt Vernhol

On 3 September 1936 the 2° Régiment de Chasse became the 2° Escadre de Chasse, comprised of Groupes de Combat 1/2, and 2/2. Then on 2 September 1938 another Groupe was added 2/3, and the Escadre was then composed of:

GC 1/2	GC 2/2	GC 3/2
Spa 3, Spa 103	Spa 57, Spa 65	Spa 83, Spa 100

The Escadre was equipped with the Morane 406 single-engined day fighters. When World War II began GC 1/2, commanded by Capitaine Daru, was based at Beauvais-Tille. Spa 3 was commanded by Capitaine Robert Williame and Spa 103 commanded by Capitaine Raoul Patureau-Miraud. From the start of hostilities until 24 June 1940, GC 1/2 was credited with a total of 23 confirmed and eight probable victories distributed as follows:

	Destroyed	Probables	Total
Me109	10	1	11
He111	3	3	6
Ju88	4	2	6
Ju87	5	–	5
Hs126	3	–	3
Me110	-	1	1
Do17	-	1	1
	25	8	33
Spa 3	12	5	17
Spa 103	11	3	14
GC Staff	2	–	2
	25	8	33

The top scoring pilot was Capitaine Robert Williame, the commanding officer of Spa 3 who had a total of nine victories (including one probable), four alone and four (and the probable) shared. He had joined Spa 3 in 1934. Another successful pilot was Raoul Patureau-Miraud who scored half a dozen victories before being shot down and killed by AA fire on 17 June 1940.

GC 1/2 was reconstituted on 1 July 1941 serving in Africa, through the Allied invasion in November 1942. Embarking for England on 26 December 1943, GC 1/2 became 329 Squadron, RAF, on 10 February 1944, equipped with Spitfires. This unit was commanded by Lieutenant Colonel P C de G Fleurquin, 'A' Flight, commanded by Lieutenant Jacques Marchelidon and 'B' Flight by Capitaine Jean Ozanne.

On 15 February 1944, 329 Squadron was joined by two other Free French Squadrons, 341 *Alsace* and 340 *Ile de France* to form 145 Wing, RAF, attached to 13 Group, RAF. During the build up to the invasion of Normandy it formed No. 145 Wing, and from August it operated from French soil during the final months of the conflict, the Wing being led by Wing Commander R W F Sampson DFC in 1945. By this time Jean Ozanne had become commanding officer of 329 Squadron and then when he was tour-expired, Marchelidon took over.

On 13 November 1945 the Groupe departed England and its designation of 329 Squadron, to become part of the 2° Escadre de Chasse de l'Armée de l'Air. During its time with the RAF the unit flew 5,073 hours against the enemy and 3,220 missions during which four pilots were killed, one missing and eight wounded, and was cited twice.

On 30 June 1946 the 2° Escadre (GC I/2 *Cigognes* and III/2 *Alsace*) departed to Indochina, beginning operations in August, and where they remained until returning to France on 1 October 1954. While there these units participated in 2,980 sorties during which two pilots were killed and three were wounded.

The *Cigognes* are still an active unit of the Armée de l'Air based at Dijon, France, flying Mirage 2000C aircraft, with an illustrious record of service over 81 years behind them.

Known Decorations of Pilots

Capitaine Alfred Auger
Chevalier de la Légion d'Honneur.
Croix de Guerre with 10 palmes.

Lieutenant Bernard Barny de Romanet
Chevalier de la Légion d'Honneur.
Médaille Militaire 23 May 1917.
Croix de Guerre with ten palmes and three étoiles de vermeil.

Lieutenant François Battesti
Chevalier de la Légion d'Honneur 29 Dec 1917.
Médaille Militaire.
Croix de Guerre with eight palmes.

Capitaine Joseph Battle
Chevalier de la Légion d'Honneur.
British Distinguished Conduct Medal (DSO?)

Adjudant Auguste Baux
Médaille Militaire.
Croix de Guerre with four palmes.

Sergent Frank Baylies
Médaille Militaire.
Croix de Guerre with six palmes and one étoile.

Adjudant-Chef François Bergot
Médaille Militaire 10 Jul 1917.
Croix de Guerre.

Sous-lieutenant Benjamin Bozon-Verduraz
Chevalier de la Légion d'Honneur 5 Apr 1918.
Croix de Guerre with eight palmes, two étoiles de vermeil and one étoile de bronze.

Chef de Bataillon Félix Antonin Gabriel Brocard
Officier de la Légion d'Honneur 18 Feb 1917.
Croix de Guerre avec palmes.

Sous-lieutenant Jean Edouard Caël
Chevalier de la Légion d'Honneur 24 Jan 1919.
Croix de Guerre with four palmes.
Belgian Croix de Guerre.

Adjudant André Chainat
Chevalier de la Légion d'Honneur 3 Aug 1916.
Médaille Militaire 5 April 1916.
Croix de Guerre with nine palmes and one étoile de bronze.

Lieutenant Louis Coudouret
>   Chevalier de la Légion d'Honneur 30 May 1918.
>   Croix de Guerre with four palmes and two étoiles de vermeil.
>   Russian Officer de Saint Georges
>   Sabre d'Ordre de Saint Georges
>   Ordre de Saint Vladimir

Chef d' Escadron Charles de Tricornet de Rose
>   Chevalier de la Légion d'Honneur 14 Oct 1911.
>   Officer de la Légion d'Honneur 13 Jul 1915.
>   Croix de Guerre.

Sous-lieutenant Noël de Rochefort
>   Chevalier de la Légion d'Honneur 10 Jun 1916.
>   Médaille Militaire 5 April 1916.
>   Croix de Guerre.

Capitaine Xavier de Sevin
>   Officier de la Légion d'Honneur.
>   Chevalier de la Légion d'Honneur 19 Apr 1917.
>   Croix de Guerre with nine palmes.

Sous-lieutenant Benjamin de Tascher
>   Chevalier de la Legion d'Honneur.
>   Croix de Guerre.

Capitaine Albert Deullin
>   Officier de la Légion d'Honneur 23 Jun 1918.
> Spa 73   Chevalier de la Légion d'Honneur 4 Jun 1916.
> MF 62   Médaille de Saint Georges 11 Feb 1916.
> GC 19   Croix de Guerre with 14 palmes.

Sergent Pierre Devaulx
>   Médaille Militaire 31 May 1917.
>   Croix de Guerre.

Capitaine Marie Jacques d'Indy
> Spa 26   Chevalier de la Légion d'Honneur 30 Jun 1918.
>   Croix de Guerre avec palmes.

Lieutenant Jean Dombray
>   Chevalier de la Légion d'Honneur.
> N 3   Croix de Guerre.

Sous-lieutenant René Dorme
>   Chevalier de la Légion d'Honneur 18 Oct 1916.
> N 3   Médaille Militaire 4 Aug 1916.
>   Croix de Guerre avec palmes.

Sergent André Dubonnet
        Médaille Militaire 9 Sept 1918.
        Croix de Guerre with three palmes and two étoiles de bronze.

Lieutenant Paul Emile Henri Dumas
        Chevalier de la Légion d'Honneur 25 Oct 1917.

Sous-lieutenant Marcel Duret
        Médaille Militaire.
Spa 67   Croix de Guerre.

Maréchal-des-Logis Georges Flachaire
        Médaille Militaire.
        Croix de Guerre.

Lieutenant René Fonck
        Officier de la Légion d'Honneur 12 May 1918.
C 47   Chevalier de la Légion d'Honneur 21 Oct 1917.
N 103   Médaille Militaire 30 Aug 1916.
        Croix de Guerre with at least 15 palmes.
        British Military Cross.
        British Military Medal.
        Belgian Croix de Chevalier de la Couronne.
        Belgian Croix de Guerre.

Lieutenant Roland Garros
        Officier de la Légion d'Honneur 7 Mar 1918.
N 26   Chevalier de la Légion d'Honneur Oct 1913.
        Croix de Guerre.

Capitaine Jean Gigodot
        Chevalier de la Légion d'Honneur 9 Nov 1918.
        Croix de Guerre with four palmes, two étoiles de bronze.
        Italian Croce Merito di Guerre.

Sergent Joseph Goux
        Médaille Militaire 19 August 1917.
N 26   Croix de Guerre.

Lieutenant Aimé Grasset
        Chevalier de la Légion d'Honneur 1 Oct 1916.
        Médaille Militaire 10 Apr 1915.
        Croix de Guerre avec palmes.
        Officer de la Croix de Saint Georges.
        Ordre de Vladimir de 3rd Classe.
        Ordre de Stanislas de 3rd Classe.
        Ordre de Sainte Anne de 4th Classe.

Sous-lieutenant Henri Guiguet
N 3   Chevalier de la Légion d'Honneur 28 Dec 1918.

Spa 167   Médaille Militaire 31 May 1916.
             Croix de Guerre with 4 palmes and 1 étoile de bronze.

Capitaine Georges Guynemer
             Officier de la Légion d'Honneur 11 Jun 1917.
N 3   Chevalier de la Légion d'Honneur 24 Dec 1915.
             Médaille Militaire 21 July 1915.
             Croix de Guerre with 26 palmes.
             Chevalier de l'Ordre de Léopold 14 Aug 1917.

Sous-lieutenant Claude Haegelen
             Chevalier de la Légion d'Honneur 19 Jul 1918.
N 103   Médaille Militaire 23 August 1917.
             Croix de Guerre with 15 palmes and three étoiles de vermeil.
             British Distinguished Service Order.

Capitaine Alfred Heurtaux
             Officier de la Légion d'Honneur 22 Oct 1917.
N 3   Chevalier de la Légion d'Honneur, 4 August 1916.
             Croix de Guerre with 15 palmes and 2 étoiles de bronze.
             Chevalier de l'Ordre de Léopold 13 Aug 1917.
             British Military Cross.

Capitaine Henri Louis Robert Jeannerod
             Chevalier de la Légion d'Honneur 31 Dec 1913.

Adjutant Charles Jeronnez
             Médaille Militaire 11 May 1917.
             Croix de Guerre.

Sous-lieutenant Auguste Constant Ledeuil
             Chevalier de la Légion d'Honneur 30 Dec 1916.
             Croix de Guerre.

Maréchal-des-Logis Adolphe Lemelle
             Médaille Militaire 31 May 1917.
             Croix de Guerre.

Lieutenant Emile Letourneau
             Chevalier de la Légion d'Honneur.
             Croix de Guerre.

Adjudant Gustave Naudin
             Chevalier de la Légion d'Honneur 8 Nov 1918.
             Médaille Militaire 13 August 1917.
             Croix de Guerre with five palmes and one étoile de vermeil.

Caporal Martin Pelhat
             Médaille Militaire Jul 1916.
             Croix de Guerre.

Sous-lieutenant Pierre Pendaries
>Chevalier de la Légion d'Honneur.
>Médaille Militaire 30 Apr 1917.
>Croix de Guerre with seven palmes.

Adjudant Edmond Pillon
>Médaille Militaire.
>Croix de Guerre.

Capitaine Armand Pinsard
>Officier de la Légion d'Honneur 30 Aug 1918.
>Chevalier de la Légion d'Honneur 7 Sep 1917.
>Croix de Guerre with 19 palmes.
>British Military Cross 17 April 1918.

Sous-lieutenant Auguste Pouchelle
>Médaille Militaire.
N 26   Croix de Guerre.

Lieutenant Jacques Puget
>Chevalier de la Légion d'Honneur.
>Croix de Guerre.

Sous-lieutenant Henri Rabatel
>Médaille Militaire 3 Mar 1916.
>Croix de Guerre avec palme.

Capitaine Georges Raymond
>Chevalier de la Légion d'Honneur 10 Jul 1917.
>Croix de Guerre with seven palmes.
>British Military Cross.

Sous-lieutenant Louis Risacher
>Chevalier de la Légion d'Honneur 1 Sep 1918.
>Croix de Guerre with four palmes and one étoile de bronze.

Adjutant Céléstin Eugène Sanglier
>Médaille Militaire 15 Aug 1916.
>Croix de Guerre.

Adjutant André Simon
>Médaille Militaire.
>Croix de Guerre with three palmes and two étoiles.

Maréchal-des-Logis Constant Soulier
>Médaille Militaire 8 March 1917.
>Croix de Guerre.

Capitaine Mathieu Tenant de la Tour
>Chevalier de la Légion d'Honneur 1 Feb 1916.

Croix de Guerre.
Chevalier de l'Ordre de Léopold 15 Aug 1917.

Adjudant Georges Toulze
Médaille Militaire 15 July 1917.
N 26   Croix de Guerre.

Adjudant Justin Usse
Chevalier de la Légion d'Honneur.
Croix de Guerre.

Sous-lieutenant Marcel Vaillet
Chevalier de la Légion d'Honneur 29 Aug 1916.
N 26   Croix de Guerre.

Lieutenant Zebau
Médaille Militaire.
Croix de Guerre.

APPENDIX B

Groupement de Combat de la Somme/ Groupe de Chasse de Cachy

Unit	Arrived
N 3	16 April 1916
N 103	28 April 1916
N 62	5 May 1916
N 26	5 June 1916
N 65	June 1916
N 37	2 July 1916
N 73	22 July 1916
N 124	19 October 1916

On 24 June 1916 this Groupe consisted of   N 3, N 26, N 62, and N 103
On 16 July 1916 this Groupe consisted of   N 3, N 26, N 37, N 62, N 65, and N 103
On 31 Aug 1916 this Groupe consisted of   N 3, N 26, N 37, N 62, N 65, N 67, N 73 and N 103

GC 12 Staff

16 Jan 1918	Groupe Commander	Capt Henri Horment
	Technical Assistant	Lt André Rouget
	Intelligence Officer	Capt Jean Varenard de Billy
	Armament Officer	Lt Joseph Point-Dumont
	Spa 3	Lt Georges Raymond
	Spa 26	Lt Xavier de Sevin
	Spa 67	Capt Marie Jacques d'Indy
	Spa 73	Capt Albert Deullin
	Spa 103	Capt Jean d'Harcourt
	Parc 112	
	CO	Capt Charles Dupuy
	Technical Assistant	Capt André Rouget
	Intelligence Officer	Capt Jean Varenard de Billy
	Armament Officer	Lt Joseph Point-Dumont

Former GC 12 pilots who Commanded other Units

Sgt Charles Biddle	Spa 73	13th USAS	22 Jun 18 – 23 Oct 18
		4th Pursuit Group	24 Oct 18 – 11 Nov 18
Lt Benjamin Bozon-Verduraz	Spa 3	Spa 94	3 Jul 18 – 11 Nov 18
Capt Pierre Cahuzac	Spa 67	Spa 73	14 Feb 18 – 24 Mar 18
Capt René Colcomb	N 3	N 38	10 Jun 16 – 24 Mar 18
Lt Raoul Echard	N 26	N 82	25 Jan 17 – 5 Jun 18
		GC 22	6 Jun 18 – 11 Nov 18
Lt Guy de la Rochefordière	Spa 3	Spa 94	30 Apr 18 – 11 Jun 18 KIA
Capt Alfred Deullin	Spa 73	GC 19	7 Feb 18 – 11 Nov 18
Lt Jean Gigodot	N 103	Spa 153	1 Jul 17 – 20 Sep 18
Capt Victor Ménard	N 26	GC 15	19 Mar 17 – 4 Feb 18
		Escadre de Combat No 1	4 Feb 18 – 17 Oct 18
Capt Jean Perrin	N 26	N 76	6 May 17 – 6 Feb 18
Lt Armand Pinsard	N 26	N 78	12 Dec 16 – 12 Jun 17 Inj
		Spa 23	Sep 17 – 11 Nov 18
Lt Guy Tourangin	N 26	N 89	18 Mar 17 – 24 Oct 18

Groupe de Combat 12, Combat Log 1916-18

NB. Because the author who compiled this list is American, the dates in the second to last column are in American order (ie: 11-4-16 is 4 November 1916).

1916

Formation

1 Nov   Pursuant to GQG, Commandant de l'Aéronautique Ordre No 17.007 of 19 October 1916, Groupe de Combat 12 was created consisting of escadrilles N 3 (Lt Alfred Heurtaux), N 26 (Capt Victor Ménard), N 73 (Lt Jean Richard), and N 103 (Capt Jean d'Harcourt). Groupe commanded by Capitaine Félix Antonin Brocard. Stationed at Cachy, about 15 km SE of Amiens, VI Armée Sector.

Date Time	Pilot	Unit	Victory	Type	Location	Confirmation*/**
1 Nov 1525	Lt Pinsard	26	2	EA	Bus-Mesnil-en-Arrouaise	
						11-04-16 3.374
2 Nov	Caporal Ravel,	103	missing in action flying a Nieuport XXI.			
3 Nov 1300	Sgt Baron	103	P	EA	NW Mesnil-Bruntel	
3 Nov 1350	S/Lt Guynemer	3	P	EA	Bertincourt	11-04-16 2.398
3 Nov 1400	Lt Heurtaux	3	11	Aviatik	Rocquigny	11-04-16 2.398
6 Nov 1530	Adj Hall	103	P	EA	Buire	11-07-16 4.945
8 Nov 1600	Sgt Baron	103	P	EA	Ligny	11-09-16 6.747
9 Nov 1015	Lt Deullin	3	P	EA	Villers Carbonnel	
9 Nov 1040	Lt Deullin	3	P	EA	Sailly-Saillisel	
9 Nov 1045	Lt Deullin	3	P	EA	Bouchavesnes	
9 Nov 1130	Adj Hall	103	P	EA	Sailly-Saillisel	
9 Nov 1140	S/Lt Ledeuil	103	2	EA	E Manancourt	11-10-16 6.524
9 Nov	Caporal L Millot	103	killed in action flying a Nieuport XVII.			
10 Nov 0750	Sgt Baron	103	P	EA	St Pierre Vaast	
10 Nov 1015	MdL Soulier	26	3	Aviatik	E Péronne	11-11-16 8.451
10 Nov 1215	Lt Guynemer	3	19	Alb C	S Nesle	11-11-16 8.451
10 Nov 1225	Lt Guynemer	3	20	Scout	Morcourt	11-11-16 8.451
10 Nov 1340	Lt Deullin	3	9	EA	Péronne	11-12-16 9.179
10 Nov	Sgt Lutzius	103	Dam	EA	St Pierre Waast	
10 Nov	Sgt Lannes	73	Dam	EA	Athies	11-11-16 8.451
10 Nov	Sgt Prou	26	Dam	EA	Athies	11-11-16 8.451
10 Nov	Sgt Bourdarie	103	seriously injured in an accident flying a Nieuport XVII.			
			Died 25 December 1916.			
10 Nov	Sgt Roxas-Elias	73	missing flying a Nieuport XXI.			
11 Nov 0900	Lt Heurtaux	3	12	Alb	W Sailly-Saillisel	11-12-16 9.179
12 Nov	Cpl Sabatier	73	2	EA		12-01-16 Cit
15 Nov 1015	Adj Jeronnez	26	1	EA	E Chaulnes	11-16-16 No #
16 Nov 0930	Lt Heurtaux	3	13	Fokker	Pressoir	11-17-16 13.286
16 Nov 1145	Sgt Sendral	26	P	EA	Barleux	11-17-16 13.285
16 Nov 1340	Lt Guynemer	3	21	Fokker	S Pertain	11-17-16 13.286
16 Nov 1516	Adj Dorme	3	16	Rumpler	E Marchélepot	12-13-16 Cit
17 Nov 0950	Adj Bucquet	3	P	EA	Laincourt-la-Fosse	
17 Nov 1525	Adj Dorme	3	P	EA	Manancourt	

Date Time	Pilot	Unit	Victory	Type	Location	Confirmation*/**
17 Nov	Sgt G Sendral	26	wounded in action.			
22 Nov 1445	Lt Guynemer	3	22	Halb	E St Christ	11-23-16 13.320
22 Nov 1510	Lt Guynemer	3	23	Halb	Falvy	11-24-16 19.347
22 Nov 1555	Lt Guynemer	3	Dam	EA	St Christ	11-23-16 13.320
23 Nov 0935	Adj Bergot	73	1	EA	Fins	11-24-16 19.347
23 Nov 1435	S/Lt Ledeuil	103	3	EA	Marchélepot	11-24-16 19.347
23 Nov 1550	Lt Deullin	3	10	EA	Bois de Vaux	11-24-16 19.347
26 Nov	Adj B Hall	103	3	EA		11-26-16 Cit
Nov	Most Nieuport XI and XVII of N 3 replaced with SPAD VII.					
4 Dec 1045	Lt Heurtaux	3	P	Aviatik	Rocquigny	12-05-16 3.434
4 Dec 1350	Adj Dorme	3	P	Aviatik	Hyencourt	12-05-16 3.434
4 Dec 1425	Adj Dorme	3	17	Fokker	N St Cren	12-06-16 4.195
8 Dec	N 3 cited by Général Foch, GAN, for having downed 36 EA between 19 August 1916 and 19 November 1916. This second citation gave N 3 the right to display the colours of the Croix de Guerre.					
11 Dec	Capt Ménard	26	P	EA	Mesnil-en-Arrouaise	
15 Dec 0925	Adj Guiguet	3	2	EA	Barleux	12-16-16 13.189
20 Dec 0910	Brig Lemelle	73	1	EA	SE Devise	12-21-16 17.264
20 Dec 1320	Adj Bucquet	3	P	EA	Chaulnes	12-21-16 17.264
20 Dec 1415	Adj Bucquet	3	P	EA	Lihons	12-21-16 17.264
20 Dec 1450	Adj Guiguet	3	3	EA	Marchélepot	12-22-16 18.076
20 Dec 1520	Sgt Baron	103	P	EA	Rancourt	12-21-16 17.264
20 Dec	Adjudant René Dorme, N 3, wounded in action flying Nieuport XVII N1720.					
24 Dec 1120	Lt Heurtaux	3	14	EA	Licourt	12-27-16 21.940
24 Dec	S/Lt Raymond	3	2	EA	Verdun	12-25-16 20.839
24 Dec	Sgt Soulier	26	P	EA	Cernay-en-Dormois	
24 Dec	Sergent Bourdarie, N 103, killed in an accident flying a Nieuport XVII.					
26 Dec 0945	Lt Heurtaux	3	15	Aviatik	Bois de Vaux	12-28-16 23.687
26 Dec 0945	Lt Guynemer	3	24	Halb	E Misery	12-28-16 23.687
27 Dec 1145	Lt Guynemer	3	25	Alb	La Maisonnette	12-31-16 1.960
27 Dec 1150	S/Lt de la Tour	3	8	Halb	Péronne	12-29-16 24.773
27 Dec 1355	Lt Heurtaux	3	16	Rump C	Misery	12-29-16 24.773
27 Dec 1445	Lt Gigodot	103	2	EA	Omiécourt	12-27-16 GC12
27 Dec	Adj Bergot	73	P	EA	St Etienne-à-Arles	

1917

Date Time	Pilot	Unit	Victory	Type	Location	Confirmation*/**
5 Jan 1130	Cpl Lemelle	73	P	EA	Nurlu	
5 Jan 1300	Adj Guiguet	3	P	EA	Roye	
5 Jan 1325	Lt Hervet	103	1	EA	Falvy	1-07-17 5.771
5 Jan 1600	Lt Ledeuil	103	P	EA	NE Manancourt	
7 Jan 1530	Lt Guynemer	3	P	EA	Ablaincourt	
23 Jan 1045	Lt Guynemer	3	26	2 seater	Maurepas	1-25-17 20.021
23 Jan 1050	Lt Guynemer	3	P	EA	Misery	
23 Jan 1134	Lt Guynemer	3	27	2 seater	Chaulnes	1-24-17 19.110
23 Jan	N 26 moved to Manoncourt-en-Vermois, about 10 km SSE of Nancy, VIII° Armée Sector.					
24 Jan 1130	Lt Heurtaux	3	17	EA	S Rocquigny	1-26-17 20.980
24 Jan 1140	Lt Guynemer	3	28	Rumpler	Goyencourt	1-27-17 21.702

Date Time	Pilot	Unit	Victory	Type	Location	Confirmation*/**
24 Jan 1150	Lt Guynemer	3	29	Rumpler	Lignières	1-26-17 20.980
24 Jan 1425	Lt Heurtaux	3	17	EA	Parvillers	1-25-17 20.021
24 Jan 1145	Lt Orlov	3	4	EA	Fresnoy-Roye	1-25-17.20.021
25 Jan 0940	Cpl Papeil	3	P	EA	Nesles	
25 Jan 1030	Lt Heurtaux	3	19	EA	E Puzeaux	1-26-17 20.980
25 Jan 1140	Adj Chainat	3	P	EA	Warlencourt	
25 Jan 1430	Capt Auger	3	P	EA	Ham	1-26-17 20.980
26 Jan 1215	Lt Guynemer	3	30	Alb C	Compiègne	1-27-17 21.702
28 Jan	N 3 & N 103 moved to Manoncourt-en-Vermois.					
29 Jan	N 73 moved to Manoncourt-en-Vermois.					
4 Feb 1530	Lt Heurtaux	3	P	EA	Emberménil	2-05-17 3.621
5 Feb 1325	Capt d'Harcourt	103	P	EA	Moyenvic	
5 Feb 1345	Capt d'Harcourt	103	P	EA	Chambrey	
6 Feb 1135	Lt Heurtaux	3	P	EA	Custines	2-07-17 5.635
6 Feb 1145	Lt Heurtaux	3	P	EA	Sivry	2-07-17 5.635
6 Feb 1205	Lt Heurtaux	3	P	EA	Bois de Faulx	2-07-17 5.635
6 Feb 1325	Lt Heurtaux	3	20	EA	Bois de Faulx	2-07-17 5.635
7 Feb 1120	Lt Guynemer	3	P	EA	Forêt de Bezanges	
8 Feb 1115	Lt Guynemer	3	31	Gotha	Bouconville	2-10-17 8.747
8 Feb 1850	Lt Gigodot	103	P	EA	Cormicy	
9 Feb 1130	Adj Bucquet	3	P	EA	Thiaucourt	
9 Feb 1530	Capt Auger	3	3	Alb	Rogéville	2-10-17 8.747
10 Feb 1340	Lt Deullin	3	11	2 seater	Champenoux	2-11-17 9.664
10 Feb 1115	Lt Guynemer	3	P	EA	NE Nomeny	2-11-17 9.664
10 Feb 1425	Capt Ménard	26	P	EA	Emberménil	
11 Feb 1315	Lt Tourangin	26	P	EA	Forêt de Bezanges	
13 Feb 1030	Sgt Soulier	26	P	EA	Cerny-en-Laonnois	
14 Feb 1000	Adj Bucquet	3	P	EA	Domèvre-Blamont	
14 Feb 1035	S/Lt Ledeuil	103	4	EA	Custines-Mory	2-15-17 13.768
16 Feb 1540	Sgt Lutzius	103	P	EA	NW Cormicy	
16 Feb	Capitaine Alfred Auger, N 3, wounded in action over Lunéville.					
22 Feb	Lieutenant Albert Deullin, N 3, assumed command of N 73, and Lieutenant Jean Richard assigned to Staff of GC 12.					
26 Feb 1325	Lt Heurtaux	3	P	EA	Bois de Faulx	
3 Mar	Sous-lieutenant Auguste Ledeuil, N 103, missing in action flying a Spad VII.					
3 Mar	Lieutenant Richard Robert, N 73, injured in an accident.					
4 Mar 1050	Capt Ménard	26	2	2 seater	Bezanges Forêt	3-17-17 13.010
6 Mar 1435	Capt Auger	3	P			
	S/Lt Raymond & }	3	P			
	S/Lt Dorme	3	P	2 seater	Forêt de Parroy	3-07-18.5.142
16 Mar	N 26 moved to Bonne-Maison, about 5 km SE of Fismes, X° Armée Sector. GAR.					
16 Mar 0908	Capt Guynemer &	3	32			
	Lt Raymond	3	3	Alb C	Courbessaux	3-17-17 13.695
16 Mar 0928	Lt Raymond	3	P	EA	Courbessaux	
16 Mar 0930	Capt Guynemer	3	33	Rumpler	Hoeville	3-17-17 13.695
16 Mar 1430	Capt Guynemer	3	34	Alb C	Regnieville	3-17-17 13.695
16 Mar 0931	Lt Deullin	73	12	EA	Einville-en-Valhay	
						3-17-17 13.695
17 Mar 1330	Capt Guynemer	3	35	EA	Attilloncourt	3-18-17 14.587

Date	Time	Pilot	Unit	Victory	Type	Location	Confirmation*/**
19 Mar		Lieutenant Mathieu Tenant de la Tour, N 3, assumed command of N 26, after Capitaine Victor Ménard was assigned to command of Groupe de Combat 15.					
23 Mar		Spa 3 moved to Bonne-Maison.					
25 Mar	1120	S/Lt Dorme	3	P	EA	Veutelay	
26 Mar		N 103 moved to Bonne-Maison.					
31 Mar	1100	S/Lt Dorme	3	18	AEG	NE Fismes	4-01-17 2.
31 Mar		N 73 moved to Bonne-Maison.					
6 Apr	1805	Adj Jeronnez	26	2	Balloon	Montchâlons	4-06-17 GC12
8 Apr	1530	Cpl Damamez (P) ⎫ Cpl Rivierre (G) ⎬ 46 MdL Theron (G) ⎭	46	P	EA	Orgeval	4-08-17 GC12
8 Apr		Maréchal-des-Logis Theron killed during this combat.					
8 Apr	1600	Sgt Gendronneau (P) ⎫ Adj de Cuypers (G) ⎬46 Lt Vilmet (O) ⎭	46	P	EA	Orainville	4-08-17 GC12
8 Apr		Sergent Gendronneau, Lieutenant Vilmet, KIA, and Adjudant de Cuypers, WIA, shot down during the above combat at Villers-Franqueux, probably by Obltn Erich Hahn, CO of Jasta 19 for his 2nd victory.					
8 Apr	1615	Lt Bloch (P) ⎫ Cpl Boye (G)) ⎬ 46 Sgt Joussen (G) ⎭	46	P	EA	Ferme de Godat	4-08-17 GC12
11 Apr		Adjudant Albert Barioz, N 73, missing in action flying Spad VII #370 during a balloon attack. Probably by pilots from Jasta 14 who claimed two Spads at 1145 S of Corbeny and a Berry-au-Bac.					
11 Apr		Sergent Paris, N 73, missing in action flying a Spad VII.					
		See above. Obltn R Berthold (11) and OfStv Hüttner (2)					
11 Apr	1050	Adj Jeronnez	26	3	EA	Cernay-en-Laonnois	4-12-17 13.539
12 Apr	1002	S/Lt Dorme	3	P	EA	Loivre	
12 Apr		Maréchal-des-Logis Benjamin de Tascher, N 26, became lost and landed in enemy lines and was taken prisoner flying Spad VII #184. He later escaped and returned to the Escadrille.					
13 Apr	1500	Capt Guynemer	3	P	EA	Béthemy	4-13-17 GAR
13 Apr	1030	MdL Soulier	26	P	EA	Cernay-en-Laonnois	4-13-17 GAR
14 Apr	1030	Capt Guynemer	3	36	Alb	La Neuville	4-17-17 15.539
14 Apr	1210	Capt Lecour-Grandmaison ⎫ Sgt Rousseau (G) ⎬ 46 Adj Vitalis (G) ⎭	46	5 5 7	EA	S Craonne	4-14-17 GAR
15 Apr	1010	Adj Jeronnez	26	P	EA	Chamouille	4-15-17 GAR
15 Apr	1010	Adj Guiguet	3	P	EA	Montchâlons	4-15-17 GAR
15 Apr	1015	Capt Guynemer	3	P	EA	Berry-au-Bac	4-15-17 GAR
15 Apr	1040	Lt Deullin	73	13	EA	Festieux	4-16-17 12.558
15 Apr	1040	Brig Rigaud	73		Dam Balloon	Festieux	4-15-17 GAR
15 Apr	1050	Capt Guynemer	3	P	EA	Berry-au-Bac	4-15-17 GAR
15 Apr		Lt Deullin	73	P	EA	Festieux	4-16-17 GAR
15 Apr		Sergent Achille Papeil, N 3, departed at 0520 hours was shot down and taken prisoner flying a Spad VII, by Vzfw Julius Buckler of Jasta 17					
16 Apr		Second Battle of the Aisne commences.					
16 Apr	1025	Brig Rigaud	73	1	EA	N Cormicy	4-17-17 13.539

Date Time	Pilot	Unit	Victory	Type	Location	Confirmation*/**
16 Apr 1445	Capt Auger	3	P	EA	Xures	4-16-17 GC12
16 Apr 1430	Brig Thomassin	26	1	EA	W Juvincourt	5-09-17 7.542
16 Apr 1505	S/Lt Dorme	3	P	2 seater	St Etienne-sur-Suippe	
						4-16-17 GAR
16 Apr 1510	Brig Rigaud	73	2	Balloon	Bruyères	4-17-17 13.539
16 Apr 1540	Sgt Lutzius	103	P	EA	N Corbeny	4-16-17 GAR
16 Apr	Brigadier Edmond Thomassin, N 26, wounded in action in a Nieuport XXIV.					
19 Apr 1451	S/Lt Dorme	3	19	Scout	NE Brimont	4-24-17 21.230
19 Apr 1450	Capt Auger	3	P	EA	Orainville	4-19-17 GC12
20 Apr	Lieutenant Jean Verdié, N 73, wounded in action.					
22 Apr 1710	Adj Bergot	73	P	EA	Auménancourt	4-24-17 21.234
22 Apr 1715	Crew	46	P	EA	Berry-au-Bac	4-22-17 GAR
22 Apr 1750	Lt Deullin	73	14	EA	W Craonne	4-23-17 20.170
22 Apr 1835	S/Lt Dorme	3	20	2 seater	Berrieux	4-24-17 21.230
22 Apr 1910	Capt Auger	3	4	2 seater	Lierval	4-24-17 21.230
23 Apr 0550	Adj Guillaumot	3	P	EA	Jouy	4-23-17 GAR
23 Apr 0715	S/Lt Dorme	3	P	Alb C	Brimont	4-23-17 GAR
23 Apr 0740	S/Lt Dorme	3	P	AEG C	Witry-les-Reims	4-23-17 GAR
23 Apr 1515	MdL Soulier	26	Dam	EA	Auménancourt	4-23-17 GAR
23 Apr 1638	S/Lt Dorme	3	P	Roland D	Forêt de Samoussy	
						4-23-17 GAR
23 Apr 1640	S/Lt Dorme	3	P	Roland D	Festieux	4-23-17 GAR
24 Apr 0930	S/Lt Dorme	3	P	Roland D	Brimont	4-24-17 GAR
24 Apr 1010	Adj Fétu	26	P	EA	Loivre-Courcy	4-24-17 GAR
24 Apr 1010	Lt Barbier ⎫ MdL Robelin ⎬	46	P	EA	Chevregny	4-24-17 GAR
	Sol Montdême ⎭					
24 Apr 1558	S/Lt Dorme	3	P	2 seater	Vaucelles-Montbavin	
						4-24-17 GAR
24 Apr 1800	S/Lt Battesti	73	1	EA	Ste Croix	5-15-17 15.298
24 Apr 1805	Capt Lecour- Grandmaison (P) ⎫ Adj Vitalis (G) ⎬	46	P	EA	Guignicourt-Juvincourt	
	Sgt Rousseau (G) ⎭					4-24-17 GAR
24 Apr 1840	S/Lt Bucquet	3	FTL	EA	Sivry-les-Etouvelles	
						4-24-17 GAR
26 Apr 1720	Sgt Grendenneau, ⎫		1			
	Asp Bruel ⎬	46	1	EA	Brimont	4-27-17 GAR
	Cpl Cadot ⎭		1			
27 Apr 0800	Capt Auger	3	FTL	EA	Bétheniville	4-27-17 GC12
28 Apr 0550	Adj Guillaumot	3	P	EA	Ecouffaux	4-28-17 GAR
29 Apr 1343	S/Lt Dorme	3	21	Alb C	Aguilcourt	5-01-17 3.
29 Apr 1025	S/Lt Dorme	3	P	Scout	N Amifontaine	4-30-17 X-410
29 Apr 1845	Lt Campion (P) ⎫ MdL Lamy (G) ⎬	46		shot down in flames near Brimont.		
	Cpl Bousque (G) ⎭					
30 Apr 1705	Capt Shigeno	26	P	EA	Juvincourt-Prouvais	
						4-30-17 GAR
2 May 0805	Sgt Haegelen	103	P	EA	NW Neufchâtel	5-02-17 GAR

Date Time	Pilot	Unit	Victory	Type	Location	Confirmation*/**
2 May 0905	S/Lt Dorme	3	P	Alb C	Montchâlons	5-02-17 GAR
2 May 1050	Adj-Chef Bergot	73	P	EA	Berrieux-Aizelles	
						5-02-17 GAR
2 May 1840	Capt Auger	3	P	EA	Réservoir	5-02-17 GAR
2 May 1915	Capt Guynemer	3	P	EA	Réservoir	
2 May 1935	Capt Guynemer	3	37	Alb	Courtecon	5-09-17 7.542
3 May 1710	Lt Barbier (P)					
	Adj Robelin (G) }	46	P	EA	Berméricourt	5-04-17 X-425
	Sol Mondême (G)					
3 May 0912	S/Lt Dorme	3	P	2 seater	Courtecon	5-04-17 X-425
3 May 0953	Capt Heurtaux	3	P	EA	Neufchâtel-sur-Aisne	
						5-04-17 X-425
3 May 1120	Capt Guynemer	3	P	EA	Malmaison	5-04-17 X-425
3 May 1935	Capt Heurtaux	3	P	EA	Aguilcourt	5-03-17 GC12
4 May 0715	Capt Heurtaux	3	21	Alb C	Berrieux	5-09-17 7.542
4 May 0910	Cpl Schmitter	103	P	EA	Bourgogne-Brimont	
						5-04-17 GAR
4 May 1400	Lt de Guibert	73	P	EA	Sivry-les-Etouvelles	
						5-04-17 GAR
4 May 1405	S/Lt Dorme	3	22	3 seater	Amifontaine	5-09-17 7.542
4 May 1508	Capt Guynemer	3	38	Alb C	Courtecon-Braye	
						5-09-17 7.542
4 May 1710	Crew	46	P	EA	Berméricourt	5-05-17 X-524
4 May 1850	Lt Raymond	3	P	EA	Juvincourt-Amifontaine	
						5-04-17 GAR

4 May — Sergent Pierre Devaulx, N 26, wounded during combat flying a Spad VII, and forced to land near Juvincourt.

5 May 0510	Adj Sanglier &	3				
	Sgt Laulhé	86	Dam	2 seater	Braye-en-Laonnois	
						5-05-17 GAR
5 May 0730	Adj Fonck	103	3	Rumpler	Berry-au-Bac	5-05-17 GAR
5 May 1915	Adj Guiguet	3	4	EA	Montchâlons	5-09-17 7.542

5 May — Capitaine Albert Heurtaux, Spa 3, severely wounded during combat with five enemy aircraft and evacuated to a hospital. Spa 3 temporarily commanded by Capitaine Alfred Auger.

6 May 1430	Adj Fonck	103	P	EA	E Neufchâtel	5-07-17 X-439
7 May 0955	Lt Tenant de la Tour	26	9	EA	Brimont	5-17-17 15.298
7 May 1045	Adj Guiguet	3	P	EA	E Ailette	5-07-17 GAR
9 May 1820	Lt Tenant de la Tour	26	P	EA	Bruyères	5-10-17 X-449

9 May — Capitaine Alfred Heurtaux wounded in combat.

10 May — Adjudant Céléstin Sanglier, N 3, killed during combat, departed at 10.40 flying a Spad VII, between Juvincourt and Brimont, probably by Leutnant Heinrich Gontermann, Jasta 15, who claimed a Spad at 12.30 N of Berry-au-Bac (19).

10 May 1007	S/Lt Dorme	3	23	Alb C	Sivry-les-Etouvelles	
						5-17-17 15.298
10 May 1120	Adj Guiguet	3	P	EA	Guignicourt	5-10-17 GC12
10 May 1310	MdL Lemelle	73	2	EA	Bièvres-Montchâlons	
						5-11-17 X-451

10 May — Capt Lecour-Grandmaison (P) KIA, Sgt Boye (G) WIA, and Cpl Crozet (G) KIA, of C 46, were shot down in the French lines. Probably by Ltn Gontermann, Jasta 15, 20th victory.

Date Time	Pilot	Unit	Victory	Type	Location	Confirmation*/**
11 May 1125	Capt Auger &	3	5			
	Lt de Sevin	12	3	2 seater	Vailly-sur-Aisne	5-12-17 X-457
11 May 0725	S/Lt Bucquet	3	P	EA	Bazancourt	5-11-17 GC12
11 May 1040	Adj Guiguet	3	P	EA	Juvincourt	5-11-17 GC12
11 May 1245	S/Lt Dorme	3	P	EA	Warmeriville	5-11-17 GC12
11 May 1430	Lt Deullin	73	15	Alb	Loivre	5-12-17 X-457
11 May 1850	Adj Fonck	103	4	Alb	Aguilcourt	5-18-17 15.298
12 May 1855	Patrol	103	Dam	EA	N Corbeny	5-12-17 X-460
13 May 1830	Adj Fonck	103	5	Fokker	Nogent l'Abbesse	
						5-22-17 GC12
14 May 1930	S/Lt Rabatel	3	P	EA	Monampteuil	5-14-17 GC12
14 May 1955	MdL Soulier	26	4	2 seater	Neuville-Chemizy	
						6-02-17 3.
14 May 1930	Lt Deullin	73	P	EA	N Réservoir	5-14-17 GC12
18 May 0820	Sgt Dedieu	26	P	EA	Berrieux	5-18-17 GC12
20 May	Second Battle of the Aisne ends.					
22 May 1840	S/Lt Dezarrois	26	P	EA	Ailles	5-22-17 GC12
23 May 1010	Sgt Barés	26	P	EA	N Craonne	5-24-17 GC12
23 May 1830	Lt Hervet	103	2	EA	Bouconville	6-01-17 X-518
23 May	Adjudant Joseph Guiguet, N 3, severely wounded by AA fire.					
24 May 0830	Capt Auger	3	P	EA	Fresnes-Reims	5-24-17 X-490
24 May 1021	S/Lt Dorme	3	P	EA	Aizelles	5-24-17 X-490
25 May 0810	S/Lt Dorme	3	P	Alb C	Berru-Epoye	5-25-17 X-494
25 May 0830	Capt Guynemer	3	39	LVG C	NW Corbeny	6-01-17 3.
25 May 0830	Capt Auger	3	P	EA	Berrieux	5-25-17 X-494
25 May 0831	Capt Guynemer	3	40	2 seater	Juzancourt	6-01-17 3.
25 May 0915	Lt Rabatel	3	2	2 seater	Berry-au-Bac	6-21-17 19.096
25 May 1215	Capt Guynemer	3	41	DFW C	Courlandon	6-01-17 3.
25 May 1830	Capt Guynemer	3	42	Fokker	Gugnicourt	6-01-17 3.
25 May	Sous-lieutenant René Dorme, N 3, flying a Spad VII, departed at 18h40, and was killed during a combat, probably by Leutnant Heinrich Kroll of Jasta 9.					
26 May 1000	Capt Guynemer	3	43	Alb C	W Condé-sur-Suippes	
						6-01-17 3.
26 May 1210	MdL Soulier	26	P	Scout	Prouvais	5-26-17 X-496
26 May 1712	MdL Soulier	26	P	2 seater	N Urcel	5-26-17 X-496
27 May 0905	Capt Guynemer	3	P	2 seater	Aubérive	5-27-17 X-502
27 May 0910	Sgt Haegelen	103	1	EA	E Nauroy	6-02-17 X-524
27 May 1835	MdL Soulier	26	5	DFW C	Pontfaverger	5-28-18 X-502
27 May 1905	Two A/C	46	Dam	EA	Brimont	5-27-17 X-502
28 May 0810	MdL Soulier	26	P	EA	Pontfaverger	5-28-17 X-505
28 May 0825	MdL Soulier	26	P	EA	Pontfaverger	5-28-17 X-505
28 May 0845	Lt Deullin	73	P	EA	Neufchâtel	5-28-17 X-505
28 May 0850	Lt de Guibert	73	P	EA	Neufchâtel	5-28-17 X-505
28 May 1045	Sgt Haegelen &	103				
	Sgt Durand	80	1	EA	Chenay	5-28-17 GC12
28 May	Sergent Marcel Haegelen, N 103, flying a Spad VII, was severely injured in the chest in a landing accident.					
29 May	Caporal Lucien Perot, N 3, departed at 18.25 flying a Spad VII, failed to return and reported as missing, thought to be a prisoner.					

Date Time	Pilot	Unit	Victory	Type	Location	Confirmation*/**
31 May	Maréchal-des-Logis Auguste Pouchelle, N 26, wounded during combat with four EA at 19.20 hours flying a Spad VII.					
1 Jun 1050	S/Lt Bucquet	3	P	EA	Monampteuil	6-01-17 GC12
3 Jun 1850	MdL Soulier,	26	6			
	Lt de Bonald &	69	3	DFW C	N Muizon	6-09-17 7.888
	Sgt Chapelle	31	3			
3 Jun 0820	Sgt Drou	73	P	EA	Brimont	6-04-17 X-527
3 Jun 1030	Capt Guynemer	3	P	EA	Craonne	6-04-17 X-527
4 Jun 0940	Lt Deullin	73	16	EA	Fismes-Bovelle	6-05-17 X-528
4 Jun 1030	Capt Guynemer	3	P	EA	Craonne	6-04-17 X-528
4 Jun 2005	Capt Auger	3	6	EA	Grandelain	6-09-17 7.888
5 Jun 1715	Capt Guynemer	3	44	Alb C	Berry-au-Bac	6-09-17 7.888
5 Jun 1730	Capt Guynemer	3	45	DFW C	Forêt de Berru	6-09-17 7.888
Jun	N 3 cited for third time, by the Commanding General, X° Armée, for having destroyed 128 EA and disabling 132 others.					
7 Jun 1033	MdL Fontaine	26	P	EA	Berry-au-Bac	6-08-17 X-537
7 Jun 1035	Adj Fétu	26	P	EA		6-08-17 X-537
11 Jun	Adj Fétu	26	1	Scout	Laon	SHAA
12 Jun 0900	Adj Fonck	103	6	Alb	Cauroy-Cormicy	6-21-17 19.096
17 Jun 0640	Lt Tenant de la Tour					
		3	P	EA	Guignicourt	6-17-17 GC12
17 Jun 1035	S/Lt Rabatel	3	P	EA	Vailly-sur-Aisne	6-17-17 GC12
17 Jun 1132	Capt Auger	3	P	EA	Chamouille	6-17-17 GC12
17 Jun	Sgt Brière	3	1	EA		7-29-17 Cit
23 Jun	Sergent Vincent Scalingi, N 73, injured in a landing accident in a Spad VII.					
24 Jun 0915	MdL Lemelle	73	FTL	EA	N Chavignon	6-25-17 X-564
24 Jun 2045	Sgt Lutzius	103	Dam	EA		6-26-17 X-565
26 Jun 1310	Sgt Tassou	73	P	EA	Bourgogne	6-26-17 GC12
27 Jun 0740	Lt Jeronnez	26	P	EA	Moulines	6-27-17 GC12
28 Jun 1700	Capt Auger	3	7	2 seater	W Pontavert	7-02-17 1.007
3 Jul 0800	S/Lt Battesti	73	P	EA	Pontavert	7-04-17 X-587
4 Jul 1600	S/Lt Battesti	73	2	EA	Berry-au-Bac	7-06-17 GC12
6 Jul 1030	Sgt Baron	103	P	EA	Brimont	7-07-17 X-599
6 Jul 1055	Capt Guynemer	3	46	DFW C	Brimont	7-13-17 12.930
6 Jul 1645	Capt Guynemer	3	P	EA	Craonne	7-06-17 GC12
6 Jul	Sergent Georges Silberstein, N 3, killed in an accident.					
6 Jul	Sergent Lecomte, N 103, was forced to land overturning his aircraft after his motor had been hit during combat.					
7 Jul 1110	Capt Guynemer	3	47	Alb	Villers-Franqueux	
	(127th Victory for N 3)					7-13-17 12.930
7 Jul 1230	Capt Guynemer	3	48	DFW C	Moussy	7-13-17 12.930
11 Jul	N 73 moved to Bergues, about 10 km SSE of Dunkerque, Flanders Sector, 1er Armée Sector.					
12 Jul	N 3 & N 26 moved to Bierne, W of Bergues, Flanders Sector.					
12 Jul	N 103 moved to Coudekerke, about 1 km S of Dunkerque, Flanders Sector.					
12 Jul	Sgt Naudin	26	1	EA	Craonne	8-13-17 Cit
21 Jul 2140	Lt Deullin	73	17	EA	NE Dixmuide	8-02-17 1.964
21 Jul	Capitaine Jean Lamon, N 73, was flying a Spad when shot down and taken prisoner. Departed at 18.15.					
22 Jul	Lieutenant Louis Pandevant, N 73, missing in action flying Spad #1543. Departed at 08.00.					

Date	Time	Pilot	Unit	Victory	Type	Location	Confirmation*/**
24 Jul		Caporal Edouard Moulines, N 3, injured in a landing accident.					
27 Jul	2030	Capt Guynemer	3	49	Alb	Langemarck	8-02-17 1.964
28 Jul	2050	Capt Guynemer	3	50	DFW C	Westroosebeke	8-02-17 1.964
28 Jul		Lieutenant Alfred Deullin, N 73, wounded in action.					
28 Jul		Capitaine Alfred Auger, N 3, killed during combat over Woesten- Zuidschoote, flying a Spad. Command of N 3 assumed by Capitaine Georges Guynemer.					
31 Jul		Third Battle of Ypres starts.					
6 Aug		Capitaine Albert Heurtaux assumed command of N 3.					
9 Aug		Adj-Chef Fonck	103	7	Fokker	NW Dixmuide	8-12-17 12.382
12 Aug		N 3, N 26 & N 103 moved to St Pol-sur-Mer at Dunkerque, Flanders Sector, 1er Armée Sector.					
14 Aug		MdL Lemelle	73	3	EA	E Forêt d'Houthulst	8-15-17 16.126
14 Aug		MdL Lemelle	73	P	EA	Forêt d'Houthulst	8-15-17 16.126
14 Aug		Caporal Oliver Chadwick, N 73, killed in combat at 09.45 near Ferme Carnot.					
15 Aug		N 73 moved to St Eloi, near Dunkerque.					
16 Aug	0832	Lt Raymond	3	4	EA	Forêt d'Houthulst	8-23-17 25.033
16 Aug		Sous-lieutenant Henri Rabatel, N 3, flying a Spad, was shot down and taken prisoner.					
16 Aug		Caporal Cornet, N 3, missing in action flying a Spad.					
16 Aug		Maréchal-des-Logis Seigneurie, N 103, flying a Spad, wounded in action by AA fire.					
17 Aug	0820	Capt Guynemer	3	51	Alb C	Vladslo	8-23-17 25.033
17 Aug	0925	Capt Guynemer	3	52	DFW C	S Dixmuide	8-23-17 25.033
17 Aug		Caporal George E Turnure, Jr, N 103, an American, injured in an accident flying a Spad.					
18 Aug		Sgt Henin	3	1	EA	Forêt d'Houthulst	8-19-17 20.395
18 Aug		Capt Guynemer	3	P	EA		8-19-17 20.395
18 Aug		Caporal Julian Biddle, an American, N 73, missing near Dunkerque.					
19 Aug		Adj-Chef Fonck	103	8	Alb C		8-23-17 25.033
20 Aug		Capt Guynemer	3	53	DFW C	Poperinghe	8-21-17 22.772
20 Aug		Adj-Chef Fonck	103	9	EA		8-21-17 22.727
21 Aug		Sous-lieutenant André Dezarrois, N 26, wounded in combat.					
21 Aug		Adj-Chef Fonck	103	10	2 seater	Dixmuide	8-22-17 24.025
21 Aug		Lieutenant Paul Dumas, N 103, wounded in action flying a Spad.					
22 Aug		Adj-Chef Fonck	103	11	EA	NE Ypres	8-24-17 25.990
3 Sep		Capt Heurtaux	3	P	EA		
3 Sep		Capitaine Albert Heurtaux, N 3, severely wounded in action, command of Spa 3 assumed by Capitaine Georges Guynemer.					
9 Sep		Sgt Pernell	103	1	EA	NE Ypres	9-10-17 9.892
10 Sep		Adjudant Pierre Petit-Dariel, N 3, wounded in action.					
11 Sep		Capitaine Georges Guynemer, N 3, killed in action in a Spad XIII.					
11 Sep		Lieutenant Gustave Lagache assumed temporary command of N 3.					
14 Sep		Adj-Chef Fonck	103	12	EA	E Langemarck	9-16-17 16.336
15 Sep		Adj-Chef Fonck	103	13	EA	Zonnebeke	9-17-17 17.537
16 Sep		Lieutenant Georges Raymond assumed command of Spa 3.					
19 Sep		Chef de Bataillon Félix Brocard, the CO of GC 12, was transferred to the Staff of the Air Ministry, and Capitaine Jean d'Harcourt assumed temporary command of the groupe until the arrival of Capitaine Henri Horment.					
20 Sep		Adj Tassou	73	P	EA	Langemarck	9-21-17 20.565

Date	Time	Pilot	Unit	Victory	Type	Location	Confirmation*/**
23 Sep		Adj-Chef Fonck	103	14	2 seater	S Houthulst	9-24-17 25.252
26 Sep		Moved to Bierne, Flanders Sector, 1er Armée.					
27 Sep		Lt Deullin	73	18	EA	Dixmuide	9-28-17 29.714
27 Sep		Adj-Chef Fonck	103	P	EA	Zonnebeke	9-28-17 29.714
27 Sep		N 73 moved back to Bergues, 1er Armée Sector.					
28 Sep		Maréchal-des-Logis Noël Fontaine, N 26, wounded flying a Spad VII.					
28 Sep		Maréchal-des-Logis Mortureux, N 26, wounded in action flying a Spad.					
29 Sep		Patrol	103	P	EA	E Dixmuide	9-30-17 31.942
30 Sep		Sgt Prou	26	1	2 seater	Poperinghe	10-01-17 3.
30 Sep		Adj-Chef Fonck &	103	15			
		Adj Dupre	102	2	2 seater	Poperinghe	10-12-17 13
5 Oct		Sergent Gaillard, N 3, killed in an accident.					
14 Oct	1400	Brig de Marcy	3	1	Alb C	Bixschoote	10-15-17 16.
		(136th victory for Spa 3)					
14 Oct		Cpl Collins	103	1	Albatros	E Langemarck	10-15-17 16.
14 Oct		Groupe Patrols downed four enemy aircraft, individual victors could not be ascertained.					
							10-15-17 16.819
14 Oct		Sergent Gaston Drou, N 73, killed in action in a Spad VII.					
15 Oct		Sgt Pietri	103	1	EA	Houthulst	10-17-17 19.03
15 Oct		Patrol	GC	P	EA		10-16-17 17.85
17 Oct		Adj-Chef Fonck	103	16	EA		10-18-17 20.23
17 Oct		Adj-Chef Fonck	103	17	EA		10-18-17 20.23
17 Oct		Sgt Lecomte &	103	1			
		Sgt Turnure	103	1	EA	Ypres	10-18-17 20.23
18 Oct		Adj-Chef Fonck	103	P	EA	Houthulst	10-19-17 21.28
18 Oct		Maréchal-des-Logis Pierre Jolivet, N 73, killed in combat flying a Spad VII.					
21 Oct		Adj-Chef Fonck	103	18	EA	Passchendaele	10-22-17 24.994
24 Oct		Sergent Robert Brière, N 3, wounded in action.					
27 Oct	1535	Capt Raymond	3	5	EA	Forêt d'Houthulst	
							10-30-17 37.068
27 Oct		Adj-Chef Fonck	103	19	EA	Westroosebeke	10-30-17 37.06
27 Oct		Adj-Chef Fonck	103	P	EA		10-28-17 34.84
27 Oct		Adj-Chef Fonck	103	P	EA		10-28-17 34.84
28 Oct		Patrol	73	P	EA	Roulers	10-29-17 36.02
29 Oct		Sgt Haegelen	103	P	EA	Westroosebeke	10-30-17 37.068
Oct		N 73 redesignated as Spa 73.					
5 Nov		Lt Dumas, Spa 103, wounded in action and evacuated.					
8 Nov		Lt Deullin	73	19	Pfalz DIII	Hollebeke	11-11-17 11.56
12 Nov		Lt Battesti	73	3	EA	W Forêt d'Houthulst	
12 Nov		Capitaine Duval, Spa 73, killed attempting to take off in a Spad.					
13 Nov		Patrol	GC	P	EA	Passchendaele	11-14-17 15.332
18 Nov		Maréchal-des-Logis Louis Paoli, Spa 73, flying Spad VII #1832, came down in Holland and was interned, later escaped and rejoined his unit.					
29 Nov		Sergent Jean Dedieu, N 26, injured in an accident.					
5 Dec		Cpl C Biddle	73	1	EA	Langemarck	12-06-17 5.387
5 Dec		Sgt Collins	103	P	EA	Houthulst	12-06-17 5.387
7 Dec		Third Battle of Ypres ends.					
8 Dec		Lieutenant Paul Tourtel, N 103, killed in an accident flying a Spad XIII.					
11 Dec		Spa 3, Spa 73 & Spa 103 arrived at Maisonneuve, NE of Villers-Cotterêts, VI° Armée Sector.					

Date Time	Pilot	Unit	Victory	Type	Location	Confirmation*/**
12 Dec	Spa 26 arrived at Maisonneuve.					
17 Dec	Capitaine Mathieu Tenant de la Tour, N 26, killed in an accident flying a Spad VII near Saint Pol.					
17 Dec	Lieutenant Daniel Dumêmes took temporary command of N 26.					
25 Dec	Lieutenant Xavier de Sevin, N 12, assumed command of N 26.					
29 Dec	Adj Naudin	26	2	EA		SHAA

1918

Date Time	Pilot	Unit	Victory	Type	Location	Confirmation*/**
3 Jan 1310	Patrol	73	P	EA	Réservoir	1-03-18 GC12
3 Jan 1510	Patrol	3	P	EA	Corbeny	1-03-18 GC12
5 Jan	By Le Général Commandant en Chef (GQG) telegram No. 2115/M, GC 12 was directed to move to Beauzée-sur-Aire, about 10 km SW of Souilly, II° Armée Sector, (G.A.E.					
10 Jan	Spa 3 and Spa 103 departed for Beauzée-sur-Aire, in accordance with VI° Armée Ordre No. 23.047.					
13 Jan	Spa 26 and Spa 73 departed for Beauzée-sur-Aire, in accordance with VI° Armée Ordre No. 23.081.					
16 Jan	Spa 67 and Parc 112 departed for Beauzée-sur-Aire, in accordance with VI° Armée Ordre No. 23.097.					
19 Jan	S/Lt Fonck	103	20	EA	Beaumont	1-20-18 21.435
19 Jan 1415	S/Lt Fonck	103	21	EA	Samogneux	1-26-18 28.538
19 Jan	Spa 67, commanded by Capitaine Marie Jacques d'Indy, assigned to GC 12.					
20 Jan 1040	Lt de Sevin	26	7			
	MdL Fontaine &	26	1	EA	Samogneux	1-21-18 26.189
	Sgt Mouton (P)(Br 35)		1			
	Lt Deublin (O)(Br 35)		1			
20 Jan	Adj Pietri	103	P	EA	E Sivry	1-20-18 II-
20 Jan	Caporal Henry A. Batchelor, Spa 103, an American, injured in an accident flying a Spad.					
25 Jan 1515	Adj Duret	67	1	EA	Béthincourt	1-30-18 33.375
25 Jan 1450	Cpl Benney	67	Dam	Albatros		1-25-18 GC 12
25 Jan	Caporal Phillip Benney, an American, Spa 67, wounded in combat, died of wound 26 January 1918.					
5 Feb 1205	S/Lt Fonck	103	22	2 seater	Clermont	2-07-18 GC12
5 Feb 1205	Lt Willemin &	67				
	Patrol	67	Dam	2 seater	Verdun	2-05-18 GC12
5 Feb	Caporal William Tailer, an American, Spa 67, killed in action near Montzéville at 13.30 hours.					
13 Feb	Capitaine Albert Deullin appointed CO of Groupe de Combat 19 taking Spa 73 with him Spa 73, now commanded by Capitaine Pierre Cahuzac, departed Beauzée-sur-Aire to join GC 19 this date in accordance with II° Armée Ordre No. 290 of 8 February 1918.					
16 Feb 1135	Lt Bozon-Verduraz &		1			
	S/Lt de la					
	Rochefordière	3	1	EA	E Damloup	2-17-18 18.967
	(138th victory for Spa 3)					
17 Feb 1215	Lt Bozon-Verduraz	3	2	2 seater	Montfaucon	2-19-18 21.192
18 Feb 1245	Patrol	103	P	EA	Bezonvaux	2-18-18 GC12
18 Feb 1306	S/Lt Fonck	103	23	Alb	Bezonvaux	2-20-18 22.389
19 Feb 1315	Cpl Baylies	3	1	EA	N Forges	2-21-18 23.401
19 Feb 1205	S/Lt Fonck	103	24	Alb C	Montfaucon	2-20-18 22.389

Date Time	Pilot	Unit	Victory	Type	Location	Confirmation*/**
20 Feb 1120	Lt Bozon-Verduraz &	3				
	S/Lt de la					
	Rochefordière	3	2	2 seater	Calonne	2-21-18 23.401
20 Feb 1640	Capt Raymond	3	6	EA	N Vauquois	2-25-18 27.004
26 Feb 1010	S/Lt Fonck	103	25	2 seater	S Montfaucon	3-04-18 3.492
26 Feb 1025	S/Lt Fonck	103	26	2 seater	Dieppe	2-27-18 30.637
2 Mar	Pursuant to Le Général Commandant en Chef telegram No. 4206/M, GC 12 is directed to proceed to Lhéry, 1er Armée Sector.					
5 Mar	Spa 3 and Spa 67 departed for Lhéry, about 25 km WSW of Reims, 1er Armée Sector, in accordance with II° Armée Ordre No. 1247 of 3 March 1918.					
6 Mar	Spa 26 and Spa 103 departed for Lhéry, in accordance with II° Armée Ordre No. 1247, of 3 March 1918.					
7 Mar	Cpl Baylies	3	2	EA	NE Courtecon	3-20-18 21.578
15 Mar 1015	S/Lt Fonck	103	27	2 seater	Berméricourt	3-16-18 16.713
15 Mar 1725	S/Lt Fonck	103	28	2 seater	N Courtecon	3-17-18 17.914
15 Mar 1730	Sgt Schmitter	103	1	2 seater	Forges-Lierval	3-16-18 16.713
16 Mar 1150	S/Lt Fonck	103	29	2 seater	Nogent l'Abbesse	3-18-18 19.103
16 Mar 1420	Adj Pendaries	67	P	2 seater	S Challerange	3-16-18 GC12
16 Mar 1735	Cpl Baylies	3	3	EA	Chevrigny	4-07-18 6.208
17 Mar 1140	Adj Mion	67	2	2 seater	Marchais-Montaigu	
						25.063
17 Mar 1820	S/Lt Fonck	103	30	Pfalz DIII	Menneville	3-21-18 22.607
17 Mar 1820	Sgt Loup	103	P	Scout	Laval	3-17-18 GC12
17 Mar 1750	S/Lt Fonck	103	P	EA	Nogent l'Abbesse	3-17-18 GC12
21 Mar 1340	Sgt Baux, ⎫	103	1			
	Adj Tasque & ⎬	103	1	Rump C	Rilly-le-Montaigu	
	Adj Baron ⎭	103	1			3-22-18 23.546
22 Mar 1515	Sgt Hoeber &	103				
	Sgt Schmitter	103	P	Scout	Berry-au-Bac	3-22-18 GC12
22 Mar 1715	Adj Naudin	26	P	Scout	Nogent l'Abbesse	
						3-22-18 GC12
22 Mar 1715	S/Lt Fonck	103	P	2 seater	Nogent l'Abbesse	
						3-22-18 GC12
22 Mar	Spa 26 departed for Mesnil-St Georges, about 3 km WSW of Montdidier, VI° Armée Sector.					
23 Mar	Adjudant Gaston Tasque, Spa 103, killed in an accident flying a Spad.					
24 Mar	Spa 3 and Spa 103 arrived at Mesnil-St Georges.					
25 Mar	Spa 67 arrived at Mesnil-St Georges, immediately moved on to Raray.					
26 Mar	Spa 3 moved to Raray, about 15 km NE of Senlis, III° Armée Sector.					
27 Mar	Sous-lieutenant André Willemin, Spa 67, departed at 16.30 flying a Spad VII failed to return and reported as missing.					
27 Mar	Capitaine Jean d'Harcourt, CO Spa 103, assigned as CO of Groupe de Combat 13; command of Spa 103 passed to Capitaine Joseph Battle from Spa 77.					
28 Mar	Spa 26 & Spa 103 moved to Raray.					
28 Mar 1030	S/Lt Fonck	103	31	EA	E Montdidier	3-29-18 29.132
28 Mar	Capitaine Joseph Battle, CO Spa 103, wounded in the foot by ground fire.					
29 Mar 1830	S/Lt Fonck	103	32	Scout	E Montdidier	3-30-18 30.097
29 Mar 1830	S/Lt Fonck	103	33	Scout	E Montdidier	3-30-18 30.097
31 Mar 0835	Sgt Schmitter	103	Dam	EA	Montdidier	3-31-18 GC12
1 Apr 1415	Capt de Sevin	26	8	EA	E Montdidier	6-20-18 23.968

Date Time	Pilot	Unit	Victory	Type	Location	Confirmation*/**
1 Apr 1445	Cpl Loup &	103				
	Cpl Mabereau	26	P	EA	Bois Tilloloy	4-01-18 GC12
3 Apr 0715	Patrol	3	P	2 seater	Piennes	4-03-18 GC12
3 Apr 1030	Sgt Vincent	26	P	EA	Fignières	4-03-18 GC12
3 Apr	Sergent Pierre Devaulx, Spa 26, MIA over Montdidier, flying a Spad VII. Departed at 10.00 hours.					
3 Apr	Caporal Claude Bernard, Spa 67, wounded in action.					
6 Apr 1135	Capt de Sevin	26	P	EA	Fignières	3-06-18 GC12
8 Apr	Spa 67 & Spa 103 moved to Hétomesnil, about 30 km NNW of Beauvais, III° Armée Sector					
9 Apr	Spa 3 moved to Hétomesnil.					
10 Apr	Spa 26 arrived at Hétomesnil.					
11 Apr 1330	Sgt Baylies	3	4	EA	Mesnil-St Georges	
						4-14-18 14.388
12 Apr 0650	Sgt Baylies	3	5	2 seater	S Moreuil	4-19-18 17.922
12 Apr 1745	Capt de Sevin &					
	Patrol	26	P	2 seater	Marcelcave	4-12-18 GC12
12 Apr 1805	S/Lt Fonck	103	34	2 seater	Moreuil	4-17-18 16.778
12 Apr 1825	S/Lt Fonck	103	35	Scout	Piennes-Montdidier	
						4-17-18 16.778
20 Apr 0940	Adj Pillon &	67	2			
	S/Lt Rougevin-Baville	67	1	EA	Moreuil-Sauvillon	
						4-22-18 23.558
20 Apr 1005	Lt Bozon-Verduraz	3	4	EA	Hangard-Thennes	
						4-23-18 24.815
21 Apr 0815	Brig Ouvrard de Linière	67	1			
	Lt Bozon-Verduraz	3	5	EA	Thory	4-23-18 24.815
	S/Lt Duret,	67	2			
	Adj Mion,	67	3			
21 Apr 1215	S/Lt Bucquet	3	3	EA	E Contoire	4-27-18 29.226
22 Apr 1745	Patrol		P	EA	Montdidier	4-22-18 GC12
22 Apr 1745	Patrol		P	EA	Montdidier	4-22-18 GC12
22 Apr 1805	S/Lt Fonck	103	36	EA	Assainvillers	4-24-18 25.915
2 May 1320	Sgt Baylies	3	6	EA	Assainvillers	5-03-18 2.734
2 May 1340	Patrol		P	EA	Montdidier	5-02-18 GC12
2 May 1755	Patrol		P	EA	Mailly-Reineval	5-02-18 GC12
2 May 1835	Patrol		P	2 seater	Montdidier	5-02-18 GC12
3 May 1725	Sgt Baylies &	3	7			
	MdL Dubonnet	3	1	EA	Montdidier	5-04-18 4.062
	(150th victory for Spa 3)					
3 May	Sergent Désiré Mabereau, Spa 26, missing in action flying Spad VII #3802 over Moreuil. Departed at 12.00 hours.					
4 May 1600	Patrol		P	EA	Fignières	5-04-18 GC12
4 May	Command of GC 12 assumed by Capitaine Charles Dupuy, replacing Capitaine Henri Horment.					
4 May	Caporal Marcel Dupont, Spa 26, flying a Spad VII when wounded in the foot during combat.					
6 May 1715	Adj Parsons	3	2	2 seater	W Montdidier	5-07-18 7.851
9 May 1455	Patrol	3	P	EA	Ayencourt	5-09-18 GC12
9 May 1600	S/Lt Fonck	103	37	2 seater	S Moreuil	5-10-18 12.142

Date Time	Pilot	Unit	Victory	Type	Location	Confirmation*/**
9 May 1600	S/Lt Fonck	103	38	2 seater	S Moreuil	5-10-18 12.142
9 May 1605	S/Lt Fonck	103	39	2 seater	S Moreuil	5-10-18 12.142
9 May 1825	S/Lt Fonck	103	40	2 seater	Montdidier	5-10-18 12.142
9 May 1855	S/Lt Fonck	103	41	2 seater	Hargicourt	5-10-18 12.142
9 May 1855	S/Lt Fonck	103	42	2 seater	Hargicourt	5-10-18 12.142
9 May 1930	Sgt Baylies	3	8	Halb C	Braches	5-10-18 12.142
9 May	Lieutenant Georges Raymond, CO Spa 3, promoted to Capitaine.					
10 May 1600	Adj Mion	67	P	EA	Wiencourt-Cayeux	
						5-10-18 GC12
10 May 1725	MdL Dubonnet	3	2	EA	Faverolles	5-12-18 14.412
10 May 1725	Sgt Baylies &	3	9			
	MdL Clément	3	1	2 seater	Montdidier	5-12-18 14.412
15 May 0825	Brig Ouvrard de					
	Linière &	67	2			5-16-18.20.334
	Capt Sabattier (GC18)		3	Scout	Montdidier-Dompierre	
15 May 1135	Lt Bozon-Verduraz &	3	6			
	MdL Molines	3	1	2 seater	Assainvillers	5-16-18 20.334
15 May 1225	Capt de Sevin ⎫	26	9			
	Adj Antoine ⎬	26	1	2 seater	Assainvillers	5-16-18 20.334
	S/Lt de Tascher ⎭	26	1			
15 May 1225	Lt Letourneau &	26	1			
	Lt Dombray	26	1	EA	Rubescourt	5-16-18 20.334
15 May 1955	Sgt Pietri	103	2	EA	Moreuil	5-17-18 21.729
15 May 2000	Patrol	103	P	EA	Demuin	5-16-18 GC12
16 May 0645	Adj Pillon	67	P	2 seater	Fontaine	5-16-18 GC12
16 May 0940	Lt Bozon-Verduraz ⎫	3	7			
	Sgt Risacher ⎬	3	1	EA	Montdidier	5-17-18 21.729
	MdL Moulines ⎭	3	2			
16 May 0945	Adj Parsons	3	3	2 seater	Montdidier	5-22-18 27.853
16 May 1000	Adj Parsons	3	P	2 seater	Rollot-Orvillers	5-16-18 GC12
16 May 1045	Capt de Sevin &	26	10			
	Lt Puget	26	1	Alb	NE Montdidier	5-23-18 29.163
16 May 1910	Adj Naudin	103	P	EA	Mezières	5-16-18 GC12
16 May	Sous-lieutenant Albanel, Spa 3, missing in action, departed at 08.00 hours flying a Spad XIII.					
17 May 1120	Adj Pillon	67	P	2 seater	Moreuil	5-17-18 GC12
17 May 1140	S/Lt Pendaries	67	4	EA	NE Moreuil	5-19-18 24.402
17 May 1330	Sgt Loup &	103	1			
	Sgt Drouillh	103	1	Pfalz	Montdidier	5-27-18 33.642
17 May 1940	Adj Baron	103	P	2 seater	Courtemanche	5-17-18 GC12
18 May 0820	Capt de Sevin ⎫	26				
	Adj Naudin ⎬	26	P	2 seater	Framicourt	5-18-18 GC12
	Lt Puget ⎭	26				
18 May 0825	Capt de Sevin ⎫	26				
	Lt Puget ⎬	26	P	Scout	Framicourt	5-18-18 GC12
	Adj Naudin ⎭	26				
18 May 0930	Adj Pillon	67	7	2 seater	E Montdidier	5-22-18 27.853
19 May 0940	Lt Fonck	103	43	EA	Montdidier	5-22-18 27.853
19 May 0950	Adj Brugère	103	1	EA	Montdidier	5-22-18 27.853
19 May 0950	Lt Fonck	103	44	EA	Montdidier	5-22-18 27.853

Date	Time	Pilot	Unit	Victory	Type	Location	Confirmation*/**
19 May	1220	Adj Parsons ⎫	3	4			
		MdL Denneulin ⎬	3	1	2 seater	Montdidier	5-21-18 26.776
		Sgt Chevannes ⎭	3	1			
19 May	1845	Lt Coudouret	103	FTL	Albatros	Rouvrel	5-19-18 GC12
20 May	0915	Adj Parsons	3	5	2 seater	Gratibus	5-22-18 27.853
20 May	1110	Adj Naudin	26	2	Scout	Orvillers	6-09-18 9.576
21 May	0807	Lt Sondermayer	3	1	EA	Montdidier	5-23-18 29.163
21 May		The Spad of Lieutenant Tadia Sondermayer, Spa 3, caught fire in the air, but he managed to land although severely burned.					
21 May	1350	Adj Baron &	103				
		Adj Pietri	103	P	2 seater	Gratibus	5-21-18 GC12
28 May	0815	Sgt Baylies	3	10	EA	Courtemanche	5-29-18 36.535
29 May	1815	Sgt Baylies	3	11	EA	Etelfay	5-31-18 38.882
29 May	1815	Lt Bozon-Verduraz	3	8	EA	Etelfay	5-31-18 38.882
30 May	1805	Capt de Sevin ⎫	26				
		S/Lt Puget ⎬	26	Dam	EA	Rollot	5-30-18 GC12
		Adj Vincent ⎭	26				
31 May	1045	Sgt Baylies &	3	12			
		MdL Dubonnet	3	3	2 seater	Montdidier	6-01-18 3.
31 May	1045	Sgt Baylies &	3	P			
		MdL Dubonnet	3	P	2 seater	Montdidier	5-31-18 GC12
2 Jun		Sgt Baux	103	2	EA	Moreuil	6-04-18 3.893
2 Jun		Sgt Hoeber &	103	1			
		S/Lt Coudouret	103	6	EA	Carlepont	6-09-18 9.576
3 Jun		Spa 26 moved to Sacy-le-Grand, about 20 km SW Compiègne, 1er Armée Sector.					
5 Jun		Spa 3, Spa 67 & Spa 103 moved to Sacy-le-Grand.					
5 Jun		Maréchal-des-Logis André Duriez, Spa 26, killed in an accident flying a Spad XIII.					
7 Jun		Spa 3, Spa 26, Spa 67 & Spa 103 moved back to Hétomesnil, 1er Armée Sector.					
11 Jun	1645	Adj Naudin	26	3	EA	Mortemer-Rollot	6-13-18 15.534
11 Jun	1830	Capt d'Indy	67	1	EA	Fécamp	6-13-18 15.534
13 Jun		Sgt Chevannes &	3	2			
		MdL Dubonnet	3	4	Balloon		6-14-18 15.886
17 Jun		Sergent Frank Baylies, Spa 3, killed in action flying a Spad XIII.					
18 Jun	0545	Adj Prétre	67	1	EA	E Frétoy	6-22-18 26.856
25 Jun	1800	Lt Fonck	103	45	Halb C	Contoire	6-28-18 34.565
25 Jun	1815	Lt Fonck	103	46	Fokker	Villers-aux-Erables	6-27-18 33.230
25 Jun		Lt Fonck	103	47	Fokker	Montdidier	6-27-18 33.230
27 Jun	0810	Lt Fonck	103	48	Halb	Morisel	6-28-18 34.565
27 Jun	0815	Lt Fonck	103	49	Pfalz DIII	Moreuil	6-30-18 37.227
28 Jun		Adj Naudin &	26	4			
		Lt Dombray	26	2	EA	Bois de Fay	6-29-18 35.874
29 Jun		Caporal Jean Mandray, Spa 103, killed in action flying a Spad VII.					
12 Jul	1750	Adj Naudin	26	5	EA	Craonne	SHAA
13 Jul		Capitaine Georges Raymond, Spa 3, crashed his Spad XIII on returning from a patrol and was lightly injured.					
16 Jul		Spa 103 moved to Trécon, about 25 km SW of Châlons-sur-Meuse, V° Armée Sector.					
16 Jul	1710	Lt Fonck	103	50	2 seater	S Dormans	7-21-18 25.674
16 Jul	1715	Lt Fonck	103	51	2 seater	S Dormans	7-21-18 25.674

Date	Time	Pilot	Unit	Victory	Type	Location	Confirmation*/**
17 Jul		Spa 3 and Spa 26 moved to Trécon.					
17 Jul		Patrol	103	P	EA		7-17-18 V-
17 Jul		Adjudant Auguste Baux, Spa 103, killed in action flying a Spad XIII; he crashed at Cachery.					
18 Jul		Spa 67 moved to Trécon.					
18 Jul	1120	Lt Fonck	103	52	EA	Cachery	7-21-18 25.674
18 Jul	1130	Lt Fonck	103	53	EA	Cachery	7-21-18 25.674
18 Jul	1635	Patrol	3	P	EA		7-19-18 V-
19 Jul	0630	Lt Fonck	103	54	EA	Châtillon	7-21-18 25.674
19 Jul	0635	Lt Fonck	103	55	EA	Châtillon	7-21-18 25.674
19 Jul	1555	Lt Fonck	103	56	EA	Dormans	7-21-18 25.674
20 Jul	1600	Patrol	3	P	EA	Vézilly	7-21-18 V-
21 Jul	1808	Adj Loup &	103	2			
		Sgt Drouillh	103	2	Fokker	Chambecy	7-22-18 27.141
21 Jul	1810	Patrol	103	P	Fokker	Bouleuse	7-22-18 V-
21 Jul		Sergent Lenoir, Spa 103, wounded in action flying a Spad XIII.					
21 Jul		Caporal F Hugues, Spa 26, missing in action flying a Spad XIII.					
22 Jul	0545	S/Lt Pendaries &	67	5			
		Adj Jaubert	67	1	EA	Ville-en-Tardenois	
							7-23-18 29.283
22 Jul	0700	Capt Battle	103	2	Balloon	E Epoye	7-23-18 29.283
22 Jul	1810	Lt Fonck	103	P	EA	Baslieux	7-23-18 V-
24 Jul	1130	Lt Fonck	103	P	EA	Châtillon	6-25-28 V-
24 Jul		Spa 67 & Spa 103 moved to Herbisse, about 45 km SSW of Châlons- sur-Marne, V° Armée Sector.					
25 Jul		Spa 3 & Spa 26 moved to Herbisse.					
28 Jul		Spa 67 & Spa 103 moved back to Hétomesnil, ler Armée Sector.					
29 Jul		Spa 3 & Spa 26 moved back to Hétomesnil.					
31 Jul	1940	Adj Naudin ⎫	26	6			
		Adj Usse ⎬	26	1	EA	Gratibus	8-03-18 3.348
		Adj Vincent ⎭	26				
1 Aug	1100	Lt Fonck	103		2 seater	E Bois de Hangard	
							8-03-18 3.348
1 Aug		Capitaine Georges Raymond reassumed command of Spa3.					
9 Aug		Lt Risacher	3	2	EA	Bouchoir	8-11-18 17.079
9 Aug		Capt Battle	103	3	EA	Etelfay	8-11-18 17.079
11 Aug		S/Lt Puget	26	2	EA	Grevillers	Cit
11 Aug		Sgt Pelletier	26	1	EA	S Roye	
11 Aug	2015	Sgt Lebroussard	26	1	EA	Grevillers	Cit
14 Aug		Lt Fonck	103	58	EA	Roye	8-15-18 23.212
14 Aug		Lt Fonck	103	59	EA	Gruny-Cremery	8-15-18 23.212
14 Aug		Lt Fonck	103	60	EA	Gruny-Cremery	8-15-18 23.212
16 Aug		MdL Dubonnet &	3	5			
		Capt Battle	103	4	EA	Carrépuis	8-19-18 29.532
16 Aug	1130	Capt de Sevin &	26	11			
		MdL Dubonnet	3	6	EA	E Roye	8-19-18 29.532
16 Aug		Adj Baron &	103	2			
		S/Lt Schmitter	103	2	EA	W Roye	8-19-18 29.532
16 Aug		Sous-lieutenant Jean Caël, Spa 3, flying a Spad XIII reported as missing; it was later learned that he was a POW.					

Date	Time	Pilot	Unit	Victory	Type	Location	Confirmation*/**
19 Aug		Maréchal-des-Logis Patay, Spa 26, missing in action flying a Spad VII.					
20 Aug	1755	MdL Lambotte &	26	1			
		Capt d'Indy	67	2	EA	Amancoeur	8-31-18 47.326
22 Aug		Caporal Gaston Sachet, Spa 67, killed in a crash landing flying a Spad VII.					
22 Aug		Escadrille Spa 167 created, commanded by Lieutenant Bernard Barny de Romanet, and assigned to GC 12.					
25 Aug	1125	Adj Usse	26	2	EA	SW Méharicourt	8-26-18 39.834
29 Aug		Adj Parsons	3	6	Fokker	Morchain	9-05-18 5.546
3 Sep		Spa 3, Spa 26 & Spa 103 Spa 67 moved to Quinquempoix, about 20 km SW of Montdidier, 1er Armée Sector.					
3 Sep		Capitaine Georges Raymond admitted to the hospital with 'Spanish' flu, where he died on 21 September; command of Spa 3 assumed by Lieutenant Aimé Grasset from Spa 150.					
8 Sep		Spa 67 moved to Lisle-en-Barrois, about 20 km SW of Souilly, II° Armée Sector, assigned to 1st Army, AEF, for the St. Mihiel Offensive.					
9 Sep		Spa 103 cited, for a third time, in l'Ordre No. 107 de la 1er Armée, for having downed 85 enemy aircraft and probably 69 others.					
9 Sep		Spa 3, Spa 26 moved to Lisle-en-Barrois.					
10 Sep		Spa 103 moved to Lisle-en-Barrois.					
14 Sep		Adjudant Aimé Vincent, Spa 26, wounded in combat.					
18 Sep		As directed by GAC Telegram #7052/B Spa 3 & Spa 26 moved from Lisle-en-Barrois, to la Noblette, between la Cheppe and St Etienne-au-Temple, IV° Armée Sector. Parc 112 moved to Châlons-sur-Marne.					
19 Sep		Spa 26 & Spa 103 moved to la Noblette.					
24 Sep	0805	Patrol	GC	P	Scout	Rouvron	9-24-18 IV-338
24 Sep	1200	Patrol	67	P	Fokker	Châlons	9-24-18 IV-338
24 Sep	1800	Patrol	26	-	EA	Massiges	9-25-18 GC12
26 Sep	1015	Adj Naudin	26	P	2 seater	Ripont	9-26-18 IV-343
26 Sep	1145	Lt Fonck	103	6	Fok DVII	Ste Marie-à-Py	9-27-18 37.621
26 Sep	1145	Lt Fonck	103	62	Fok DVII	St Souplet	9-27-18 37.621
26 Sep	1210	Lt Fonck	103	63	Halb C	Perthes-les-Hurlus	9-27-18 37.621
26 Sep	1720	Lt de Romanet	167	P	Scout	Navarin	9-26-18 IV-343
26 Sep	1745	Adj Parsons	3	P	Scout	Aubérive-Souain	9-26-18 GC12
26 Sep	1800	Adj Parsons	3	7			
		MdL Denneulin }	3	2	2 seater	S Tahure	10-14-18 18.77
		S/Lt Pendaries	67	6			
26 Sep	1810	Lt Fonck	103	64	Fok DVII	St Souplet	9-27-18 37.621
26 Sep	1820	Lt Fonck	103	65	Halb	E Souain	9-27-18 37.621
26 Sep	1820	Lt Fonck	103	66	DFW C	E Souain	9-27-18 37.621
26 Sep	1820	Adj Brière	103	P	Scout	N Souain	9-27-18 IV-345
27 Sep	1730	S/Lt Coudouret	103	P	EA	NE Somme-Py	9-27-18 IV-345
28 Sep	1030	Lt Fonck	103	67	2 seater	NE Somme-Py	10-04-18 4.504
28 Sep	1130	Sgt Chauffaux	3	P	2 seater	Ste Geneviève	9-28-18 IV-346
29 Sep	1135	Patrol	67	P	EA	Somme-Py	9-29-18 IV-350
29 Sep		Adjudant Gustave Naudin, Spa 26, wounded in action.					
1 Oct	1245	Sgt Sansom &	103	1			
		Adj Drouillh	103	3	Scout	NW Somme-Py	10-04-18 4.504
1 Oct	1245	Sgt Sansom &	103				
		Adj Drouillh	103	P	Scout	NW Somme-Py	10-01-18 GC12

Date	Time	Pilot	Unit	Victory	Type	Location	Confirmation*/**
1 Oct	1405	Cpl de Lombardon	167	1	2 seater	N Bétheniville	10-02-18 IV-363
1 Oct	1510	Adj Parsons	3	8	2 seater	N Somme-Py	10-04-18 4.504
2 Oct	0910	Lt Garros	26	4	Fokker DVII	St Marie-à-Py	10-04-18 4.504
2 Oct		Lt Garros	26	P	EA	Somme-Py	10-02-18 IV-363
3 Oct	1010	Cpl de Lombardon &	2				
		Lt de Romanet	167	11	Fokker DVII	Mont Blanc	10-03-18 4.504
3 Oct	1435	Sgt Brillaud	26	1	Fokker DVII	E Somme-Py	10-04-18 4.504
3 Oct	1450	Lt le Petit	67	1	Fokker DVII	Moronvillers-Dontrien	
							10-04-18 4.501
3 Oct		Sergent Robert Brillaud, Spa 26, wounded in action.					
5 Oct		Lieutenant Roland Garros, Spa 26, missing in action.					
5 Oct	1600	Patrol	26	FTL	2 seater	Bétheniville	10-05-18 IV-374
5 Oct	1710	Patrol	26	P	2 seater	Manre-Aure	10-05-18 IV-374
5 Oct	1730	Lt Fonck	103	68	2 seater	Liry-Marvaux	10-06-18 7.071
5 Oct	1740	Lt Fonck	103	69	Scout	Hauvine-St Clément	
							10-06-18 7.071
10 Oct	0700	Lt de Romanet	167	12	2 seater	Bignicourt	10-11-18 14.434
10 Oct	1535	Patrol	GC	P	Scout	N Somme-Py	10-10-18 IV-386
14 Oct	1310	Lt Dumas &	167	2			
		Lt de Romanet	167	13	2 seater	Alleux	10-15-18 20.111
15 Oct	1345	Patrol	GC	P	Scout	E Novy	10-15-18 IV-398
16 Oct		Escadrille Spa 173 created, commanded by Lieutenant Jacques Allez, and assigned to GC 12.					
18 Oct	1430	Lt Dumas &	167	3			
		Lt de Romanet	167	14	Fok DVII	Civry-sur-Aisne	10-19-18 25.317
18 Oct	1625	Sgt Sansom &	103	2			
		Adj Drouillh	103	4	Fok DVII	Arnicourt-Sery	10-19-18 25.317
18 Oct	1430	Sgt de Lombardon	167		2 seater	Allend'Huy	10-19-18 GC 12
23 Oct	0825	Sgt Brière	3	P	2 seater	Novy	10-23-18 IV-417
23 Oct	1210	Lt de Romanet	167	15	2 seater	Le Chesne	10-24-18 32.883
23 Oct	1215	S/Lt Le Chevalier &		1			
		Lt de Romanet	167	16	2 seater	Attigny	10-24-18 32.883
23 Oct	1625	Lt de Romanet	167	P	EA	Attigny	10-24-18 IV-419
24 Oct	1150	Lt le Petit	67	P	2 seater	N Rethel	10-24-18 IV-419
24 Oct	1400	Capt de Sevin	26	12	EA	NE Vouziers	10-25-18 34.342
24 Oct	1500	S/Lt Guiguet &	167	5			
		Lt de Romanet	167	17	2 seater	N Attigny	10-25-18 34.342
27 Oct	1545	Adj Vincent	26	P	Fokker	NE Vouziers	10-27-18 IV-424
28 Oct	1530	Adj Usse	26	3	EA	N Rethel	11-06-18 6.943
28 Oct	1545	Lt Letourneau	26	2	EA	Méry-Cogny	10-29-18 40.479
28 Oct	1545	Sgt Dard	26	1	EA	Vitry	10-29-18 40.479
29 Oct	1030	Sgt de Lombardon &	3				
		Asp Villars	167	1	2 seater	N Attigny	11-02-18 IV-439
29 Oct	1317	S/Lt Pendaries	67	7	2 seater	Lametz	11-01-18 3.
29 Oct	1330	Sgt Lebroussard	26	P	2 seater	Longwy	10-29-18 IV-428
29 Oct	1355	Sgt Sansom &	103				
		Brig Ouvrard de Linière		P	2 seater	Le Chesne	10-29-18 IV-428
29 Oct	1500	Lt de Romanet	167	18	2 seater	Bois de Loges	10-30-18 42.171
30 Oct	1020	Sgt Brière	3	2	2 seater	Vouziers	11-06-18 6.943
30 Oct	1105	Patrol	3	P	Scout	N Rethel	10-30-18 GC12

Date	Time	Pilot	Unit	Victory	Type	Location	Confirmation*/**
30 Oct	1145	MdL Plessis &	26	2			
		S/Lt de Tascher	26	1	2 seater	E Vouziers	11-06-18 6.943
30 Oct	1300	Adj Baron	167	P	2 seater	N Rethel	10-30-18 IV-431
30 Oct	0815	S/Lt Guiguet	167	P	2 seater	NE Rethel	10-30-18 IV-431
30 Oct	1440	Lt de Romanet	167	P	2 seater	NW Rethel	10-30-18 IV-431
30 Oct	1525	Lt Fonck	103	70	2 seater	Falise-Vouziers	11-06-18 6.943
30 Oct	1540	Lt Fonck	103	71	Scout	Semuy-Terron	11-06-18 6.943
30 Oct	1540	Lt Fonck	103	72	Scout	Semuy-Terron	11-06-18 6.943
30 Oct		Patrol	103		Balloon	NE Vouziers	11-01-18 3.
31 Oct	0945	Patrol	67	P	2 seater	Alland'Huy-Voncq	
							10-31-18 IV-433
31 Oct	1120	Lt Fonck	103	73	2 seater	N Vouziers	11-01-18 3.
31 Oct	1130	Patrol	103	P	2 seater	Ballay	10-31-18 GC12
31 Oct	1135	Lt Fonck	103	74	Scout	E Vouziers	11-01-18 3.
31 Oct	1403	Patrol	26	P	2 seater	Vouziers	10-31-18 GC12
31 Oct	1420	Patrol	26	P	2 seater	Quatre-Champs	10-31-18 GC12
1 Nov		Spa 3, Spa 26 & Spa 103 moved to Hauviné, about 30 km ENE of Reims.					
1 Nov	1235	Lt Schmitter &	103	3			
		MdL Guy	103		EA	La Croix-Bois	11-02-18.1.336
1 Nov	1420	Lt Fonck	103	75	Halb C	La Croix-Bois	11-02-18.1.336
1 Nov	1435	Lt Fonck	103	P	2 seater	Semuy	11-01-18.V-435
2 Nov		Spa 67 moved to Hauvine.					
3 Nov	0915	Patrol	3	P	2 seater	Doux	11-03-18 IV-440
3 Nov	1340	Patrol	26	P	Fokker	Le Chesne	11-03-18 IV-440
3 Nov	1420	Patrol	26	P	2 seater	Le Chesne	11-03-18 IV-440
4 Nov	1025	Patrol	GC	P	EA	Bairon	11-04-18 IV-442
4 Nov	1100	Patrol	GC	P	EA	Le Chesne	11-04-18 IV-442
4 Nov		Sergent Beroulle, Spa 26, missing in action; departed at 09.45.					
4 Nov		Command of Spa 103 passed to Capitaine Charles Dupuy, who also retained command of GC 12.					
11 Nov		Armistice					
5 Dec		Spa 3 cited for the fourth time, by the Commanding General, IV° Armée. The citation stated that Spa 3 had destroyed 171 enemy aircraft and 4 balloons and disabled another 160. This fourth citation gave Spa 3 the right to display the colours of the fourragère of the Médaille Militaire on the unit's colours.					

Notes

*   Date of Confirmation in the Résumé des Opérations Aériennes, Compt Rendu, etc.

**   Number of Résumé, Compt Rendu, etc. by which that victory was confirmed.

Under Brocard GC 12 was granted four shared victories in 11½ months, while under other commanders GC 12 was permitted 32 shared victories in less than 12½ months.

     CR = Compte Rendu

     II, IV, V, X = Indicates the Armée Compte Rendu in which the victory was confirmed.

     GC12 = Groupe de Combat 12 Compte Rendu in which victory was confirmed.

     GAR = Groupe d'Armées de Reserve Compte Rendu in which victory was confirmed.

Pilot Victories 1916-18

Total Squadron Victories in WWI

Spa 3	171 aircraft and 4 balloons	175
Spa 26	48 aircraft and 3 balloons	51
Spa 67	45 aircraft and 0 balloons	45
Spa 73	29 aircraft and 1 balloon	30
Spa 103	108 aircraft and 3 balloons	111
Spa 167	10 aircraft and 0 balloons	10
Spa 173	0 aircraft and 0 balloons	0
	411 aircraft and 11 balloons	422

Total Victories with GC 12

Spa 3	106 aircraft and 1 balloon	107
Spa 26	31 aircraft and 0 balloons	31
Spa 67	14 aircraft and 0 balloons	14
Spa 73	20 aircraft and 1 balloon	21
Spa 103	105 aircraft and 3 balloons	108
Spa 167	10 aircraft and 0 balloons	10
Spa 173	0 aircraft and 0 balloons	0
	286 aircraft and 5 balloons	291

Headquarters Staff, Groupe de Combat 12

Commanding Officers

Chef de Bataillon Félix Brocard	1 Nov 1916 – 13 Sep 1917
Capitaine Jean d'Harcourt	13 Sep 1917 – 30 Sep 1917
Capitaine Henri Horment	30 Sep 1917 – 4 May 1918
Capitaine Charles Dupuy	4 May 1918 – 11 Nov 1918

Adjoint Technique (Technical Assistant)

Lieutenant Max Benoit	1 Nov 1916 – 22 Feb 1917
Lieutenant Jean Richard	22 Feb 1917 – 4 Oct 1917
Capitaine André Rouget	4 Oct 1917 – 11 Nov 1918

Officier de Renseignements (Intelligence Officer)

Capitaine Jean Varenard de Billy	– 11 Nov 1918

Armament Officier (Armament Officer)

Capitaine Joseph Point-Dumont   8 Jul 1917 – 11 Nov 1918

Commander Parc 112

Capitaine Joseph Peralda   1 Dec 1916 – 25 Sep 1917
Capitaine Pierre Barbey   25 Sep 1917 –

APPENDIX H

Personnel Known to have Flown with Spa 3

Commanding Officers

Name[2]	From	Dates	To/Comment
Lt Bellenger		Jul 12 – Dec 12 14	
Capt Georges Bellemois		Dec 12 – 11 Apr 15	
Capt Félix Brocard		11 Apr 15 – 1 Nov 16	CO GC 12
Capt René Colcomb		4 Feb 16 – 16 Apr 16	Acting
Capt Albert Heurtaux		1 Nov 16 – 17 Mar 17	WIA
Capt Alfred Auger		17 Mar 17 – 28 Jul 17	KIA
Capt Georges Guynemer		28 Jul 17 – 6 Aug 17	
Capt Albert Heurtaux		6 Aug 17 – 3 Sep 17	WIA
Capt Georges Guynemer		3 Sep 17 – 11 Sep 17	KIA
Lt Gustave Lagache		11 Sep 17 – 15 Sep 17	
Capt Georges Raymond		16 Sep 17 – 13 Jul 18	INJ
?		13 Jul 18 – 31 Jul 18	
Capt Georges Raymond		1 Aug 18 – 3 Sep 18	Hosp/Died
Lt Aimé Grasset	GC 16	3 Sep 18 – 28 Oct 18	CIACB
Lt Jean Dombray	Spa 26	28 Oct 18 – 11 Nov 18	

Other Flying Personnel

Lt Adam,			
S/Lt Albanel, Charles		– 16 May 18	MIA
Adj Ambroise-Thomas			
Sgt Andras de Marcy, Xavier			
Capt Auger, Alfred	N 31	– 17 Mar 17	CO N 3
Sgt Barbotte,			
Adj Barouillet,			
Adj Bartholle,	(O) [1]		
MdL Battesti, François		9 Aug 14 – 10 Aug 14	Hosp
Sgt Baylies, Frank (American)	Spa 73	18 Dec 17 – 17 Jun 18	KIA
Adj Bégou, Lucien		1 Aug 14 – 12 Mar 15	RGAé
Lt Benoit, Max		– 1 Nov 16	GC 12
Sgt Bernard,			
Adj-Chef Bertolle, Léon	(O)	3 Feb 15 –	

[1] Observer.
[2] NB. The reader will find some pilots' names repeated in each Squadron as the pilot leaves and re-joins the Squadron for the reason given in the last column.

Cpl Bloch, Marcel		19 Jan 15 – 3 Jul 15	WIA
Cpl Bloch, Marcel		20 Jan 16 – 25 May 16	N 62
Sgt Bonnard, Etienne Charles		12 Apr 15 – 3 Nov 15	Serbia
Sgt Boscher, Louis	Spa 167		
Sgt Bouet,			
Adj Bourgeois,			
Lt Bozon-Verduraz, Jean		15 Jun 17 – 3 Jul 18	CO Spa 94
Sgt Brière, Robert		– 11 Nov 18	
Lt Brocard, Félix	Dep 6	18 Mar 15 – 11 Apr 15	CO N 3
Sgt Brou, Georges		25 May 15 – 21 Aug 15	MF 62
Capt Bruyère, (O)			
S/Lt Bucquet, Louis		29 Oct 15 – 18 Jun 18	
S/Lt Caël, Jean	Spa 102	15 Jun 18 – 16 Aug 18	KIA
Sgt Caron,		1 Aug 14 – 19 Aug 14	RGAé
Sgt Chainat, André		Mar 16 – 7 Sep 16	WIA
Cpl Chassin, Antoine		27 Apr 16 – 30 Apr 16	MIA
Sgt Chauffaux,			
Sgt Chevalier,		– 1918	
Sgt Chevannes, Maurice			
MdL Clément,		3 Aug 15 – 1 Sep 15	MF 62
Lt Colcomb, Alphonse René (O)		29 Apr 15 – 1 Oct 15	MF 62
Capt Colcomb, Alphonse René		11 Feb 16 – 9 Jun 16	CO N 38
Cpl Cornet,		– 16 Aug 17	POW
Cpl David,			
Lt de Bazelaire de Ruppière, Marie Joseph Robert (O)		27 Mar 15 – 3 Oct 15	42 InfRgt
Lt Varenard de Billy, Jean (O)		27 Jun 16 –	
Sgt Decatoire,			
Lt de Fontenaillet,			
S/Lt de Guibert, Charles		1 Oct 15 – 9 Oct 15	
S/Lt de Guibert, Charles		19 Jan 16 – 25 May 16	N 62
S/Lt de Guibert, Louis	N 62	3 Apr 17 –	
S/Lt de la Fressange, (O)		9 Nov 15 – 2 May 16	
S/Lt de la Rochefordière, Guy		– 30 Apr 18	CO Spa 94
Lt de Lavalette, (O)		3 Feb 15 – 27 Sep 15	Serbia
S/Lt Demarze,		– 19 Sep 18	KIAcc
S/Lt de Moulignon,		11 Mar 16 –	
MdL Denneulin,			
Capt de Serre, Gaston		1 Aug 14 – 18 Apr 15	RGAé
Lt Deullin, Albert	MF 62	2 Jul 15 – 22 Feb 17	CO N 73
Sgt Devienne, Emile		22 Mar 15 – 16 Jul 15	
Sol Dineaux, (G) [3]		– 9 Apr 15	KIA
Lt Dombray, Jean	Spa 26	11 Oct 18 – 28 Oct 18	CO Spa 3
S/Lt Dorme, René		27 May 16 – 25 May 17	KIA
MdL Dubonnet, André		29 Apr 18 –	
Sol Dufresne, (G)		– 3 Jul 16	Inj
Lt Dumont,			
Sgt Duran,		1 Aug 14 – 21 Dec 14	
Lt Duval, (O)			

[3] Gunner.

Name			Dates	
Sgt Faucon,				
Adj Faure,				
Adj Faure, René			6 Aug 14 – 15 Apr 15	RGAé
Capt Ferguson, Henry C. USAS (American)			May 18 – Jul 18	WIA
Lt Foucault, Gabriel			– 16 May 16	KIAcc
Adj François,				
Lt Fremond,			1915 –	
Sgt Gaillard,			– 5 Oct 17	KIAcc
Adj Genet,				
Adj Genevois,			6 Aug 14 – 14 Aug 14	
Adj Genevois			22 Mar 15 – 13 Apr 15	RGAé
Sgt Georges,				
S/Lt Graff, Henri	(O)	MF 62	11 Mar 16 – 31 Mar 16	C 43
Sgt Granger,				
Lt Grassel,	(O)		– 3 Feb 16	MIA
Sgt Grivotté, Victor			21 Nov 15 – 3 Feb 16	MIA
Sol Guerder, Charles	(G)		15 –	
Adj Guiguet, Joseph			18 Jun 16 – 23 May 17	WIA
S/Lt Guiguet, Joseph			– Sep 18	Spa 167
Adj Guillamet,				KIA
Sgt Guilleau,				
Capt Guynemer, Georges			9 Jun 15 – 28 Jul 17	CO N 3
Capt Guynemer, Georges			7 Aug 17 – 3 Sep 17	CO N 3
Adj Hatin, Paul Emile	(O)	C 46	22 Apr 15 – 30 Apr 16	MIA
Sgt Hénin, André		Spa 167		
Lt Heurtaux, Albert			5 Jun 16 – 3 Sep 17	WIA
Adj Houssemand, Charles			25 Mar 15 –	
Lt Hugel, E.L.	(O)		24 Mar 15 –	
S/Lt Jaulin, Julien	(O)		22 Jul 15 – 1 Sep 15	MF 62
Cpl Judd, David E. (American)			18 Dec 17 – 22 Jul 18 218	RAF
Cpl Labarre,			1 Aug 14 – 7 Aug 14	
Lt Lagache, Gustave			1 Apr 17 – 8 Oct 17	N 112
Adj Lartigue, Paul			1 Aug 14 – 21 Apr 15	RGAé
Adj Laulhé,				
Lt Lecour-Grandmaison, Henri			22 Apr 16 – 25 May 16	N 62
S/Lt Le Fèbvre,				
Adj Legros,				
Adj Lemarie, Etienne			11 Mar 16 – 19 Mar 16	RGAé
Adj Lemarie, Etienne			25 Apr 16 –	
Cpl Madon, Georges			6 Aug 14 – 14 Aug 14	
Adj-Chef Marinkovitch, Michel			22 May 15 – 3 Aug 15	MF 19
Adj Martin,				
S/Lt Moineville,	(O)	MF 62	1 Oct 15 – 31 Mar 16	C 43
Cpl Moulines,				
S/Lt Moulines, Eduoard			– 24 Jul 17	WIA
Sgt Mourey,				
Sgt Moreau,				
Lt Mouronval, François			– 25 May 15	MF 62

Capt Münch, Max		19 Aug 14 – 7 Apr 15	RGAé
Cpl Nautré, Georges		9 May 16 – 25 May 16	N 62
Lt Nogues, Maurice		– 19 Sep 17	N 73
Lt Orloff, Ivan			
(Russian)		Nov 16 – Mar 17	
S/Lt Pandevant, Louis	(O)	27 Aug 15 – 8 Mar 16	WIA
Sgt Papeil, Achille		– 15 Apr 17	POW
Sgt Papineau,			
Sgt Parent, François		– 21 Aug 15	MS 62
Adj Parsons, Edwin	N 124	26 Feb 18 – 11 Nov 18	
(American)			
Lt Peretti, Jean	N 26	2 Jan 16 – 27 Feb 16	N 67
Lt Peretti, Jean	N 67	21 Mar 16 – 28 Apr 16	WIA/DOW
Cpl Pérot, Lucien		– 29 May 17	MIA
Adj Petit-Dariel, Pierre		– 10 Sep 17	WIA
Sol Pillon, Etienne	(G)	– 8 Mar 16	KIAcc
Sgt Rabat,			
Lt Rabatel, Henri		– 16 Aug 17	WIA/POW
Lt Raymond, Georges		– 2 Aug 17	N 73
Lt Raymond, Georges	N 73	2 Sep 17 – 13 Jul 18	INJ/DOW
Sgt Revol-Tissot, Charles		6 Sep 14 –	
Cpl Ribardière,			
Lt Richard, Jean		7 Jun 15 – 31 Jun 16	CO N 73
MdL Richard, Raymond		14 Oct 15 – 8 Mar 16	KIAcc
Sgt Rigaud,			
Sgt Risacher, Louis		27 Jun 17 – 17 Aug 18	Spa 159
S/Lt Robert,	(O)	13 Oct 15 –	
Lt Rougevin-Baville, Alfred	Spa 67	14 May 18 – 4 Jun 18	CO Spa 99
Sgt Rousse,			
S/Lt Sainflou,	(O)	16 Mar 15 –	
Adj Sanglier, Céléstin	N 62	3 Apr 17 – 10 May 17	KIA
Sgt Schmitt,			
Sgt Silberstein, Georges		6 Jul 17 – 6 Jul 17	KIAcc
Capt Siméon, Louis	(O)	MF 62	20 Jun 15 – 1 Sep 15	MF 62
Adj Simon,		9 Aug 14 – 19 Aug 14	
Lt Sondermayer, Tadia		– 21 May 18	WIA
(Serbian)			
Sol Soreau, Paul	(G)	– 16 May 16	KIAcc
Adj Strohl,		– 6 Apr 16	RGAé
Adj Tarascon, Paul		4 May 16 – 25 May 16	N 62
Lt Tenant de la Tour, Mathieu	Hosp	5 Jun 16 – 21 Mar 17	CO N 26
Cpl Thézé, Joseph		– 17 Sep 18	Spa 103
Lt Thobie, Jean	(O)	3 Feb 15 – 15 Feb 15	
Lt Thobie, Jean	(O)	– 14 Jan 16	N 62
Capt Tiersonnier,		– 6 Aug 14	WIA Flak
Lt Trétare,		1 Aug 14 – 5 Sep 14	KIAcc
Lt Trichard,			
Adj Védrines, Jules		11 Apr 15 – 2 Jun 16	
S/Lt Venson,		28 Mar 15 – 12 Oct 15	N 67

Personnel Known to have Flown with Spa 26

Commanding Officers

Name	From	Dates	To/Comment
Capt Jeannerod, Robert		26 Aug 14 – 6 Feb 15	
Lt de Malherbe, Marie Paul René		6 Feb 15 – 25 Nov 15	
Capt Thobie, Marcel	RGAé	25 Jan 16 – May 16	
Capt de Sieyes de Veynes, Jacques		May 16 – 3 Jul 16	POW
Capt Ménard, Victor		15 Jul 16 – 19 Mar 17	CO GC 15
Capt Tenant de la Tour, Mathieu		21 Mar 17 – 17 Dec 17	KIAcc
Lt Dumênes, Daniel		17 Dec 17 – 25 Dec 17	
Capt de Sevin, Xavier	Spa 12	25 Dec 17 – 11 Nov 18	

Other Flying Personnel

Name		From	Dates	To/Comment
Adj Antoine, Julius			24 Jul 17 – 11 Nov 18	
Lt Barbier,	(O)		Aug 14 – 27 Aug 14	KIAcc
Sgt Barault, Lucien			19 Jan 15 – 9 Apr 15	RGAé
Adj-Chef Barés, Léon		GDE	12 Feb 17 – 24 Jul 18	
Sgt Barra, François		RGAé	6 Feb 16 –	
Capt Becques,			1914 –	
Lt Bernard, Marcel			– 15 Feb 17	Hosp
MdL Beroule, Albert			14 Apr 18 – 4 Nov 18	MIA
Lt Berthin,	(O)		16 Dec 14 –	
S/Lt Bielouvucic, Jean			26 Aug 14 – 20 Sep 14	
S/Lt Bielouvucic, Jean			28 Jul 15 – 19 Oct 15	
MdL Boileau, Marcel			– 29 Jun 17	
Lt Bouvars,	(O)		31 May 16 –	
Cpl Brady, Lester S.			23 Feb 18 – 13 Apr 18	USAS
Sgt Brillaut, Robert			24 Jul 18 – 11 Nov 18	
Adj Bruneau,			28 Jun 16 –	
Capt Brunet,	(O)		19 Jan 15 –	
Lt Cahuzac, Pierre			15 Nov 14 – 25 Sep 15	CO N 91
Sgt Caponay, Maurice				
Adj Casale, Jean				
S/Lt Chayane de Dalmassy	(O)		16 Dec 14 –	
Sol Chedeville, Henri	(O)			
Sgt Chenal,			26 Jun 16 – 5 Jul 16	
Adj Constantini, Dominique			16 Jun 15 – 26 Sep 15	
S/Lt Couche,	(O)	GDE	4 Mar 16 –	
Cpl Couderc,			19 Jan 17 – 21 Jan 17	GDE
Sgt Dard, René			18 Jun 18 – 11 Nov 18	
S/Lt de Barneville,			– 22 Sep 16	POW/DOW
S/Lt de Blomac, Jean			– 11 Jan 17	
Sgt Dedieu, Jean			– 13 Jul 18	INJ
Adj Dedieu, Jean			2 Feb 18 – 13 Jul 18	GDE
Lt Dalaplane,			26 Aug 14 – 27 Aug 14	KIAcc

MdL de Linière, Jacques			13 Oct 18 – 11 Nov 18	
Sgt Delrieu,				
Sgt Dely,			5 Sep 16 –	
Lt de Moulignon,			9 May 17 – 27 Aug 17	Conval
Sgt de Rochefort, Noël			25 Oct 15 – 15 Sep 16	POW
MdL de Tascher, Benjamin			31 Dec 16 – 12 Apr 17	POW
S/Lt de Tascher, Benjamin			19 Nov 17 – 11 Nov 18	
Sgt Devault, Pierre			1916 – 4 May 17	WIA
Sgt Devaulx, Pierre			18 Mar 18 – 3 Apr 18	MIA
S/Lt Dezarrois, André			– 21 Aug 17	WIA
Capt d'Indy, Marie Jacques			– 25 Jul 17	CO Spa 67
Lt Dombray, Jean			5 Oct 17 – 11 Oct 18	CO Spa 3
Lt Dumêmes, Daniel	(O)	RGAé	19 Oct 15 – 7 May 16	
Lt Dumêmes, Daniel			– 1 Mar 18	GC 11
Cpl Dupont, Marcel			10 Apr 18 – 4 May 18	WIA
MdL Duriez, André			17 May 18 – 5 Jun 18	KIAcc
Lt Echard, Raoul			7 Aug 16 – 25 Jan 17	CO N 82
Cpl Eldon, Jean			– 3 Nov 18	Spa 173
Adj Faure, Maurice			1915 – 9 Jan 16	WIA
Cpl Ferraz, Jean			1 Sep 18 – 11 Sep 18	
Adj Fétu, Adrien			26 May 17 – 19 Jan 18	
Lt Fontaine,			5 Dec 15 – 1 Feb 16	
MdL Fontaine, Noël			25 May 17 – 28 Sep 17	WIA
S/Lt Fontaine, Noël			1 Jan 18 – 11 Nov 18	
S/Lt Garros, Roland			3 Feb 15 – 18 Apr 15	POW
S/Lt Garros, Roland			23 Aug 18 – 5 Oct 18	MIA
Cpl Gaucher, Léon			21 Oct 18 – 11 Nov 18	
S/Lt Gaut,			26 Jun 16 –	
Sgt Gérard, Victor			1 Sep 18 – 11 Sep 18	
S/Lt Gérard,			16 Dec 14 –	
Cpl Gestry,			24 Jul 18 – 30 Jul 18	GDE
Capt Glaize, François			11 Nov 16 – 5 Dec 16	CO N 80
Sgt Guerin,		GDE	5 Oct 17 – 30 Nov 18	GDE
Lt Guillery,			16 Dec 14 –	
S/Lt Gullerot,			27 Jul 15 – 1915	
Asp Haller,	(O)		5 Jul 16 –	
Lt Happe,			– 20 Oct 14	Interned
Cpl Heliot, Maurice			29 Nov 15 – 1 Feb 16	
S/Lt Heurtaux,			15 Dec 14 –	
Cpl Hugues, François			15 Jun 18 – 21 Jul 18	MIA
S/Lt Islac,	(O)		26 Aug 14 –	
Cpl Jaubert,			26 May 16 –	
S/Lt Jeronnez, Charles			– 30 Oct 17	
S/Lt Joly de Bamerville, Eric			6 Sep 16 – 21 Sep 16	POW/DOW
MdL Lambotte, Hubert			17 May 18 – 11 Nov 18	
Sgt Lebroussard, Armand			7 May 18 – 11 Nov 18	
MdL Lemaitre, Emmanuel			28 Dec 15 –	
MdL Le Quellec, Yves		GDE	29 Jul 17 – 7 Feb 18	CRP
Lt Letourneau, Emile			24 Apr 17 – 11 Nov 18	
Capt Lhôtel, Pierre	(O)		29 Jan 17 – 20 Feb 17	Dijon

Name			Dates	Status
Sgt Mabereau, Désiré			17 Feb 18 – 3 May 18	MIA
S/Lt Mallet, Robert			31 Dec 15 –	
Lt Marchand, Gaston	(O)		1 May 15 – 17 Mar 16	
S/Lt Maria, Joseph	(O)		16 May 15 – 19 Dec 15	WIA
S/Lt Maria, Joseph	(O)		16 Feb 16 –	
Brig Messier,			5 Jul 16 – 5 Jul 16	MIA
S/Lt Micheletti, Charles			26 Jun 16 –	
S/Lt Momet, Georges			19 Oct 15 – 17 Jan 16	WIA/DOW
Cpl Monier, Léon			11 Jan 15 – 25 Mar 15	
Sgt Montels, Marius			30 Jul 18 – 11 Nov 18	
Sgt Montmain, Jean			26 Aug 14 – 14 Jan 15	KIAcc
MdL Mortureux,			27 Jul 17 – 13 Jan 18	GDE
Adj Moutach, Henri			9 May 15 –	
Sol Murat,	(G)			
Adj-Chef Naudin, Gustave			16 Nov 17 – 3 Nov 18	Hosp
Cpl Nugue, Charles			1 Sep 18 –	
Cpl Parieu, François			9 Dec 15 – 1 Feb 16	
Sgt Parent, Robert			29 Nov 15 – 10 Jan 16	MIA
MdL Patay,			29 Jul 18 – 17 Aug 18	MIA
Cpl Pelhat, Martin			28 May 16 – 6 Jul 16	POW
Cpl Pelissier, Joseph		CIACB	16 Oct 18 – 11 Nov 18	
Sgt Pelletier, Jean			15 Jun 18 – 11 Nov 18	
Capt Perrin, Jean	(O)	RGAé	27 Jan 16 –	
Capt Perrin. Jean			18 Mar 17 – 6 May 17	CO N 76
MdL Picard, Emile			14 Oct 17 – 4 Jan 18	GDE
Lt Pinsard, Armand			8 Jul 16 – Nov 16	CO N 78
S/Lt Plantey,	(O)		26 Aug 14 –	
MdL Plessis, Marcel			17 May 18 – 11 Nov 18	
Cpl Poublan, Jean			15 Jun 18 – 5 Jul 18	GDE
Brig Pouchelle, Auguste			1 Jul 16 – 18 Aug 16	WIA
Adj Pouchelle, Auguste			31 Dec 16 – 31 May 17	WIA
S/Lt Pouchelle, Auguste			9 Dec 17 – 12 Jun 18	Spa 67
Capt Pouderoux,	(O)		1 May 15 – 6 Aug 15	
Sgt Prou, Marcel			1916 – 17	
Sgt Prou, Pierre			16 Jun 17 – 1 Mar 18	RGAé
Lt Puget, Jacques			5 Nov 17 – 11 Nov 18	
MdL Quellec,			8 Aug 17 –	
Lt Radisson,			26 Aug 14 – 6 Nov 14	KIA
Lt Robert,			31 Dec 15 – 5 Feb 16	
Sgt Rose,			26 Aug 14 –	
Sgt Rosenlecker,			– 23 Sep 16	MIA
Lt Sarda,	(O)		25 Feb 15 – 23 Aug 15	
Sgt Sendral, Jean Georges			29 May 16 – 17 Nov 16	WIA
Capt Shigeno, Kiyotake (Japanese)			17 Sep 16 – 13 Aug 17	Hosp
Adj Simon, André			9 Jan 15 – 19 Dec 15	KIAcc
Cpl Soulier, Constant			18 Jun 16 – 10 Aug 17	Hosp
Brig Thomassin, Edmond			12 Apr 17 – 16 Apr 17	WIA
Lt Tourangin, Guy			– 18 Mar 17	Pau
S/Lt Tournier,	(O)		29 May 16 –	

Sgt Treille de Grandseigne, Georges		29 Nov 15 – 1 Feb 16	
Adj Usse, Justin		17 May 18 – 18 May 18	Hosp
Adj Usse, Justin		20 Jul 18 – 3 Nov 18	Spa 173
Capt Varaigne,		1914 –	
Cpl Vatta, Raoul		28 Mar 18 – 14 Apr 18	GDE
Cpl Vermonet,		14 Apr 16 –	
MdL Vilain,	(G)	17 Dec 15 –	
Adj Vincent, Aimé		11 Nov 17 – 11 Nov 18	
Lt Vuillet,		24 Aug 15 – 26 Sep 15	
S/Lt Walckenaer, François	(O)	16 Apr 16 –	
Capt Yence,		16 Dec 14 –	
MdL Zambotte,			

Personnel Known to have Flown with Spa 67

Commanding Officers

Name	From	Dates	To/Comment
Capt Galouzeau de Villepin, Olivier	C 47	21 Jul 15 – 25 Feb 16	
Capt Constans de Saint Sauveur, Henri		25 Feb 16 – 25 Jul 17	
Capt d'Indy, Marie Jacques		25 Jul 17 – 11 Nov 18	

Other Flying Personnel

MdL Alibert, Henri		– 11 Nov 18	
Sgt-Maj Armenault, Jules	(O)	9 Jun 17 – 17 Aug 17	C 46
Lt Arnoux de Maison Rouge, Antoine		22 Sep 16 – 28 May 17	N 124
S/Lt Bailly,	Spa 173	13 Oct 18 – 11 Nov 18	
Cpl Benney, Philip P. (American)		12 Dec 17 – 25 Jan 18	WIA/DOW
Cpl Bernard, Claude		23 Jan 17 – 3 Apr 17	WIA
Capt Bernon,		15 Jan 17 – 12 Jun 17	Hospital
Capt Bernon,		3 Aug 17 – 18 Aug 17	SFA
MdL Bouillet, Joseph		23 Jan 18 – 11 Nov 18	
S/Lt Boisseau,		2 Mar 16 – 8 Mar 16	Parc 11
S/Lt Bourget,	Spa 173	22 Oct 18 – 11 Nov 18	
Sgt Bouzinard,	RGAé	10 Aug 15 – 28 Aug 15	C 28
Sgt Brixon,		–	KIA
2/Lt Brown, Jasper USAS		13 Feb 18 –	
Adj Bucquet, Louis	N 3	24 Feb 16 – 21 Mar 16	N 3
Capt Cahuzac, Pierre		23 Oct 17 – 12 Feb 18	CO Spa 73
MdL Casale,	MS 23	20 Jan 16 – 29 Feb 16	MS 23
Sgt Chainat, André	N 3	15 Mar 16 – 21 Mar 16	N 3
Sgt Colcombe,		23 Jan 16 – 24 Jan 16	WIA
Cpl Cordelier,			

Cpl Courcenet, Robert			25 Jul 18 – 19 Sep 18	
Sgt Courtel,	(O)		25 Mar 17 – 11 Jun 17	GC 13
Sgt de Dampierre,			25 Apr 17 – 30 Apr 17	N 79
S/Lt de Fouquet, Maxime			3 May 16 – 14 Jan 17	
Lt de Fouquet, Maxime			9 Apr 17 – 11 Sep 17	RGAé
Lt de Goyé de Castelet,	(O)	N 48	14 Mar 16 – 9 Jun 16	MF 63
Sgt de Laveliette, Jean		GDE	29 May 16 – 18 Jun 16	N 102
Sgt de Marolles, Robert		N 48	14 Mar 16 – 24 May 17	
Lt Derode, Jean			21 Feb 16 – 17 Jun 16	Hosp
Lt Derode, Jean			– 10 Jan 17	CO N 102
Lt de Rose,				
MdL Déry, Louis		MS 23	20 Jan 16 – 29 Feb 16	MS 23
Capt de Saint Sauveur, Henri			22 Feb 16 – 25 Feb 16	CO N 67
S/Lt Des Brunes,	(O)		24 Jul 15 –	
Sgt Deschamps, Maurice			17 Mar 18 – 11 Nov 18	
S/Lt Devienne,			31 May 16 – 18 Jun 16	
Lt d'Harcourt, Jean		N 38	11 Jun 16 – Jul 16	CO N 103
Lt Duchesne,	(O)	RGAé	24 Jul 15 – 16 Aug 15	
S/Lt Durand, Antoine	(O)		4 Sep 15 – 7 Jun 16	C 104
S/Lt Duret, Marcel			9 Jun 17 – 11 Nov 18	
S/Lt Ferru, Charles		RGAé	29 Aug 15 – 22 May 16	
Chef de Escad Feugère des Forts,	(O)	RGAé	24 Jul 15 – 16 Aug 15	
MdL Flachaire, Georges		RGAé	4 Aug 15 – 31 Aug 17	
Lt Fournier,			1916 –	
MdL Fumat, Emile			22 Jan 18 – 11 Nov 18	
S/Lt Guignand, Urbain Gaston		N 37	22 May 16 –	
Lt Gond,	(O)		24 Jul 15 – 28 Aug 15	C 28
Sgt Goux, Marie Joseph			1916 – 19 Aug 17	WIA
Cpl Hegy,		GDE	11 Jun 17 – 24 Jun 17	MIA
Adj Houssemand, Charles			28 Feb 16 – 21 Mar 16	N 3
S/Lt Hudelet.,			29 Feb 16 –	
Lt Jacaud,	(O)	RGAé	24 Jul 15 – 28 Aug 15	C 28
Adj Jaubert, Marcel			17 Mar 18 – 11 Nov 18	
Sgt Kalvelage, Edouard			Jan 18 – 12 Jul 18	GDE
Capt Lamy,			16 Mar 17 – 19 Mar 17	N 65
Cpl Lebroussard, Armand			18 Apr 18 – 6 May 18	Spa 26
Lt Le Petit, Robert			29 Jul 18 – 11 Nov 18	
S/Lt Leps, Jacques	(O)		4 Sep 15 – 7 Jun 16	N 23
MdL Loiseau, Jean		CIACB	16 Sep 18 – 11 Nov 18	
Sgt Luling, Jean Marie			26 Apr 17 –	
Lt Malice,	(O)	RGAé	21 Jan 16 – 11 May 16	
S/Lt Marchand,			23 Jul 18 – 28 Jul 18	Spa 3
Cpl Margarit, Etienne			30 Jul 18 – 11 Nov 18	
Adj Martin-Reinert, Charles			26 Mar 17 – 7 Feb 18	CRP
Cpl Massot,			19 Feb 16 –	
Sgt Massot, Henri		Hosp	24 Jan 17 – 12 Aug 17	Hospital
MdL Ménard, René			16 Sep 17 – 11 Nov 18	
S/Lt Merlant,	(O)	RGAé	20 Jan 16 – 1 Jun 16	WIA
S/Lt Merlant,	(O)		– 4 Sep 17	C 46

Brig Mermet, Raymond			– 12 Apr 18 GDE	
S/Lt Michel, Joseph	(O)		4 Sep 15 – 25 Mar 16	MIA
S/Lt Mion, Adrien			– 11 Nov 18	
Sgt Moulais, Jules			22 Jul 15 – 5 May 16	RGAé
S/Lt Navarre, Jean			24 Feb 16 – 17 Jun 16	WIA
S/Lt Navarre, Jean			3 Mar 17 – 15 Apr 17	
Cpl Neveu, Joseph			Jan 18 – 11 Nov 18	
MdL Ouvrard de Linières, Max			1918 – 11 Nov 18	
S/Lt Pendaries, Pierre			2 Feb 18 – 11 Nov 18	
S/Lt Peretti, Jean			28 Feb 16 – 21 Mar 16	N 3
Adj Pillon, Edmond			15 Apr 18 – 18 Jun 18	CIACB
Sgt Poisard,		RGAé	8 Oct 15 –	
S/Lt Pouchelle, Auguste			17 Jun 18 – 11 Nov 18	
Cpl Poublanc,			– 28 Jul 18	GDE
Cpl Ponder, William T. (American)			30 Jan 18 – 21 Feb 18	
S/Lt Prétre, Henri			1917 – 12 Jul 18	Spa 91
Adj Prou, Pierre		RGAé	16 Sep 18 – 11 Nov 18	
Adj Quinchez, Fernand			12 Sep 17 – 9 Sep 18	Spa 173
Lt Richard, Paul	(O)	RGAé	20 Jan 16 – 3 Sep 16	MIA
Cpl Richard,		RGAé	21 Jul 15 – 12 Oct 15	N 3
Lt Rougevin-Baville, Alfred			28 Apr 16 – 13 May 18	Spa 3
Sgt Rousseau, Edouard			2 Feb 16 – 21 Mar 16	WIA
Sgt Rousseau, Edouard			– 3 Sep 16	MIA
Cpl Sachet, Gaston		GDE	6 Aug 18 – 23 Aug 18	KIA
S/Lt Schurck, René			17 May 18 – 4 Jul 18	Trans
Cpl Sedillon, Robert			– 31 Jan 18	
S/Lt Serre,	(O)	RGAé	24 Jul 15 – 28 Aug 15	C 28
Cpl Tailer, William (American)		GDE	14 Dec 17 – 5 Feb 18	KIA
S/Lt Tenant de la Tour, Mathieu		RGAé	17 Jul 15 – 1 Oct 15	
MdL Thibaudet, Marcel		RGAé	21 Jul 15 – 25 Apr 16	Hosp
Lt Thobie, Jean			1917 – 13 Feb 18	CO Spa 48
Adj Toulze, Georges			21 Feb 16 – 1917	
Cpl Trochon, Amédée			1916 –	
S/Lt Vailet, Marcel			Jul 16 – 18 Sep 17	RGAé
S/Lt Venson, Fernand		N 3	14 Aug 15 – 24 Feb 16	
Adj Verwicht, Louis		RGAé	21 Jul 15 – 25 Jan 16	
Cpl Vitalis, Marie Gaston	(G)			
Lt Wibault,	(O)	Parc 11	2 Mar 16 – 21 Mar 16	Parc 11
S/Lt Willemin, André			25 Apr 17 – 27 Mar 18 MIA	

Personnel Known to have Flown with Spa 73

Commanding Officers

Name	From	Dates	To/Comment
S/Lt Bouny, Pierre		31 Mar 16 – 18 Apr 16	MF 59
Capt Baillardel de Larienty-Tholozan, Honoré	F 14	18 Apr 16 – 5 May 16	KIAcc
?		6 May 16 – 31 May 16	
Lt Richard, Jean	N 3	1 Jun 16 – 22 Feb 17	EM GC 12
Capt Deullin, Albert	N 3	22 Feb 17 – 14 Feb 18	CO GC 19
Capt Cahuzac, Pierre	Spa 67	14 Feb 18 – 22 Mar 18	GDE
Lt Nogues, Maurice	Spa 73	22 Mar 18 – 27 Apr 18	WIA
Lt Gerdes, Robert	Spa 73	27 Apr 18 – 10 Jul 18	Acting CO
Capt Jaille, Pierre	Spa 75	10 Jul 18 – 11 Nov 18	

Other Flying Personnel

Name	From	Dates	To/Comment
2/Lt Ackermann, J.H. (American)		– 11 Jun 18	WIA
MdL Amigues,	GDE	30 Apr 16 –	
MdL Arrighi, Paul	CIACB	12 Sep 18 – 11 Nov 18	
Sgt Baillardel de Lareinty-Tholozan, Foulques	F 14	31 Jul 16 –	
Adj Baroiz, Albert	GDE	12 Mar 17 – 11 Apr 17	MIA
Adj Barroil, Fernand	GDE	3 Jan 18 – 11 Nov 18	
Lt Battesti, François	GDE	12 Mar 17 – 11 Nov 18	
Cpl Baylies, Frank (American)	GDE	17 Nov 17 – 18 Dec 17	Spa 3
Adj-Chef Bergot, François		Jul 16 – 6 Jan 17	N 38
S/Lt Bergot, François	N 38	30 Jan 17 – 11 Nov 18	
Sgt Biddle, Charles (American)	GDE	28 Jul 17 – 10 Jan 18	N 124
Cpl Biddle, Julian (American)	GDE	11 Aug 17 – 18 Aug 17	MIA
Sgt Bordes,		Jul 16 – 7 Sep 16	MIA
Asp Bouchard, Joseph	CIACB	30 Aug 18 – 11 Nov 18	
Sgt Boulay, Paul	GDE	24 Apr 18 – 11 Nov 18	
Adj Bruneau, Robert		Jul 16 – 20 Oct 16	WIA
Cpl Buchet, Aimé	CIACB	1 Oct 18 – 11 Nov 18	
Cpl Bush, Philip (American)	GDE	19 Jan 18 – 21 Jul 18	USAS
Sgt Cacheux,		Jul 16 –	
Cpl Chadwick, Oliver (American)	GDE	28 Jul 17 – 14 Aug 17	KIA
S/Lt Claude-Fontaine, Gaston		23 Jul 17 – 11 Nov 18	
MdL Clouard, Joseph	N 49	31 Mar 16 – 21 Apr 16	GDE
S/Lt Constantinowich, Vladimir	RGAé	4 Jun 17 – 24 Jul 17	Hospital
MdL Courtieu, André	GDE	1 Feb 18 – 3 Mar 18	Spa 96

MdL Daladier, Gustave		27 Apr 16 – 16 Jul 16	F 14
Capt de Pierre de Bernis, Pons Raymond		26 Jul 18 – 26 Jul 18	EM GC 19
Lt de Girval, Bernard	GDE	25 Dec 17 – 30 Jun 18	KIA
Lt de Guibert, Charles	N 3	9 Apr 17 – 5 Sep 17	
MdL Delestre, Paul (O)	N 77	19 Sep 17 – 25 Sep 17	VB 109
S/Lt de Lignières, Jacques	GDE	9 Mar 17 – 26 Jun 17	N 153
Lt de Limier, Jean		1916 – 22 Jan 17	Trans
Lt Depasse,	GDE	8 May 16 –	
Sgt Drou, Gaston	GDE	25 Apr 17 – 14 Oct 17	KIA
Cpl du Maroussem, Robert		31 Mar 16 – 22 Apr 16	GDE
Lt Dumas, Paul	GDE	4 Feb 18 – 14 Feb 18	EM GC 19
Lt Dumas, Paul		14 Feb 18 – 24 Jul 18	Spa 85
Sol Durieu, (G)		– 15 Jun 16	MF 59
Cpl Dussaut,		Jul 16 –	
Capt Duval,	GDE	30 Oct 17 – 12 Nov 17	KIAcc
Adj Fieux, André	CIACB	4 Nov 18 – 11 Nov 18	
Sol Fleurot, (G)		– 15 Jun 16	N 49
Sgt Funck-Bretano, Théophile		22 Apr 16 – 25 Jun 16	KIA
Lt Gerdes, Robert	GDE	26 Jul 17 – 27 Apr 18	CO Spa 73
Asp Girod, Marcel	CIACB	16 Jul 18 – 18 Sep 18	Inf Rgt 101
Cpl Gobe, Charles	GDE	21 Dec 17 – 30 Apr 18	GDE
Lt Grenes, François (O)		1916 – 30 Apr 17	Pilot Sch
Adj Hamel, Jean		19 Apr 16 –	
MdL Huruguen, Marcel	CIACB	16 Jul 18 – 11 Nov 18	
MdL Jolivet, Pierre	GDE	25 Apr 17 – 18 Oct 17	KIA
Cpl Jones, Charles (American)	0GDE	15 Aug 17 – 21 Jan 18	N 124
Cpl Judd, David (American)	GDE	1 Dec 17 – 18 Dec 17	Spa 3
Sgt Labrely, Jean	Spa 155	30 Aug 18 – 11 Nov 18	
Adj Laguel,		Jul 16 –	
Capt Lamon, Jean		5 Jan 17 – 16 Jan 17	N 103
Capt Lamon, Jean	N 103	30 Jan 17 – 13 Feb 17	Hosp
Capt Lamon, Jean	Hosp	1 Apr 17 – 21 Jul 17	POW
S/Lt Lannes, André		1916 – 19 Mar 17	N 88
Capt Lanron, Jean	GDE	5 Jan 17 – 13 Feb 17	Hospital
Adj-Chef Larmande, André	GDE	14 Nov 17 – 11 Sep 18	Bourget
Cpl Le Geurn,	GDE	1 Jul 16 –	
Adj Lemelle, Adolphe		16 Nov 16 – 26 Sep 17	Hospital
Sgt Leurelle, Adolphe			
S/Lt Mamy, André (O)	Spa 62	14 Mar 18 – 14 Mar 18	EM GC 19
S/Lt Mamy, André (O)	GC 19	14 Mar 18 – 2 Apr 18	Spa 62
Sgt Maugeard,	GDE	1 Jul 16 –	
Sgt Mauger, Georges	GDE	23 Jul 17 – 12 Jul 18	CIACB
Sgt Millo, Honoré		11 Jul 18 – 11 Nov 18	
Lt Mimaud-Grandchamp, Robert	V114	18 Jul 17 – 1 Aug 17	
Lt Nogues, Maurice	N 3	19 Sep 17 – 22 Mar 18	CO Spa 73
Lt Pandevant, Louis	GDE	16 Mar 17 – 22 Jul 17	MIA
MdL Paoli, Louis	GDE	23 Oct 17 – 19 Nov 17	POW

MdL Paoli, Louis	Escaped	7 Mar 18 – 12 Aug 18	KIA
Sgt Paris, Marcel		Jul 16 – 4 Mar 17	N 82
Adj Paris, Marcel	N 82	23 Mar 17 – 25 May 18	Instructor
Cpl Perrin, Georges	GDE	26 Jul 18 – 1 Aug 18	MIA
S/Lt Prejean, Albert	CIACB	16 Jul 18 – 17 Oct 18	Spa 85
Lt Raymond, Georges	N 3	2 Aug 17 – 2 Sep 17	N 3
MdL Rehm, Eugène	CIACB	29 Jul 18 – 11 Nov 18	
Cpl Rigaud, Roger		1916 –	
Lt Robert, Roger		– 3 Mar 17	Injured
Sgt Roger,		Jul 16 –	
Brig Ropital, Georges	GDE	23 Aug 18 – 29 Aug 18	Spa 155
Cpl Rouen, André	CIACB	16 Oct 18 – 11 Nov 18	
Adj Rouzet, René	CIACB	16 Sep 18 – 11 Nov 18	
Sgt Roxas-Elias,		– 10 Nov 16	MIA
Sgt Roy, Roger		1916 – 25 Jan 17	Russia
Cpl Sabatier, Robert		29 Apr 16 –	
Sgt Scalingi, Vincent		1916 23 Jun 17	Inj-Hosp
MdL Scalingi, Vincent	Hosp	29 Sep 17 – 21 Nov 17	GDE
S/Lt Tasd'homme, Léon		31 Mar 16 – 28 Feb 17	RGAé
Adj Tassou, Roger		Jul 16 – 26 Jul 18	Instructor
Adj Trampitch, Armand	GDE	3 Feb 18 – 15 Oct 18	CIACB
Sgt Travet, Marcel	GDE	22 Feb 18 – 20 Jun 18	Hospital
Adj Vaillet, Georges	CIACB	7 Nov 18 – 11 Nov 18	
Sol Varlet (O)		– 15 Jun 16	N 49
Cpl Vasseur, Alfred	GDE	1 May 18 – 21 Jul 18	Hospital
Lt Verdie, Jean	GDE	10 Feb 17 – 20 Oct 17	Artil.Sch

Personnel Known to have Flown with Spa 103

Commanding Officers

Name	From	Dates	To/Comment
Capt Benoist, Georges		2 Aug 14 – 1 Jul 15	
Capt Boucher, Max		1 Jul 15 – 23 Oct 15	Avord
Lt Gaborit de Montjou, Guy		23 Oct 15 – 16	
Capt Gallet, Henri	V 114	16 – 12 Jul 16	
Lt Barbey, Pierre		12 Jul 16 – Jul 16	
Capt d'Harcourt, Jean		Jul 16 – 27 Mar 18	GC 13
Capt Battle, Joseph	Spa 77	27 Mar 18 – 4 Nov 18	
Capt Dupuy, Charles		4 Nov 18 – 11 Nov 18	

Other Flying Personnel

Sgt Ageorges,			
Sgt Astor,			
Sol Badeau, (G)			
Sgt Baillard,			
Adj Barault, Lucien		21 Aug 17 – 14 Dec 17	Spa 88

Lt Barbey, Pierre		1 Oct 16 – 20 Aug 17	Parc 4
Sgt Bardel,		1916 – 27 Jan 17	Russia
Lt Barny de Romanet, Bernard		19 Sep 18 – 1 Oct 18	CO Spa 167
S/Lt Baron, Joseph		1916 – 11 Nov 18	
Cpl Batchelor, Henry A.		26 Dec 17 – 20 Jan 18	Hosp
(American)			
Adj Baux, Auguste	GDE	16 Jan 18 – 17 Jul 18	MIA
Sgt Bazot, Alfred		– 27 Sep 16	Injured
Cpl Bernard,			
Sgt Besson,		24 Jan 15 –	
Adj Bonneau,		12 Sep 15 –	
S/Lt Bordas, Lucien		2 Sep 15 – 5 Oct 15	SFA
Sgt Boscher, Louis		17 Sep 18 – 1 Oct 18	Spa 167
Sgt Bourdarie		– 24 Dec 16	KIAcc
Lt Bouvier,			
Sgt Bridou, André		– 13 Aug 14	KIAcc
Sgt Brion,		1915 – 24 Oct 15	N 65
Cpl Briquet,			
Adj Brugère, Jean	GDE	8 Jan 18 – 11 Nov 18	
Sgt Buanu-Varilla, Etienne		1914 –	
Sgt Butruille,		27 Dec 17 – 21 Mar 18	Pau
Sgt Carrier,		1915 – 23 Oct 15	
S/Lt Casel,	(O)	19 Apr 17 – 16 May 17	
MdL Chapel,		1916 – 5 Aug 17	GDE
Adj Chastin,	(O)	25 Jan 15 – 10 Jul 15	
Cpl Cnudde,			
S/Lt Colcombet,	(O)	18 Feb 15 – 27 Jul 15	
Sgt Collins, Phelps		18 Sep 17 – 7 Jan 18	N 124
(American)			
Cpl Colomies, René		19 Sep 18 – 1 Oct 18	Spa 167
S/Lt Cournier,	(O)	1916 – 25 Dec 17	Spa 3
Lt Courtel,		6 Oct 17 – 9 Dec 17	KIAcc
S/Lt Coudouret, Louis Fernand	GDE	18 May 18 – 11 Nov 18	
Sgt Debaud,	GDE	13 Jul 18 – 11 Nov 18	
Sgt Debrod,		– 3 Aug 16	MIA
Sgt de Chambannes,			
Sgt de Coucelles,		1915 – 24 Oct 15	
S/Lt de Dompierre,	(O)	1915 – 16 Jul 15	
Sgt de Dreux-Brézé,		1915 – 15 Oct 15	
Sgt Degorce,		1916 – 24 May 17	Hosp
Sgt de Lagerie,	(O)	1915 –	
Adj Delaître,		1915 – 8 Nov 15	SFA
S/Lt de Landrian,	(O)	1915 – 22 Jul 15	RGAé
Sgt de Linière, Pierre		1915 –	
Cpl de Lombardon, Jean		19 Sep 18 – 1 Oct 18	Spa 167
Sgt de Mortemart,		1915 –	
Sol Deneschaud,	(G)		
Cpl Descamps,			
Lt Desquenne,		26 Jun 17 – 5 Dec 17	Spa 313
Sgt Doux, Emile		1915 – 24 Oct 15	

Name		Dates	Note
Adj Drouillh, Henri		26 Dec 17 – 11 Nov 18	
S/Lt Dumas, François		16 Sep 18 – 1 Oct 18	Spa 167
Lt Dumas, Paul		26 Jun 17 – 21 Aug 17	WIA
Lt Dumas, Paul		21 Oct 17 – 5 Nov 17	WIA/Hosp
MdL Dupuy,		1915 –	
Cpl Ebendinger,			
S/Lt Esperon du Tremblay, Victor		19 Sep 18 – 1 Oct 18	Spa 167
Cpl Faure,			
Sgt Fay,		1915 – 18 Oct 15	
Cpl Ferraz, Jean		22 Sep 18 – 1 Oct 18	Spa 167
Cpl Flint,			
Lt Fonck, René		26 Apr 17 – 11 Nov 18	
Lt Fontaine,	GDE	27 Nov 17 – 6 Oct 18	CIACB
Adj Frobert,		1914 – 17 Nov 15	
Lt Gaborit de Monthou, Guy		1915 – 23 Oct 15	CO VB 103
S/Lt Gaillard,			
Sgt Garnier,		25 Jan 15 –	
Sol Garnier,	(G)		
Lt Garros, Roland	GDE	21 Aug 18 – 23 Aug 18	Spa 26
Sgt Gervais,		1915 – 24 Oct 15	
Sgt Giclat,			
Lt Gigodot, Jean		21 Jun 16 – 16 Jun 17	CO N 153
Sgt Girard, Victor		21 Sep 18 – 1 Oct 18	Spa 167
Lt Gonnet-Thomas, Louis		1 Sep 15 – 21 Oct 15	CO N 65
Sgt Guers, Spa 3		11 Aug 18 – 11 Nov 18	
Sgt Gui,	GDE	22 Jul 18 – 11 Nov 18	
Sgt Guillet,			
Sgt Haegelen, Marcel	GDE	8 Mar 17 – 28 May 17	WIA
Sgt Haegelen, Marcel	Hosp	21 Sep 17 – 7 Feb 18	Spa 100
Adj Hall, Weston (Bert) (American)		18 Nov 16 – 20 Dec 16	
Adj Hecfeuille,		1914 –	
Sgt Hénon, André		22 Sep 18 – 1 Oct 18	Spa 167
Lt Hervet, Pierre		8 Aug 16 – 25 Dec 17	Gun Sch
Sgt Hoeber, Robert (American)		19 Dec 17 – 11 Nov 18	
Sgt Hourlier,		1915 – 17 Oct 15	
Lt Houssin, René	(O)	18 Aug 15 – 29 Oct 15	Avord
Sgt Huc,		– 16 Oct 18	Spa 173
Cpl Hugues,			
Sgt Jacquelin,			
MdL Laffray,	GDE	17 May 18 – 31 Aug 18	Hosp
MdL Laffray,		9 Oct 18 – 3 Nov 18	Spa 173
Lt Lamon, Jean	N 73	16 Jan 17 – 30 Jan 17	N 73
Sgt Léau,		1915 – 24 Oct 15	
S/Lt Lechevallier, Marcel		19 Sep 18 – 1 Oct 18	Spa 167
Cpl Leclerc,			
S/Lt Lecomte, René		1916 – 1 Jan 18	Hosp
S/Lt Lecomte, René		6 Mar 18 – 13 Jun 18	Spa 88

S/Lt Ledeuil, Auguste		1916 – 3 Mar 17	MIA
Lt le Forestier	(O)	23 Jul 15 – 26 Dec 15	Pau
Sgt Lenoir,	GDE	17 Apr 18 – 11 Nov 18	W/21 July
Sgt Leroy,		1915 – 24 Oct 15	
Cpl Lévêque,			
Adj Loup, Gilbert	GDE	16 Jul 17 – 11 Nov 18	
Sgt Lutzius, Georges		1916 – 30 Jun 17	N 153
Cpl Maffert, Jean		– 3 Aug 16	MIA
Sgt Malherbe,		1914 – 11 Feb 15	
Cpl Mandray, Jean	GDE	16 Jun 18 – 29 Jun 18	KIA
Sgt Maréchal, Maurice		16 Oct 18 – 11 Nov 18	
Sgt McCall, George A. (American)		24 Oct 18 – 11 Nov 18	
Sgt Mellinger,		– 31 Jul 15	MIA
Sgt Mérignac,		1914 –	
Sgt Mérital,		20 Oct 15 –	
Lt Migaud, Gabriel		2 Aug 14 –	
Sgt Miguel,		1916 – 5 Mar 17	N 315
Sgt Millot, Léon		1916 – 9 Nov 16	KIA
Adj Miserolle,			
Cpl Misery,			
S/Lt Moineau,		2 Aug 14 – 1914	
Cpl Nugues, André		22 Sep 18 – 1 Oct 18	Spa 167
Cpl Ollagnier,			
Brig Ouvrard de Linière, René	Spa 85	13 Oct 18 – 11 Nov 18	
Sgt Padieu		1915 – 4 Oct 15	
Sgt Pasieux,			
Sgt Papineau,	GDE	19 Jul 18 – 7 Oct 18	Hosp
Cpl Pelletier,			
Sgt Pernelle, André		1916 – 10 Dec 17	GDE
Sgt Petit,			
Sgt Pichery,	CIACB	5 Oct 18 – 11 Nov 18	
Cpl Pichon,		6 Apr 18 – 10 May 18	Hosp
Adj Piétri, Camille		10 May 17 – 3 Aug 18	Hosp
Adj Poggi,		1914 –	
Cp[Potelet,			
Cpl Ravel,		– 2 Nov 16	MIA
Asp Renaud,		1915 –	
Cpl Reno, Leonard (American)		23 Jul 17 – 19 Sep 17	Hosp
Sgt Roman, François		– 24 Sep 16	MIA
Sgt Romanel,	GDE	28 Mar 18 – 11 Nov 18	
Capt Salel, Henri		13 Feb 15 – 1 Apr 15	
Sgt Sansom,	GDE	17 May 18 – 11 Nov 18	
S/Lt Schmitter, Pierre		12 Apr 17 – 11 Nov 18	
MdL Seigneurie, André		– 2 Jul 16	MIA
MdL Seigneurie,		26 Jul 17 – 17 Aug 17	WIA
S/Lt Seigneurie,	Hosp	12 Sep 17 – 14 May 18	
Sol Simon,	(G)		
Lt Skadousky,	(O)	1 Sep 15 – 21 Oct 15	N 65

Sgt Soudin, Robert		17 Sep 18 – 1 Oct 18	Spa 167
Sgt Steuer, André		– 24 Sep 16	MIA
S/Lt Suberive,		1 Dec 15 –	
Sgt Tardres,		5 Nov 15 – 8 Nov 15	
Adj Tasqué, Gaston	Spa 67	16 Jan 18 – 23 Mar 18	KIAcc
Cpl Thézé, Joseph		17 Sep 18 – 1 Oct 18	Spa 167
S/Lt Thouzellier, Léon	GDE	5 Feb 18 – 11 Nov 18	
S/Lt Tournier, (O)		1916 – 25 Dec 17	
Lt Tourtel, Paul	N 85	6 Oct 17 – 8 Dec 17	KIAcc
Cpl Trouillet, Paul		1 Sep 18 – 1 Oct 18	Spa 167
Sgt Turnure, George E, Jr (American)		27 Jul 17 – 16 Dec 17	
Adj Vaurin,		1914 – 5 Aug 15	
Cpl Vailatoux, (B)		– 31 Jul 15	MIA
Adj Villard, Emile		4 Sep 18 – 1 Oct 18	Spa 167
Sol Vinel, (B)		– 13 Aug 14	KIAcc
Cpl Virolet,			
Sgt Voisin,		1914 – 19 Dec 14	
Sgt Watrin,		1916 – 14 Oct 17	GDE

Personnel Known to have Flown with Spa 167

Commanding Officer

Name	From	Dates	To/Comment
Ltn Barny de Romanet, Bernard	Spa 37	22 Aug 18 – 11 Nov 18	

Other Flying Personnel

MdL Boscher, Louis	Spa 103	10 Oct 18 – 11 Nov 18	
Cpl Colomies, René	Spa 103	14 Sep 18 – 11 Nov 18	
Sgt de Lombardon, Jean	Spa 103	19 Sep 18 – 11 Nov 18	
S/Lt Dumas, François	Spa 12	16 Sep 18 – 11 Nov 18	
S/Lt Esperon du Tremblay, Victor	GDE	19 Sep 18 – 11 Nov 18	
Cpl Ferraz, Jean	Spa 103	22 Sep 18 – 11 Nov 18	
Sgt Gerard, Roger	Spa 168	9 Sep 18 – 11 Nov 18	
Sgt Girard, Victor	Spa 103	21 Sep 18 – 11 Nov 18	
S/Lt Guiguet, Joseph	Spa 3	Sep 18 – 11 Nov 18	
Cpl Henon, André	Spa 103	22 Sep 18 – 11 Nov 18	
S/Lt Lechevallier, Marcel	CIACB	19 Sep 18 – 11 Nov 18	
Cpl Marcon, Raymond René	CIACB	16 Oct 18 – 11 Nov 18	
Sgt Nugues, André	Spa 103	22 Sep 18 – 11 Nov 18	
Sgt Soudin, Robert	Spa 103	17 Sep 18 – 11 Nov 18	
Cpl Thézé, Joseph	Spa 103	17 Sep 18 – 11 Nov 18	
Sgt Trouillet, Paul Louis	Spa 103	1 Sep 18 – 11 Nov 18	
S/Lt Villard, Emile Antoine	Spa 103	4 Sep 18 – 11 Nov 18	

Personnel Known to have Flown with Escadrille Spa 173

Commanding Officer

Name	From	Dates	To/Comment
Lt Allez, Jacques	Spa 65	16 Oct 18 – 11 Nov 18	

Other Flying Personnel

Name	From	Dates	To/Comment
S/Lt Bailly,		Oct 18 – 13 Oct 18	Spa 67
Sgt Bloyard,		16 Oct 18 – 11 Nov 18	
S/Lt Bourgeot		16 Oct 18 – 22 Oct 18	Spa 67
Sgt Brenier,		16 Oct 18 – 11 Nov 18	
Adj Chambrelan,		16 Oct 18 – 11 Nov 18	
Cpl Eldon, Jean	Spa 26	3 Nov 18 – 11 Nov 18	
Cpl Filaine,		16 Oct 18 – 11 Nov 18	
Cpl Granger,		16 Oct 18 – 11 Nov 18	
Lt Grasset,		16 Oct 18 – 11 Nov 18	
Cpl Huc,	Spa 103	16 Oct 18 – 11 Nov 18	
MdL Laffray	Spa 103	3 Nov 18 – 11 Nov 18	
Cpl Meunier,		16 Oct 18 – 11 Nov 18	
Sgt Plancoulene,		16 Oct 18 – 11 Nov 18	
Adj Quinchez, Fernand	Spa 67	9 Sep 18 – 11 Nov 18	
Brig Schmitt,		16 Oct 18 – 11 Nov 18	
MdL Tournaire,		16 Oct 18 – 11 Nov 18	
Adj Usse, Justin	Spa 26	3 Nov 18 – 11 Nov 18	

Abbreviations

CIACB   Centre d'Instruction Aéronautique de Chasse et de Bombardement.

EM   Staff Appointment.

GB   Groupe de Bombardement.
Bombing Group.

GC   Groupe de Combat de Chase
Pursuit Group.

GDE   Groupe Divisionaire d'Entrainement.
Divisional Training Group.

RGAé   Reserve Générale Aéronautique.
Aeronautical General Reserve.

SFA   Service des Fabrications de l'Aviation Militaires.
Military Aviation Construction Service.

Equivalent Ranks

Maréchal	General of the Army
Général d'Armée	General

Général de Division	Lieutenant General
Général de Brigade	Major General
	Brigadier General
Colonel	Colonel
Lieutenant Colonel	Lieutenant Colonel
Chef de Bataillon	Major (Infantry)
Chef d'Escadron	Major (Artillery)
Chef d'Escadrons	Major (Cavalry)
Commandant	Major
Capitaine	Captain
Lieutenant	1st Lieutenant
Sous-lieutenant	2nd Lieutenant
Aspirant	Officer Candidate
Adjudant-Chef	Chief Warrant Officer
Adjudant	Warrant Officer
Maréchal-des-Logis-Chef	Sergeant-Major (Artillery-Cavalry)
Sergent-Major	First Sergeant
Maréchal-des-Logis-Fourrier	Quartermaster Sergeant (Art-Cav)
Maréchal-des-Logis	Sergeant (Artillery-Cavalry)
Sergent	Sergeant
Sergent-Fourrier	Quartermaster Sergeant
Brigadier	Corporal (Artillery-Cavalry)
Caporal	Corporal
Caporal-Fourrier	Quartermaster-Corporal
Soldat de 1er Classe	Private First Class
Soldat de 2° Classe	Private

APPENDIX I

Pilots Credited with Victories with Groupe de Combat 12

	Unit	Alone	Shared	GC 12 Total	Other		War Total
Lt René Fonck	103	72	1	73	2	(a)	75
Capt Georges Guynemer	3	34	1	35	18	(b)	53
Sgt Frank Baylies	3	9	3	12	-		12
Capt Albert Deullin	3 & 73	12	-	12	8	(c)	20
Capt Alfred Heurtaux	3	11	-	11	10	(d)	21
Lt Bernard Barny de Romanet	167	3	5	8	10	(e)	18
S/Lt René Dorme	3	8	-	8	15	(f)	23
Lt Jean Bozon-Verduraz	3	3	5	8	3	(g)	11
Adj Edwin Parsons	3	5	2	7	1	(h)	8
Capt Xavier de Sevin	26	2	4	6	6	(i)	12
Adj Gustave Naudin	26	4	2	6	-		6
Sgt André Dubonnet	3	1	5	6	-		6
Capt Alfred Auger	3	4	1 +	5	2	(j)	7
Capt Georges Raymond	3	4	1	5	1	(k)	6

	Unit	Alone	Shared	GC 12 Total	Other		War Total
Adj Henri Drouillh	103	-	4	4	-		4
S/Lt Louis Guiguet	3	3	1	4	1	(l)	5
S/Lt Pierre Pendaries	67	2	2	4	3	(m)	7
Sgt Constant Soulier	26	3	1 ++	4	2	(n)	6
Lt François Battesti	73	3	-	3	4	(o)	7
Capt Joseph Battle	103	2	1	3	1	(p)	4
Sgt Jean de Lombardon	167	1	2	3	-		3
Adj Charles Jeronnez	26	3	-	3	-		3
Adj Adolphe Lemelle	73	3	-	3	-		3
S/Lt Pierre Schmitter	103	1	2	3	-		3
Adj Justin Usse	26	2	1	3	-		3
S/Lt Joseph Baron	103	-	2	2	-		2
Adj Auguste Baux	103	1	1	2	-		2
Sgt Charles Biddle	73 & 103	2	-	2	5	(q)	7
Sgt Robert Brière	3	2	-	2	-		2
Sgt Maurice Chevannes	3	-	2	2	-		2
Capt Marie d'Indy	67	1	1	2	-		2
Lt Guy de la Rochefordière	3	-	2	2	-		2
MdL Denneulin	3	-	2	2	-		2
2S/Lt Benjamin de Tascher	26	-	2	2	-		2
Lt Jean Dombray	26	-	2	2	-		2
Lt François Dumas	167	-	2	2	1	(r)	3
S/Lt Marcel Duret	67	1	1	2	-		2
Sgt Marcel Haegelen	103	2	-	2	20	(s)	22
Lt Pierre Hervet	103	2	-	2	-		2
Lt Robert Le Petit	67	2	-	2	-		2
S/Lt Auguste Ledeuil	103	2	-	2	2	(t)	4
Lt Emile Letourneau	26	1	1	2	-		2
Adj Gilbert Loup	103	-	2	2	-		2
S/Lt Adrien Mion	67	1	1	2	1	(u)	3
S/Lt Moulines	3	-	2	2	-		2
MdL Max Ouvrard de Linière	67	-	2	2	-		2
Sgt Camille Pietri	103	2	-	2	-		2
Adj Armand Pillon	67	1	1	2	6	(v)	8
Lt Jacquews Puget	26	1	1	2	-		2
Brig Rigault	73	2	-	2	-		2
Sgt Louis Risacher	3	1	1	2	3	(w)	5
Sgt Sansom	103	-	2	2	-		2
Capt Mathieu Tenant de la Tour	3 & 26	2	-	2	7	(x)	9
Adj Julius Antoine	26	-	1	1	-		1
S/Lt François Bergot	73	1	-	1	-		1
Sgt Robert Brillaud	26	1	-	1	-		1
Adj Jean Brugère	103	1	-	1	-		1
S/Lt Louis Bucquet	3	2	-	2	1	(y)	3
MdL Clement	3	-	1	1	-		1
Sgt Phelps Collins	103	1	-	1	-		1
S/Lt Louis Coudouret	103	-	1	1	5	(z)	6
Sgt René Dard	26	1	-	1	-		1

Name	Sqn						Total
Sgt Jacques de Linière	103	1	-	1	-		1
Sgt Xavier de Marcy	3	1	-	1	-		1
Adj Adrien Fétu	26	1	-	1	-		1
MdL Noël Fontaine	26	-	1	1	-		1
S/Lt Roland Garros	26	1	-	1	3	(aa)	4
Lt Jean Gigodot	103	1	-	1	3	(bb)	4
Sgt Gui	103	-	1	1	-		1
Adj Bert Hall	103	1	-	1	3	(cc)	4
Sgt André Henon	3	1	-	1	-		1
Sgt Robert Hoeber	103	-	1	1	-		1
Adj Marcel Jaubert	67	-	1	1	-		1
MdL Hubert Lambotte	26	-	1	1	-		1
Adj Armand Lebroussard	26	1	-	1	-		1
S/Lt Marcel Lechavelier	167	-	1	1	-		1
S/Lt René Lecomte	103	-	1	1	2	(dd)	3
Capt Victor Ménard	26	1	-	1	3	(ee)	4
Lt Ivan Orlov	3	1	-	1	4	(ff)	5
Sgt Jean Pelletier	26	1	-	1	-		1
Agt André Pernelle	103	1	-	1	-		1
Lt Armand Pinsard	26	1	-	1	26	(gg)	27
MdL Marcel Plessis	26	-	1	1	-		1
S/Lt Henri Prétre	67	1	-	1	3	(hh)	4
Sgt Pierre Prou	26	1	-	1	-		1
Lt Henri Rabatel	3	1	-	1	1	(ii)	2
Lt Alfred Rougevin-Baville	67	-	1	1	-		1
Cpl Robert Sabatier	73	1	-	1	1	(jj)	2
Lt Tadia Sondemayer	3	1	-	1	-		1
Adj Gaston Tasque	103	-	1	1	-		1
Brig Edmond Thomassin	26	1	-	1	-		1
Sgt George Turnure	103	-	1	1	2	(kk)	3
Asp Emile Villard	167	-	1	1	-		1
Adj Aimé Vincent	26	-	1	1	-		1

(a)   C 47 (2)
(b)   N 3 (18) before GC 12
(c)   MF 62 (1); GC 19 (7)
(d)   N 3 (10) before GC 12
(e)   Spa 37 (10)
(f)   N 3 (15) before GC 12
(g)   Spa 94 (3)
(h)   N 124 (1)
(i)   N 12 (6)
(j)   N 31 (2)
(k)   N 3 (1) before GC 12
(l)   N 95 (1)
(m)   N 69 (3)
(n)   N 26 (2) before GC 12
(o)   Spa 73 (4) after GC 12
(p)   Spa 77 (1)
(q)   13th USAS (5)

(r)   unknown unit
(s)   Spa 100 (20)
(t)   N 103 (2) before GC 12
(u)   unknown unit
(v)   N 102 (1), N 82 (4) & Spa 98 (1)
(w)   Spa 159 (3)
(x)   N 57 (1); N 3 (6)
(y)   N 3 (1) before GC 12
(z)   N 57 (1), N 102 (1) & Russia (3)
(aa)   MS 26 (3)
(bb)   N 103 (1) before GC 12 & Spa 153 (2)
(cc)   N 124 (3)
(dd)   Spa 88 (2)
(ee)   GC 15 (3)
(ff)   Russia (4)
(gg)   Spa 78 (15), Spa 23 (11)
(hh)   Spa 91 (3)
(ii)   N 3 (1) before GC 12
(jj)   N 73 (1) before GC 12
(kk)   103rd USAS (2)

+   Shared with N 12.
++   Shared with Lt de Bonald, N 69, 3 & Sgt Chapelle, N 31, 3.

Spa 3 had 110 victories with GC 12
Spa 26 had 36 victories with GC 12
Spa 67 had 13 victories with GC 12
Spa 73 had 19 victories with GC 12
Spa 103 had 101 victories with GC 12
Spa 167 had 10 victories with GC 12

APPENDIX J

Airfields Occupied by Groupe de Combat 12

1 Nov 1916 – 28 Jan 1917	Cachy	VI° Armée
	Approx. 15 km SE Amiens	
28 Jan 1917 – 16 Mar 1917	Manoncourt-en-Vermois	VIII° Armée
	Approx. 10 km ESE Nancy	
16 Mar 1917 – 11 Jul 1917	Bonne-Maison	VI° Armée
	Approx. 5 km SE Fismes	
11 Jul 1917 -	Bergues	1er Armée
	Approx. 10 km S Dunkerque	
	Bierne	1er Armée
	Approx. 10 km S Dunkerque	
	Coudekerque-Branche	1er Armée
	Approx. 5 km S Dunkerque	

	St Pol-sur-Mer	1er Armée
	West Dunkerque	
– 11 Dec 1917	St Eloi	1er Armée
	Near Dixmuide	
11 Dec 1917 –	Maisonneuve	VI° Armée
	Near Villers-Cotterêts	
12 Jan 1918 – 7 Mar 1918	Beauzée-sur-Aire	II° Armée
	Approx. 12 km SW Souilly	
7 Mar 1918 – 22 Mar 1918	Lhéry	V° Armée
	Approx. 20 km WSW Reims	
22 Mar 1918 – 26 Mar 1918	Mesnil-St Georges	VI° Armée
	Approx. 2 km W Montdidler	
26 Mar 1918 – 8 Apr 1918	Raray	VI° Armée
	Approx. 10 km NE Senlis	
8 Apr 1918 – 3 Jun 1918	Hétomesnil	VI° Armée
	Approx. 40 km W Montdidier	
3 Jun 1918 – 7 Jun 1918	Sacy-le-Grand	X° Armée
	Approx. 20 km SW Compiègne	
7 Jun 1918 – 17 Jul 1918	Hétomesnil	X° Armée
17 Jul 1918 – 24 Jul 1918	Trécon	V° Armée
	Approx. 30 km SW Châlons-sur-Marne	
24 Jul 1918 – 28 Jul 1918	Herbisse	V° Armée
	Approx. 45 km SSW Châlons-sur-Marne	
28 Jul 1918 – 3 Sep 1918	Hétomesnil	1er Armée
3 Sep 1918 – 8 Sep 1918	Quinquempoix	1er Armée
8 Sep 1918 – 18 Sep 1918	Lisle-en-Barrois	1st Army AEF
18 Sep 1918 – 1 Nov 1918	La Noblette	IV° Armée
	Between La Chesne and St Etienne-au-Temple	
1 Nov 1918 – 11 Nov 1918	Hauviné	IV° Armée
	Approx. 25 km ENE Reims	

The Markings of Groupe de Combat 12

by Greg Van Wyngarden

While the official designation of the grouping of Escadrilles N 3, N 26, N 73 and N 103 would be Groupe de Combat 12, this unit is more popularly known as *les Cigognes* due to the famous stork emblems adopted by the component squadrons. It was Escadrille N 3 that began the use of the stork as a unit badge, the choice relating to the Alsatian origins of the escadrille. This escadrille was founded in 1912, located at Belfort along the Franco-German border next to Alsace. The stork was the traditional symbol of Alsace, due to the fact that the birds nest among the chimneys and rooftops of the region. However, the need for unit markings was not realised until well after the beginning of World War One, and it was not until almost two years into the war that the emblem of a stork in flight was painted on the fuselage sides of N 3 aircraft.

Even before the stork emblem was devised, however, pilots with N 3 were making use of strictly personal markings, some of which were retained after the unit marking was adopted. The most famous of these was the name *Vieux Charles* so associated with Georges Guynemer. Actually, this name first appeared on a Nieuport X flown by Sergent Charles Bonnard which was inherited by Guynemer after Bonnard was transferred to Serbia; Guynemer would apply it to most of the aircraft he flew thereafter. Another personal marking was the winged cow's head on a shield used by Vedrines on his Nieuport XI. Dorme marked most of his aircraft with the legend *Père Dorme* as well as a green cross of Lorraine, and André Chainat applied the name *L'Oiseau bleu* to the series of machines he flew. Sergent André Dubonnet carried a cat symbol emblematic of his family's wines on at least one of his Spads.

The classic *cigogne* emblem was probably the first applied to Nieuport XVI machines of N 3 in the late spring or early summer of 1916. It is obvious that a stencil or a series of very similar stencils was used to apply the symbol, as it remained unchanged in size, shape and detail throughout the war. The Nieuport XVIs and early XVIIs were camouflaged on their upper surfaces in dark shades of green and brown, thus the stork was generally painted in white with red beak and legs on these dark aircraft, for the best visibility. Later this was altered slightly to a white stork with black feathers and red beak and legs, which became the 'standard' colouration of the classic image.

However, on light-coloured aircraft such as silver-finished Nieuport XVII fighters and on some early beige-coloured Spads, the stork was painted entirely red. When the later five-coloured factory camouflage appeared on late model Spad VII and XIII machines, the white stork with red and black details was revived. There were the inevitable exceptions; for instance, Dorme seems to have used a uniquely personal rendition of the emblem, a red bird with white feathers, on some of his aircraft.

In addition to the unit marking each aircraft was usually marked with a large individual number on the rear fuselage and often on the upper wing as well. Initially these numbers were red, later changed to green by official decree; when the five-colour camouflage began appearing on Spads, the colour of the number reverted to red for the sake of contrast. It was common for a pilot to retain 'his' number through a succession of machines: Guynemer was identified by a 2, Dorme used 12, Raymond had 9 and so on.

GC 12 was created on 19 October 1916 under the command of Félix Brocard, and N 3 was joined by escadrilles 26, 73 and 103. Each adopted a different aspect of the stork in flight as their escadrille emblem. In fact, both Escadrille Spa 26 and Spa 103 would go through more than one kind of stork badge as time progressed. In early 1918, Spa 73 was transferred to GC 19 when its CO, Capitaine Albert Duellin, was given command of that Groupe. Escadrille Spa 67 therefore became part of GC 12 to replace it. Very late in the war, the four escadrilles of GC 12 were joined by Spa

167, formed in August 1918. Both Spa 67 and 167 would take new forms of the stork as their unit emblems to stay with the established pattern of GC 12, but photographic documentation of their aircraft has proven difficult to locate – at least for this writer/artist.

Escadrille N 26 had originally adopted a flaming torch upheld by a hand as its unit emblem as early as 1915. This torch insignia was painted in a variety of colours and styles on the fuselage sides of their Nieuport XI and XVII fighters throughout much of 1916. After its incorporation into GC 12, the unit emblem was changed to a stork in a 'landing' configuration, with legs and head stretched downward and wings upraised in a 'V' shape; this insignia was usually placed on a red and white riband which wrapped over the fuselage. Later this configuration was modified to the classic Spa 26 form, with head pointing straight ahead and wings and legs stretched behind to form a rather narrow shape. Both formats of the stork insignia were painted white with black feathers at the tip of the wings and tail, with red beak and legs. As usual in French escadrilles, the individual identifications consisted of large numbers painted on the aft fuselage (and sometimes the upper wing), apparently in red.

Escadrille Spa 73 adopted a unique form of the stork insignia when they became part of the Groupe. The bird had its wings outstretched to both sides with the head facing the viewer, rendered delicately in white with red beak and legs, and black feather details with blue shading. This emblem (and consequently the unit) was informally known as *La Cigogne qui fait face*, or even *La Cigogne japonaise* due to its oriental styling. Almost invariably the bird insignia was placed on a blue and white riband which extended over the fuselage. Again, individual numbers were painted in red on the aft fuselage.

Escadrille Spa 103 originated as Bréguet Escadrille 17 in August 1914, and later became Escadrille VB 3 equipped with Voisin bombers. The unit designation was again changed in March 1915, becoming VB 103; at this time the unit marking was a red five-pointed star painted on the nacelle. This red star insignia was retained for a period after the unit changed to an Escadrille de Chasse in February 1916, becoming N 103; the most famous example of this star marking appeared on the Spad VII of S/Lt August Lendeuil which was captured on 3 March 1917 and well-photographed by the Germans. After the formation of GC 12, the unit adopted an early form of a stork insignia, with wings stretched upward and placed on a red-white riband. By autumn 1917 the stork had assumed its final form, so familiar from photographs of Fonck's various Spads, with raised wings and legs trailing behind. Individual identification in this unit was achieved with Roman numerals painted on the fuselage after of the stork, generally in red with white outlines. In addition to his numeral, Fonck often marked his aircraft with the old five-pointed star on the upper and lower wings, again in red outlines in white.

As stated above, both Spa 67 and Spa 167 utilised other formats of the *Cigogne* emblem after their respective incorporations into GC 12. Spa 67 used a stork identical to that of Spa 3, but somewhat smaller and placed against a two-tone pennant. The leading half of the pennant was a dark-brownish red, while the trailing half was bright red-orange. There was, apparently, at least one variant of this emblem with a different style of stork on a red and orange pennant. In its brief time at the Front, Spa 167 devised a stork emblem with upraised wings and head and neck pointed straight ahead. Unfortunately neither information nor good photographs, which would reveal more about the personal markings used by these latter two units, have been located.

The author (G V W) would be at fault if he did not acknowledge the research on *Cigogne* markings carried out by the very knowledgeable Jon Gutman, and also the very useful work of markings historians Dr Glen K Merrill and Ty Smith. The foregoing text is based very largely on their marvellous work. Obviously, any investigation of French unit markings is built on the vital pioneering research of Commandant E Moreau-Berillon, the leading authority in this field.

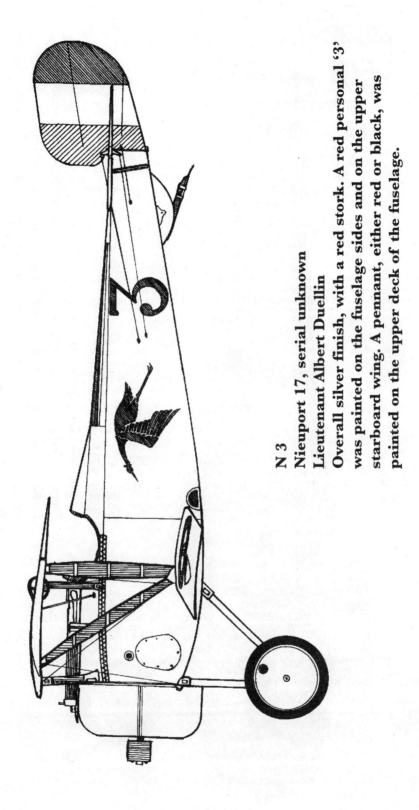

N 3
Nieuport 17, serial unknown
Lieutenant Albert Duellin
Overall silver finish, with a red stork. A red personal '3' was painted on the fuselage sides and on the upper starboard wing. A pennant, either red or black, was painted on the upper deck of the fuselage.

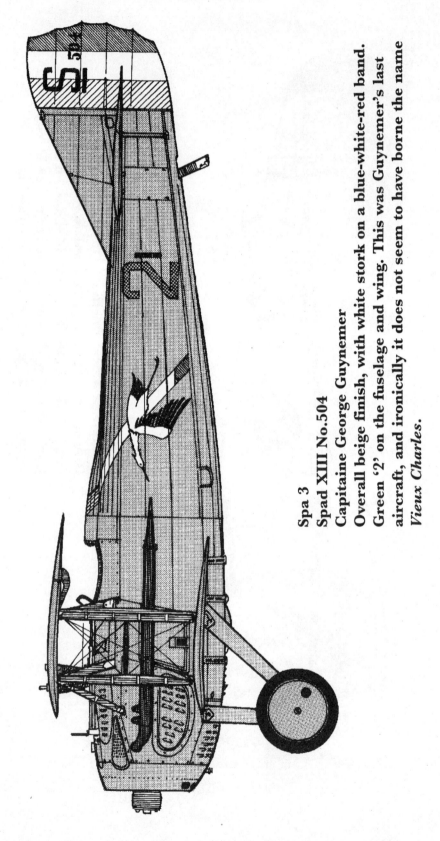

Spa 3
Spad XIII No.504
Capitaine George Guynemer
Overall beige finish, with white stork on a blue-white-red band.
Green '2' on the fuselage and wing. This was Guynemer's last
aircraft, and ironically it does not seem to have borne the name
Vieux Charles.

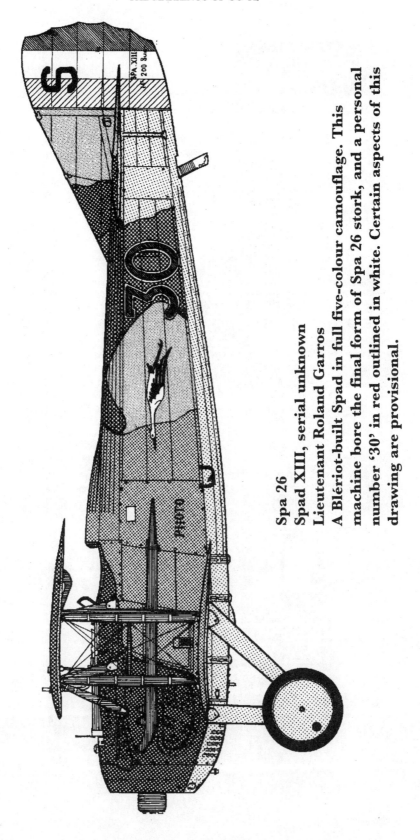

Spa 26
Spad XIII, serial unknown
Lieutenant Roland Garros
A Blériot-built Spad in full five-colour camouflage. This
machine bore the final form of Spa 26 stork, and a personal
number '30' in red outlined in white. Certain aspects of this
drawing are provisional.

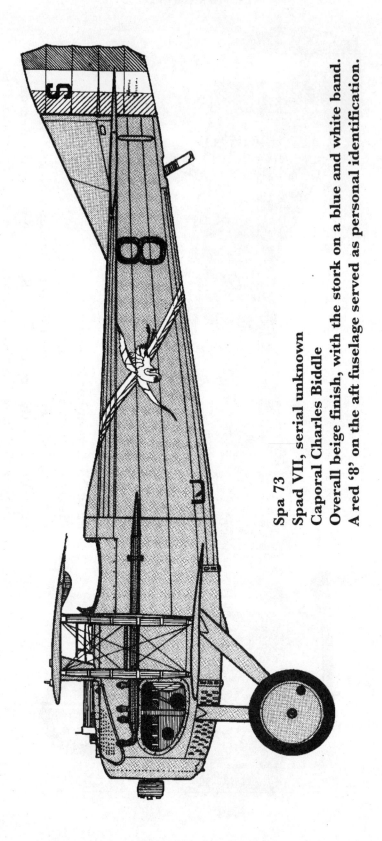

Spa 73
Spad VII, serial unknown
Caporal Charles Biddle
Overall beige finish, with the stork on a blue and white band.
A red '8' on the aft fuselage served as personal identification.

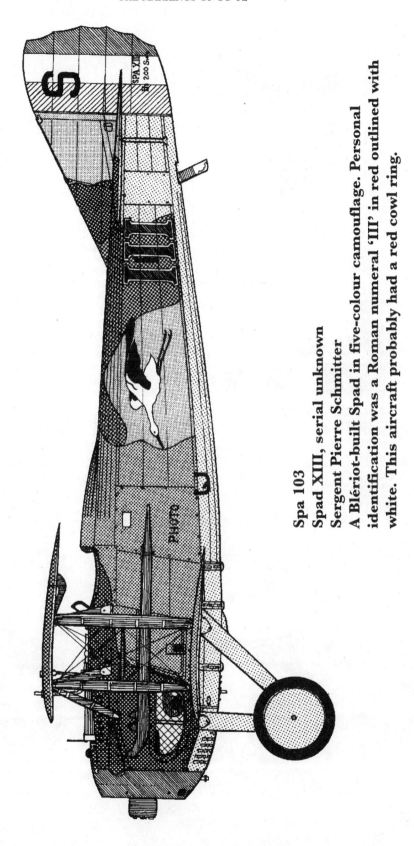

Spa 103
Spad XIII, serial unknown
Sergent Pierre Schmitter
A Blériot-built Spad in five-colour camouflage. Personal identification was a Roman numeral 'III' in red outlined with white. This aircraft probably had a red cowl ring.

Spa 3

Spa 26

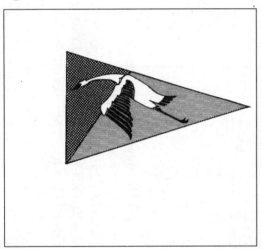

Spa 67

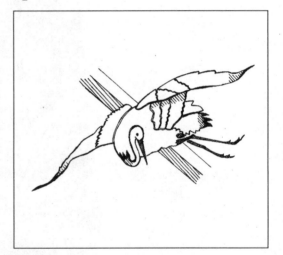

Spa 73

Spa 103

Spa 167

Glossary

FA	Flieger-Abteilung
FA(A)	Flieger-Abteilung Artillerie
Kek	Kampfeinsitzer Kommando
RFV	Région Fortifiée du Verdun
GQG	Grand Quartier Général (Headquarters of the Commander Chief of the Armées)
CIACB	Centre d'Instruction de l'Aviation de Chasse et de Bombardement
GDE	Groupe Division d'Entraînement
SFA	Service des Fabrications de l'Aéronautique
AéCF	Aéro-Club de France
Hussard	Light Cavalry
Cuirassier	Cavalryman
Dragon	Mounted Infantry
Artillerie Lourde	Heavy Artillery
Artillerie de Campagne	Field Artillery (Horse and Mounted)
Artillerie à Cheval	Horse Artillery
Spahis	Algerian Cavalry

(See also pp. 143-144.)

Bibliography

Battesti, François *Les Cigognes de Brocard au Combat*

Biddle, Charles J *Fighting Airman – The way of the Eagle*, Scribner's and Sons, 1919.

Bordeaux, Henry *Guynemer, Knight of the Air*, Yale University Press, 1918.

Christienne, Charles & Lisarrague, Pierre *A History of French Military Aviation* Charles-Lavauzelle, 1980

Cuich, Myrone N *Guynemer et ses avions*

Demaizière, Louis *Un Grand Pilote – Romanet*

Fonck, René *Mes Combats*, (Ace of Aces) Doubleday & Co, 1967

Franks N L R & Bailey F W *Over The Front*, Grub Street 1992

Franks, N L R, Bailey F W & Guest, R *Above the Lines*, Grub Street, 1993

McEntee, Girard *Military History of the World War*

Mortane, Jacques *Carré des As*

Mortane, Jacques *Sentinelles de l'Air*

Mortane, Jacques *Les Mystères de la Guerre Aérienne*

Mortane, Jacques *La Guerre des Ailes-Navarre, Sentinelle de Verdun*

Mortane, Jacques & Dacay, Jean *La Guerre des Nues*

Hall, James N. & Nordhoff, Charles B. *The Lafayette Flying Corps*

Ministère de la Défense Nationale Revue *Historique de l'Armée – L'Aviation Militaire Française*

Parsons, Edwin C *I Flew with the Lafayette Escadrille*

Service Historique de l'Armée de l'Air Historique du Groupe de Chasse I/2 'Les Cigognes'

Index of Personnel in Narrative